INTRODUCTION TO ISLAMIC **MARITAL** COUNSELING

INTRODUCTION
TO ISLAMIC
MARITAL
COUNSELING

IMAM ABDUL-RAHMAN YAKI

Library of Congress Control Number:		2018902320
ISBN:	Hardcover	978-1-5434-8480-9
	Softcover	978-1-5434-8481-6
	eBook	978-1-5434-8482-3

Print information available on the last page.

Rev. date: 03/13/2018

To order additional copies of this book, contact:
Xlibris
1-888-795-4274
www.Xlibris.com
Orders@Xlibris.com
770857

No man is exempted from making mistakes.
—Prophet Muhammad ﷺ

As the great Islāmic scholar, Imam Mālik of Madinah, once said,

كُلُّ كَلَامٍ فِيهِ مَقْبُولٌ وَ مَرْدُودٌ إِلَّا كَلَامُ صَاحِبِ هَذَا الْقَبْرِ

"Every statement will either be accepted or rejected except for the speech
of the inhabitant of this grave (of the Prophet Muhammad ﷺ)."[1]

This saying is echoed by many righteous scholars devoted to conveying the
message sent by Allāh, the Almighty, to the Prophet; peace be upon him.
May Allāh have mercy on them all.

This book is dedicated to *you*, the reader, and to leaders and families
everywhere who need encouragement in helping to build marital
relationships effectively, especially within the Muslim community.
However, perfection only belongs to Allāh. For this reason, we ask Allāh
for His forgiveness. Surely that which is right is from Him. Errors and
mistakes are mine, and I pray that Allāh forgives me of my shortcomings
and that He forgives all of us, in general. As a reader, keep us in your
prayers. We pray all benefit from this.

رَبَّنَا تَقَبَّلْ مِنَّا إِنَّكَ أَنتَ السَّمِيعُ الْعَلِيمُ

Our Lord, accept [this] from us.
Indeed, You are the Hearing, the Knowing.
—Qur'an 2:127

Amīn.

---

[1] Imam Ad-Dhahabi, Siyar A'lām al-Nubala'a (2003), 49.

CONTENTS

CONTENTS

ACKNOWLEDGMENTS

First and foremost, my appreciation is to Allāh, who has guided me with His mercy.

To my parents, who have raised me well
To my teachers, who have educated me patiently
To my family, who have generously and patiently supported me
To the beautiful and supportive community of the Islāmic Center of the Capital District
To all those who have contributed to my development and upbringing, past and present

May Allāh bless you all.

This book is a practical work of *imamship* of more than a decade of learning, teaching, reflecting, and counseling in the United States; in other words, it is lessons learned. I have been influenced by many, but ideas that have impacted me the most have an Islāmic coloring. Always keep in mind that proper knowledge does not contradict divine guidance enshrined in the Qur'an and the Sunnah.

Thanks to my students Khalafalla Osman and 'Esa Hassan for their time, dedication, and energy with regard to their assistance in helping me to organize and articulate this book. Additionally, many thanks to my student Alaudeen Umar for his phenomenal work on the graphic design of the book cover. May Allāh bless them all.

I am truly grateful to my dear friend and retired colleague Will Aitcheson, whom I call Professor. His generosity and insight as a professional psychologist is greatly appreciated. My gratitude also goes to Omar Elkassed and his wife, Rhonda Ragab, in Los Angeles, and many more. Thank you, and may God bless you all.

PREFACE

In the name of Allāh, the Beneficent, the the Merciful.

All praises are due to Allāh. We praise Him; we seek His help; we seek His forgiveness and His guidance. We seek refuge in Allāh from the evil of our souls and the wrongdoings of our actions. Whoever Allāh guides, no one can misguide. And whoever Allāh leaves astray, none can guide him. I bear witness that there is no deity worthy of worship except Allāh ﷻ. And I bear witness that Muhammad ﷺ is His servant and messenger. Allāh ﷻ says in the Qur'an,

$$ يَا أَيُّهَا الَّذِينَ آمَنُوا اتَّقُوا اللَّهَ حَقَّ تُقَاتِهِ وَلَا تَمُوتُنَّ إِلَّا وَأَنتُم مُّسْلِمُونَ $$

"O you who believe! Fear Allāh as He should be feared. And die not except in a state of Islām" (Qur'an 3:102).

Allāh ﷻ also says,

$$ يَا أَيُّهَا النَّاسُ اتَّقُوا رَبَّكُمُ الَّذِي خَلَقَكُم مِّن نَّفْسٍ وَاحِدَةٍ وَخَلَقَ مِنْهَا زَوْجَهَا وَبَثَّ مِنْهُمَا رِجَالًا كَثِيرًا وَنِسَاءً وَاتَّقُوا اللَّهَ الَّذِي تَسَاءَلُونَ بِهِ وَالْأَرْحَامَ إِنَّ اللَّهَ كَانَ عَلَيْكُمْ رَقِيبًا $$

People, be mindful of your Lord, who created you from a single soul, and from it created its mate, and from the pair of them spread countless men and women far and wide; be mindful of God, in whose name you make requests of one another. Beware of severing the ties of kinship: God is always watching over you. (Qur'an 4:1)

يَا أَيُّهَا الَّذِينَ آمَنُوا اتَّقُوا اللَّهَ وَقُولُوا قَوْلًا سَدِيدًا - يُصْلِحْ لَكُمْ أَعْمَالَكُمْ وَيَغْفِرْ لَكُمْ ذُنُوبَكُمْ ۗ وَمَن يُطِعِ اللَّهَ وَرَسُولَهُ فَقَدْ فَازَ فَوْزًا عَظِيمًا

Believers, be mindful of God, speak in a direct fashion and to good purpose, and He will put your deeds right for you and forgive you your sins. Whoever obeys God and His Messenger will truly achieve a great triumph. (Qur'an 33:70–71)

After thanking Allāh, I ask that He accept my humble effort, and I pray that He forgives our mistakes. The following pages are indeed an attempt to address some of the societal issues of marital life that confront the modern-day Muslim. The modern-day imam, to understand the needs of his community, must primarily understand himself, his environment, and the time in which we live. Ours is the age of science and technology. Directly or indirectly, these fields have influenced and affected our lives. Any resistance to either is irresponsible and sometimes catastrophic. Pretending to live in the twentieth century is not only unrealistic but also nonsensical. To be an effective imam in the twenty-first century, one must be equipped in terms of Islāmic sciences and in the knowledge of the environment, time, and the society in which we live in. Allāh says in Surah Ibrahim,

وَمَا أَرْسَلْنَا مِن رَّسُولٍ إِلَّا بِلِسَانِ قَوْمِهِ لِيُبَيِّنَ لَهُمْ ۖ فَيُضِلُّ اللَّهُ مَن يَشَاءُ وَيَهْدِي مَن يَشَاءُ ۚ وَهُوَ الْعَزِيزُ الْحَكِيمُ

"And We have not sent a messenger except with the language of his people, in order that he might make (the message) clear to them" (Qur'an 14:4).

Here, the "language of his people" is a comprehensive phrase that denotes the tools needed for an effective propagation through proper communication. I once heard a wise man say, "If you have a tool, you can endure all kinds of problems. Without a tool, you are vulnerable." Therefore, Allāh, the all-Aware, will never send us to emulate the legacy of His messengers through calling people to His way without equipping us with the proper, effective, and necessary tools. These tools also are our standard criteria for this book, and in our toolbox are two very essential resources: the Qur'an and the Sunnah. Moreover, these resources have manuals for understanding, written by the most knowledgeable and righteous of generations, our predecessors. Similarly, in this humble work there happens to be data that are very useful and informative from scholars of different spheres of expertise. In Islām, we take from all sources of knowledge as long as it does not contradict our theological foundation. It has been jurisprudentially accepted that "wisdom is a lost treasure of a believer, he takes it wherever he finds it."[2]

This work is a result of more than a decade of counseling families within Muslim communities in the United States and even worldwide, thanks to the power of modern communication. Also, a few visits to Ghana have contributed to the success of this work. Although most of my friends and colleagues have called these visits "a working visit," I have called them "training experiences." I was encouraged by many seminar participants to develop a resource tool for imams and leaders at the Islamic Council for Development and Humanitarian Services (ICODEHS) in Accra, back in April 2009, which was a successful achievement. The *Ghanaian Times* wrote in its April 15, 2009, edition "100 Muslim scholars go to school." After the seminar, I received such encouragement from leaders such as Sheikh Umar Ibrahim Imam, the national imam of ASWAJ in Ghana; Sheikh Mustapha Ibrahim, director of ICODEHS; and others. May Allāh bless them all. In addition, each of the participants made a significant

---

[2] Although this hadīth is weak in chain, the message is still resonant within Islamic scholarship because of the virtue in the words. As academics, however, we need to point out that this is, in fact, a weak hadīth found in Ibn Majah, Hadīth #4169.

contribution to the success of this work. Their questions and concerns are part of it, and to all of them I say, may Allāh reward you.

Also, thanks to my colleagues, who spent their precious hours discussing issues of importance pertaining to the family and other social issues. To all I say, may Allāh protect you. My family has always been caring, responsible, and generous to me. What else should I say, other than may Allāh continue to bless you. My teachers, past and present, who have taught me and showed me the light are numerous. May Allāh have mercy over them. Most importantly, my parents, who have taken their responsibilities seriously and have given me discipline colored with love, may the paradise be your abode, Muhammed and Nana Hawwa.

It is also worth noting that one cannot rely only on the self when writing a book; other scholars and works are always consulted. Therefore, their valuable assistance cannot be overemphasized. I personally acknowledge their help in making this dream come true. May the Almighty God reward them.

Finally, I pray that all of us will benefit from this work by improving it with constructive criticism. This is an introductory part, hopefully, of our next project, *Al-Bishirinmu Ma-Aurata,* a much more comprehensive book on marital matters and how to improve marital relationships. The title is inspired by our very successful radio program, hosted by our dear sister, Hafsat Kadir English, in Hausa, Accra, Ghana. All these successes come from Allāh, and all praise is due to Him.

In this document, I have used the words *Allāh* and *God* interchangeably. I also have tried to perfect transliteration of some Islāmic words or concept into English. This can be tough for one reason in particular—certain Arabic letters have no equivalent in Latin script. Also, we can disagree and not be disagreeable. A great number of our *fiqh* practices are understood from the text, *mafhum* and not *mantuq,* which is clear-cut and explicitly proven through the text. The solution is our reliance on Allāh, based on authentic teachings of the Prophet ﷺ and proper understanding based on the understanding of our predecessors. With that mind-set, when there is disagreement—and there will be disagreement—we will be able to appreciate and celebrate our scholarly diversity. May Allāh help us and forgive us of our sins. *Wassalāmu Alaikum.*

بِسْمِ اللهِ الرَّحْمٰنِ الرَّحِيْمِ

A Note from the Author

Muharram 10, 1439 AH
September 30, 2017 CE

I thank Allāh ﷻ for His enormous blessings, which are innumerable, and may the peace and blessings be upon His Prophet ﷺ, his household, and all those who followed his footsteps. We begin with the attitude of gratitude—being grateful for all that Allāh ﷻ has given us. This book is the revised edition; the first edition was published in my home country of Ghana during a working visit in May 2017. However, publishing mistakes were detected, and as soon as I returned to the States, I began to revise the book, day and night.

In this edition, I would like to thank my humble student Khalafalla Osman. You have been with me every step of the way in organizing this book. I appreciate your generosity. Keep up the good work. You have challenged me on certain occasions, but that shows your maturity. May Allāh ﷻ continue to bless you.

To Omar Elkassed and his wife, Rhonda Ragab: You have contributed greatly in the success of this book. I was quite impressed when I saw suggestions made with regard to classical Arabic grammar. To both of you, may Allāh ﷻ continue to bless your lives.

To Will Aitcheson: Your positive and constructive criticism in the making of this book was unimaginable, and your generosity has been remarkable.

To the many others who have contributed to this book: Your contributions made the book a better read. Your feedback was invaluable. Thank you all, and may Allāh ﷻ bless this humble effort.

—Imam A. Yaki

Transliteration Tables

ء	'		ض	d̲
ب	b		ط	t̲
ت	t		ظ	dh̲
ث	th		ع	'
ج	j		غ	gh
ح	h̲		ف	f
خ	kh		ق	q
د	d		ك	k
ذ	dh		ل	l
ر	r		م	m
ز	z		ن	n
س	s		ه	h
ش	sh		و	w
ص	s̲		ي	y

Short Vowel		Long Vowel	
َO	a	أ	ā
ِO	e	اِ	ī
ُO	u	وُ	ū

there may be times that we also transliterate
long vowels using aa/ee/oo format.

Explaining Arabic References

ﷺ: **Salal Lāhu 'Alaihi Wa Sallam,** meaning "May Allāh's peace and blessings be upon him." This will always be used in regard to the Prophet Muhammad.

﷾: **Jalla Jalāluh**, meaning "His glory is great." This statement will always be used in reference to Allāh (God). Other ways Muslims praise Allāh are by saying 'Azza wa Jall and Subhānahu Wa Ta'āla. Due to the beautiful and easy symbol ﷾, we chose that format. However, all phrases are within the tradition of Islām.

Regarding Names and Attributes of Allah

'Affirmation without Comparison' – Nothing resembles Him in His Being and Attributes.

Based on His affirmation in the Qur'an:

$$\text{لَيْسَ كَمِثْلِهِ شَيْءٌ وَهُوَ السَّمِيعُ الْبَصِيرُ}$$

"There is nothing like Him: He is the All Hearing, the All Seeing" (Qur'an 42:11).

Allah's Names and Attributes are not compared with the attributes of His creation.

His Hearing, Seeing, Knowledge, Power, Will, Mercy, Hands, are His – alone. Trying to compare it with His creation is anthropomorphism, an act of disbelief.

Nothing resembles Him in His Being and Attributes.

Therefore, in this humble work, when it comes to Allah's Names and Attributes, whether capitalized or not. Our belief or position is, Names and Attributes of Allah are not to be compared with His creation.

He is One without partners.

-Imam A. Yaki

CHAPTER 1

What Is the Islāmic Perspective?

I am a Muslim. Thus, when I counsel, I do not divorce Islām from my methodology. This position makes me a better counselor because I follow the principles of Islām. Upholding principles such as mercy, justice, and goodness enhances my abilities as a counselor. One must understand what the Qur'an and the Sunnah are to fully appreciate this introductory book on marriage counseling. What is the science that helps us understand these two sources? What are the basic tenets of Islām? Although anyone may read this book, I wrote it while guided by and viewed through the lens of Islām's main sources.

The Two Main Sources of Islām

Al-Qur'an

Ours is a nation of uncompromised monotheism, unified under the umbrella of Islām and guided through the microscope of the Qur'an and the Sunnah. In his farewell address to humanity, Muhammad, may peace be with him, stressed the importance of following the Qur'an and the Sunnah, which offer the only guidance that guarantees the *ummah*, the community, full protection and safety in both lives. Therefore, the ummah must achieve a proper understanding of these main sources as protection from the intellectual bankruptcy and agony that it faces today. We Muslims believe in the divine books, which include Torah, the Gospels, and the Qur'an. The Qur'an, however, bears the stamp of finality and perfection and serves as a witness over previous books. If you wish, read Surah Al-Maidah:

وَأَنزَلْنَا إِلَيْكَ الْكِتَابَ بِالْحَقِّ مُصَدِّقًا لِّمَا بَيْنَ يَدَيْهِ مِنَ الْكِتَابِ وَمُهَيْمِنًا عَلَيْهِ ۖ فَاحْكُم بَيْنَهُم بِمَا أَنزَلَ اللَّهُ ۖ وَلَا تَتَّبِعْ أَهْوَاءَهُمْ عَمَّا جَاءَكَ مِنَ الْحَقِّ ۚ لِكُلٍّ جَعَلْنَا مِنكُمْ شِرْعَةً وَمِنْهَاجًا ۚ وَلَوْ شَاءَ اللَّهُ لَجَعَلَكُمْ أُمَّةً وَاحِدَةً وَلَٰكِن لِّيَبْلُوَكُمْ فِي مَا آتَاكُمْ ۖ فَاسْتَبِقُوا الْخَيْرَاتِ ۚ إِلَى اللَّهِ مَرْجِعُكُمْ جَمِيعًا فَيُنَبِّئُكُم بِمَا كُنتُمْ فِيهِ تَخْتَلِفُونَ

And We have revealed to you, [O Muhammad], the Book in truth, confirming that which preceded it of the Scripture and as a criterion over it. So judge between them by what Allāh has revealed and do not follow their inclinations away from what has come to you of the truth. To each of you We prescribed a law and a method. Had Allāh willed, He would have made you one nation [united in religion], but [He intended] to test you in what He has given you; so race to [all that is] good. To Allāh is your return all together, and He will [then] inform you concerning that over which you used to differ. (Qur'an 5:48)

What is the source of the Qur'an? The word *Qur'an* is derived from, *qara-a*, to "read" or to "recite," and *Qur'an* means "the reading" or "the recitation." In the terms of Islām, *Qur'an* means "the Word of Allāh, revealed to Prophet Muhammad ﷺ, in the richest form of the Arabic language and is considered the eternal miracle of Islām to humanity." The Qur'an contains 114 chapters and is not compiled in chronological order of revelation. Rather, it is organized in the way in which the Prophet ordered the scribes to arrange it. Some of its chapters are very long; others are quite short. For example, Surah Al-Baqarah (chapter 2) reigns as the longest chapter, with 286 verses, and Surah Al-Kauthar (chapter 108) is the shortest, with three verses. It is worth noting that the entire Book has been preserved in the hearts and minds of many Muslims, both past and present. The importance of memorizing it cannot be overemphasized; it is the ultimate goal of all devout Muslims.

Indeed, unlike other holy texts, the Qur'an is not only to be read ritualistically but also—most importantly—to be understood and implemented. The Qur'an addresses humanity in all walks of life, regardless of time and space. Our predecessors held the view that the best methodology of Qur'anic explanation entails understanding gained in four ways:

1. The Qur'an through the Qur'an
2. The Qur'an through the Sunnah
3. The Qur'an through the companions and their students
4. The Qur'an through classical Arabic language

As-Sunnah

Etymologically, Sunnah derives its meaning from the root *sanna*, meaning "line of conduct," "mode of life," "behavior," "example," "precedence," and "dispensation." In the life of Islām, multiple definitions of this word rest on different disciplines, but it is agreed that it is "the guidance upon which the Prophet and his companions were on." The antonym of *sanna* is *bid`a*, or innovation. Therefore, Sunnah is the practical demonstration of the Qur'an by the Prophet in words and deeds. *Hadīth* is the vehicle by which Sunnah is transported to the community for consumption. Hadīth means "recent," "information," and "new." In the Islāmic context, hadīth is "the statement, action, approval, manner, and physical characteristics of the Prophet."

Hadīth comprises two elements:

1. *Sanad*, or chain of narration
2. *Matn*, or text

For a hadīth to be reliable and accepted, both its sanad and matn need to go through a process of scrutiny and authentication. Here is a list of some of the great imams of hadīth and their literature that the scholarship of Islām greatly celebrates:

1. *Al-Jāmi' As-Sahīh* by Imam Muhammad bin Ismā'il Al-Bukhāri: Popularly known as *Sahīh Al-Bukhāri*, this work is celebrated as the most important of all the hadīth collections because it is completely authentic in both chain and text.
2. *Al-Musnad As-Sahīh* by Imam Muslim Bin Al-Hajjāj: Popularly known as *Sahīh Muslim*, this is a highly celebrated work in the world of hadīth collections, second only to *Sahīh Al-Bukhāri*.
3. *Sunan Abi Dawūd* by Imam Abi Dawūd Sulaiman bin Al-Ash'ath.
4. *Sunan At-Tirmidhi* by Imam Abu 'Īsa Muhammad bin 'Īsa At-Tirmidhi.
5. *Sunan An-Nasāi* by Imam Abu Abdur-Rahmān Ahmad bin Suh'aib An-Nasāi.
6. *Sunan Ibnu-Mājah* by Imam Ibnu-Mājah Muhammad bin Yazīd bin Mājah
7. *Musnad Ahmad* by Imam Ahmad bin Muhammad bin Hanbal.
8. *Al-Muwatta* by Imam Mālik bin Anas bin Mālik, the earliest substantial work in the field of hadīth collections.
9. *Al-Umm* by Imam Muhammad bin Idrīs Ash-Shāf'ie.

The last three scholars mentioned are among the greatest of scholars and are known collectively (with one other) as the Four Great Imams. The contributions in the field of hadīth collections of the three scholars mentioned above gave them legacies carved in stone by the Muslim community. The first of the four great imams, however, is the eminent scholar Imam Abu Hanifa An-Nu'man bin Thābit. His contributions to the field of *fiqh* (Islāmic jurisprudence) are beyond description.

The Order of Allāh to Obey the Prophet

When you review what was just mentioned, please acknowledge and reflect upon how dutiful and dedicated Prophet Muhammad ﷺ was in conveying Allāh's message. Allāh, through His Qur'an, emphasized the necessity of obeying the Prophet, so much so that it is mentioned side by side with the obedience of Allāh:

قُلْ أَطِيعُوا اللَّهَ وَالرَّسُولَ ۖ فَإِن تَوَلَّوْا فَإِنَّ اللَّهَ لَا يُحِبُّ الْكَافِرِينَ

"Say, obey God and the Messenger but if they turn away God loves not the disbelievers" (Qur'an 3:32).

وَأَطِيعُوا اللَّهَ وَالرَّسُولَ لَعَلَّكُمْ تُرْحَمُونَ

"And obey God and the Prophet so that you may be given mercy" (Qur'an 3:132).

وَأَطِيعُوا اللَّهَ وَرَسُولَهُ وَلَا تَنَازَعُوا فَتَفْشَلُوا وَتَذْهَبَ رِيحُكُمْ ۖ وَاصْبِرُوا ۚ إِنَّ اللَّهَ مَعَ الصَّابِرِينَ

"Obey God and His Messenger, and do not quarrel with one another, or you may lose heart and your spirit may desert you" (Qur'an 8:46).

مَّن يُطِعِ الرَّسُولَ فَقَدْ أَطَاعَ اللَّهَ ۖ وَمَن تَوَلَّىٰ فَمَا أَرْسَلْنَاكَ عَلَيْهِمْ حَفِيظًا

"Whoever obeys the Messenger obeys God. If some pay no heed, We have not sent you to be their keeper" (Qur'an 4:80).

قُلْ إِن كُنتُمْ تُحِبُّونَ اللَّهَ فَاتَّبِعُونِي يُحْبِبْكُمُ اللَّهُ وَيَغْفِرْ لَكُمْ ذُنُوبَكُمْ ۗ وَاللَّهُ غَفُورٌ رَّحِيمٌ

"Say, If you love God, follow me, and God will love you and forgive you your sins; God is most forgiving, most merciful" (Qur'an 3:31).

A good Muslim needs a clear understanding of Islām, and that cannot be achieved without a proper understanding of the authentic and practical Sunnah demonstrated in our faith. I cited the verses above as a response to those who believe that Islām can be practiced while divorcing the tradition of the Prophet ﷺ (Sunnah) from the Words of Allāh ﷻ (Qur'an). This sacred methodology did not come from my imagination; it was passed down from the Prophet ﷺ to his companions and, furthermore, to their students. These generations are known as *As-Salaf As-Sālih*, "the Righteous Predecessors." Some notable scholars from that period include Imam Abu Hanifa, Imam Mālik, Imam Ash-Shāfi'e, and Imam Ahmad bin Hanbal (may Allāh be pleased with them all). These scholars dedicated their lives to establishing an authentic understanding of this religion, causing them to be held in great regard as the fathers of mainstream Islām. Their methodology? Qur'an and Sunnah.

What happens if you deviate from this methodology? Well, the result would be akin to the medical school student prescribing medication without certification. Would you allow that person to diagnose you? Let us say, God forbid, you receive a speeding ticket. If you are found guilty, then you will suffer the consequences, even if you do not believe that you were speeding! Would you allow the legal intern to represent you in court? I didn't think so. Now, if we would not entrust amateurs with our health or our legal standing, then how could we trust a layman with our relationship to Allāh? As a student in Islāmic law, I must echo the teachings of all mainstream Islāmic scholarship; that is, obedience to the Prophet ﷺ is actually obedience to Allāh ﷻ. Similarly, one cannot understand Allāh properly except through the Prophet ﷺ. So let it be clear: the Qur'an and Sunnah are inseparable.

Both the Qur'an and the Sunnah are divinely oriented. The Qur'an and the Sunnah represent the divine speech in its recited and nonrecited forms, respectively. Allāh says,

$$وَمَا يَنطِقُ عَنِ الْهَوَىٰ - إِنْ هُوَ إِلَّا وَحْيٌ يُوحَىٰ$$

"Nor does he speak from [his own] inclination. It is not but a revelation revealed" (Qur'an 53:3–4).

Imam Abu Zuhra, one of the twentieth century's best Muslim minds in the field of hadīth, wrote, "Sunnah completes the Qur'an." The word used in his original Arabic text is *Mukmilah*, meaning "completes."[3]

Also, Al-Imam Ash-Shafi'e, one of the best minds of all time and the originator of *Usūl Al-Fiqh* (*The Principles of Islāmic Jurisprudence*), wrote in his classic work, *Ar-Risālah*, regarding the Sunnah:

a) When Allāh uses the word Al-Hikmah in the Qur'an, he argues that Allāh is referring to the Sunnah itself.

b) Imam Ash-Shafi'e distinguishes between three kinds of rulings that come from Allāh:

1- **Clear-cut in the Qur'an**: Rulings such as these occur where the Prophet ﷺ himself does not interject because what Allāh says in the verse is explicitly clear. (Examples include verses pertaining to the prohibition of the consumption of dead animals and pork.)

2- **Clear-cut in the Qur'an but requiring prophetic input**: These ruling occur where Allāh ﷻ is clearly commanding His believers something that requires additional explanation from His Messenger ﷺ regarding the technicalities and context. An example is prayer. Allāh says clearly in many verses of the Qur'an that prayer is prescribed upon the believers, but only through the Prophet ﷺ's explanation can we gather the logistics of when, where, and how.

3- **Ruling explained solely by the Prophet ﷺ**: There are instances where the Prophet will communicate to us what Allāh ﷻ decrees, directly from his tradition. As Muslims, we believe that anything that comes from the Prophet ﷺ comes from Allāh ﷻ. Therefore, when the Prophet legislates anything, it is surely from Allāh, and we are obligated to follow it. An example for this is when Allāh ﷻ revealed the verse in Surah Al-Baqarah:

---

[3] Imam Abu Zuhra, Usūl Al-Fiqh (1997), 95.

كُتِبَ عَلَيْكُمْ إِذَا حَضَرَ أَحَدَكُمُ الْمَوْتُ إِن تَرَكَ خَيْرًا الْوَصِيَّةُ لِلْوَالِدَيْنِ وَالْأَقْرَبِينَ بِالْمَعْرُوفِ ۖ حَقًّا عَلَى الْمُتَّقِينَ

"It is prescribed that he should make a proper bequest to parents and close relatives—a duty incumbent on those who are mindful of God" (Qur'an 2:180).

Following this ayah, the Messenger ﷺ explained by stating,

بَابِ لَا وَصِيَّةَ لِوَارِثٍ

"A legal heir has no right to inherit through a will."[4]

Ibn Hajar states in his book *Fat-hul Bāri* that the imams Abu Dawūd, At-Tirmidhi, and others have connected this chain from a hadith narrated by Abu Umāmah, who said, "I heard the Messenger ﷺ saying in the Farewell Sermon that 'Indeed, Allāh has given each deserving relative their right, and therefore there is no bequest for he who inherits.'"[5] Although this statement seems to be contradictory to the aforementioned Qur'anic verse through the third principle we mentioned, it has been determined that the Prophet ﷺ's statement is an abrogation of the verse. In summary, this principle exemplifies the belief that whatever is in the Qur'an and whatever is in the authentic Sunnah are both from Allāh and are inseparable.[6]

As-Shafi'e continues by expressing that he is just echoing what he has heard from the scholarly authorities in the field of Qur'an when he declares that *Al-Hikmah* in the Qur'an is the Sunnah. To bring the point home, the eminent scholar argued that "therefore, [the Prophet] taught with the Book of Allāh and also taught that which is not textually mentioned in the Book. Whatever he the Prophet taught, we are obligated by Allāh to follow. Because Allāh has made following of the Prophet, an act of obedience to

---

4   Explanation of Hadīth 2747 in Sahīh Al Bukhāri.

5   Al-Asqalāni, *Fat-hul Bāri*, vol. 6, 23–24.

6   Ar-Risālah, Al-Imam Ash-Shafi'e, 32–33.

Him; moreover, disobeying the Prophet is an act of disobedience to Him."[7] He follows his words with a saying of the Prophet: "Let me not find one of you reclining on his couch when he hears something regarding me which I have commanded or forbidden and saying: We do not know. What we found in Allāh's Book we have followed."[8]

So What Went Wrong?

Rhetorical abuse is one of the ummatic problems, past and present. Almost every movement that has begun in different generations within the Muslim community has sought legitimization in the Qur'an and Sunnah and, in some cases, has caused a dizzying atmosphere of talk and emotion. To save us from our current state of agony, there must be a relentless attack on false eloquence, which is composed of ignorance and self-centeredness.

Here is a summarized case for the Sunnah:

1. Sunnah derives its validity from Qur'an itself.

Allāh said,

$$ يَا أَيُّهَا الَّذِينَ آمَنُوا أَطِيعُوا اللَّهَ وَأَطِيعُوا الرَّسُولَ وَأُولِي الْأَمْرِ مِنكُمْ ۖ فَإِن تَنَازَعْتُمْ فِي شَيْءٍ فَرُدُّوهُ إِلَى اللَّهِ وَالرَّسُولِ إِن كُنتُمْ تُؤْمِنُونَ بِاللَّهِ وَالْيَوْمِ الْآخِرِ $$

"O you who believe! Obey Allāh and obey the Messenger and those of you who are in authority. And if you differ in anything amongst yourselves, refer it to Allāh and His Messenger, if you believe in Allāh and in the Last Day ..." (Qur'an 4:59).

---

[7] Ar-Risālah, Al-Imam Ash-Shafi'e, 88–89.

[8] Sunan Abi Dawūd, Hadīth #4605, graded *Sahīh* (authentic).

Also Allāh says,

$$وَمَا آتَاكُمُ الرَّسُولُ فَخُذُوهُ وَمَا نَهَاكُمْ عَنْهُ فَانتَهُوا$$

"And whatsoever the Messenger gives you, take it, and whatsoever he forbids you, abstain from it." (Qur'an 59:7).

In the light of the aforementioned verses, one can conclude that the adherence of the Sunnah is binding and has legislative power with the Qur'an.

2. The scholars of Islām exerted a profound and unimaginable amount of effort regarding hadīth scrutiny; they accomplished separating the genuine from forgery and authentic from weak.

3. All acts of worships without the Sunnah are incomplete.

4. The Prophet ﷺ through his Sunnah unfolded the truth revealed in the Qur'an and taught it practically to his companions; may Allāh be pleased with them all.

5. Al-Hikmah (wisdom) and Al-Bayān (clear proof) mean the Sunnah of the Prophet; this is the opinion of our predecessors, including Imam Ash-Shāfi'ie, who was the originator of Usūlul-Fiqh (The Legal Maxims of Islāmic Jurisprudence), as mentioned earlier.

Please read the following verses as evidence for this claim:

$$كَمَا أَرْسَلْنَا فِيكُمْ رَسُولًا مِّنكُمْ يَتْلُو عَلَيْكُمْ آيَاتِنَا وَيُزَكِّيكُمْ$$
$$وَيُعَلِّمُكُمُ الْكِتَابَ وَالْحِكْمَةَ وَيُعَلِّمُكُم مَّا لَمْ تَكُونُوا تَعْلَمُونَ$$

"Just as We have sent among you a Messenger from yourselves reciting to you Our verses and purifying you and teaching you the Book and wisdom and teaching you that which you did not know" (Qur'an 2:151).

وَأَنزَلْنَا إِلَيْكَ الذِّكْرَ لِتُبَيِّنَ لِلنَّاسِ مَا نُزِّلَ إِلَيْهِمْ وَلَعَلَّهُمْ يَتَفَكَّرُونَ

And We revealed to you the message that you may make clear to the people what was sent down to them and that they might give thought (Qur'an 16:44).

In brief, it is time for us all to honestly rededicate ourselves to the authentic teachings of the Prophet ﷺ. It is the only way to the obedience of Allāh. If we want to get closer to Allāh, we should adopt the methodology of the closest to Allāh, the Prophet ﷺ. We are not calling for every Muslim to go overseas and become a scholar, but it is important, before using any Islāmic text, to first and foremost understand its authenticity grading and context. Islām encourages seeking beneficial knowledge that not only feeds us spiritually but also intellectually and universally. Therefore, we must all strive to improve ourselves in our critical thinking while remaining humble. As a community, we must absolutely avoid both the deification and the demonization of our scholars. This is because they are all human and worthy of our respect and prayers. At the end of the day, we seek these human beings for their knowledge of Allāh through their understanding of the prophetic tradition.

How Do the Commandments of Allāh Work?

Al-Amr, meaning "commandment," is a lot more comprehensive than laypeople might think. Scholars argue that Al-Amr is the centerpiece of the laws of Islām. Muslim scholars, for centuries, have debated on the following question: If Allāh states a command, is it an obligation that you must fulfill or just a declaration of its permissibility? Al-Jamhoor, the majority of Muslim scholarship, are in agreement that a command from Allāh is to be treated as an obligation that must be fulfilled, unless followed with an attachment. For example, "marriage to he who can afford it." This means that if you have the financial, spiritual, physical, and psychological means to get married, then get married. Otherwise, keep fasting!

Knowledge of the Qur'an and Sunnah is a necessity and not an option, but knowledge of the Qur'an is extremely comprehensive. One could get it from *'Uloom al-Qur'an* (the sciences of the Qur'an). Examples are as follows:

1. *An-Naskh*, which is the law of abrogation. Yes, even the Qur'an has discontinuations of some previous laws. A popular example and also the first example in Qur'anic history, according to Ibn 'Abbas, is the changing of the *Qibla* (the direction of prayer). Formerly, it was located in Baitul Maqdis, which is the Sacred Sanctuary in Palestine. Then, almost a year or so after Hijrah, Allāh ﷻ sent down an ayah revealing that the Qibla is the House of Allāh in Makkah.[9]

2. *'Ām* (general) vs. *Khās* (specific) rulings in the Qur'an: In the Qur'an, Allāh ﷻ makes general commands, but there also are some commands that have specifications before implementation. Example of '*Ām* is in Surah Hud, Ayah 6. Allāh says, "There is not a creature that moves on earth whose provision is not His concern. He knows where it lives and its [final] resting place: it is all [there] in a clear record." An example of Khās is in Surah Āl-Imran, Ayah 97. Allāh says, "Pilgrimage to the House is a duty owed to God by people who are able to undertake it."

3. *Mantooq* (proven by the text) vs. *Mafhoom* (understood from the text): Many rulings are understood from the text but not explicitly addressed, causing differences in opinion by Muslim scholars. For example, Allāh ﷻ in chapter 23 of the Qur'an begins by stating that the believers are successful. Following that, he addresses a few qualities, and one of those characteristics is those "who shun idle talk."[10] Now, what constitutes idle talk? That is what scholars refer to as *mafhoom*. Then, there are ayahs that say, "You are forbidden to eat carrion; blood; pig's meat; any animal over which any name other than God's has been invoked." This command is clearly stated, with no room for misunderstanding. This is what the scholars refer to as *mantooq*.

---

9 Tafsīr Ibn Kathīr, Surah Al-Baqarah, Ayah 144.

10 Quran 23:3.

Likewise, knowledge of the Sunnah necessitates the ability to separate the authentic and the weak. Narrations in both Bukhāri and Muslim are authentic; other books of hadīth require the authentication process of great hadīth scholarship. Not all hadīth, however, termed by a scholar or two as weak is actually weak. Scholars have different tools in their authentication process. May Allāh reward them tremendously.[11]

وَالَّذِينَ جَاءُوا مِن بَعْدِهِمْ يَقُولُونَ رَبَّنَا اغْفِرْ لَنَا وَلِإِخْوَانِنَا الَّذِينَ سَبَقُونَا بِالْإِيمَانِ وَلَا تَجْعَلْ فِي قُلُوبِنَا غِلًّا لِّلَّذِينَ آمَنُوا رَبَّنَا إِنَّكَ رَءُوفٌ رَّحِيمٌ

> Those who came after them say, "Lord, forgive us our sins and the sins of our brothers who believed before us, and leave no malice in our hearts towards those who believe. Lord, You are truly compassionate and merciful." (Qur'an 59:10)

None of the five pillars of Islām can be performed properly without Sunnatic input or clarification; therefore, rejecting the Sunnah is cataclysmic. To save the ummah from its current state of agony, teachers are needed who are well trained in different spheres of Islāmic knowledge—ones who are humble, disciplined. and understand not only their environment but also the importance of time. Qur'an and Sunnah are not limited to time and space; therefore, these basic main sources are important tools in navigating the crises of our twenty-first century.

Lord! Grant us knowledge, wisdom, and a blessed life to please you and serve humanity.

---

[11] Summarized from Dr. Mustafa Saīd Khan's thesis, *Athar al-Ikhtilāf fi al-Qawā'id Al-Usūliyyah*, 295–307.

The Major Principles of Fiqh (Islāmic Jurisprudence)

After discussing Qur'an and Sunnah, one also must learn the *fiqhi* principles that assist scholars with navigating through the Qur'an and the Sunnah. So what does *fiqh* mean?

Fiqh

The word, etymologically defined, means "understanding." When understood in the Islāmic context, *fiqh* is the science and application of Islāmic law. Fiqh is what truly keeps Islām with the times. Through fiqh, scholars constantly improve their understanding of the two main sources so that laymen Muslims can apply it in their everyday lives. A greater understanding of practicing Islām brings not only success to the individual but also to the larger community. For this reason, our predecessors have sacrificed their precious time not only in spreading the science of fiqh but also, of equal importance, in the structuring and standardization of it, based on the two main sources: Qur'an and Sunnah.

In the field of fiqh, there are many principles that scholars use to understand all matters of Islām. However, there are *five reputable basic principles* that scholars use to understand matters related to Islām:

الأمور بمقاصدها Principle No. 1
Al-Umooru Bi-maqaasidihaa
Actions are judged, based on intention.

This principle is the most important of all in the field of fiqh. Scholars past and present have given much attention to its explanation, due to its importance. Most of the rulings, if not all, revolve around this principle.

Its origin is from the hadīth of Umar bin Khattāb, may Allāh be pleased with him, found in the *Sahīhain* (the two authentic books of hadīth, Sahīh Al-Bukhāri and Sahīh Muslim) that the Prophet ﷺ said,

إِنَّمَا الأَعْمَالُ بِالنِّيَّاتِ، وَإِنَّمَا لِكُلِّ امْرِئٍ مَا نَوَى

14

"The reward of deeds depends upon the intentions and every person will get the reward according to what he has intended."[12] This hadīth is agreed upon. Its meaning is self-explanatory—that Allāh, the Almighty, will judge our actions based on our intent. However, what it means in the world of fiqh is that when an issue comes to the attention of the scholar, the first thing that needs to be assessed is the intention of the action in question. This is because before we begin anything, we must always ask ourselves, "Why are we doing this?" Action is defined by its purpose.

So if someone commits a crime, the jurist has to first analyze the state of mind of the doer. Did this individual intend to commit this crime? Was it an accident, or was it premeditated? Was the individual insane or sane? These are some of the factors that need to be understood when the jurist makes a decision. And that's what's so special about fiqh—one cannot make a blanket judgment for all perpetrators. Scholars of fiqh often have to look at cases individually because every case is different.

From a spiritual perspective, this principle can be explained in the example of those who sought Islāmic knowledge. Why did they seek this knowledge? If it was for the people, congratulations; Allāh will give them temporary respect and prestige. Their deeds on the day that actually matters, however—the day of judgment—will be unacknowledged, just as Allāh ﷻ was not acknowledged when they sought that knowledge. However, if they chose to seek knowledge to purify their hearts and become closer to Allāh, then Allāh will grant them respect and prestige of this life. And on the day of judgment, Allāh will reward them with the presence to which they intended to be close. This is what the principle means.

Scholars of hadīth and fiqh are in agreement on the importance and greatness of this hadīth. Ibn Rajab, one of the great scholars of the Hanbali school of jurisprudence, said, "This hadīth is a comprehensive principle that is unique to all actions; nothing is exempted."

There are many textual evidences from Qur'an and Sunnah that testify to this:

---

[12] Sahīh Al-Bukhāri, Hadīth #1, and Sahīh Muslim, Hadīth #1907.

وَمَن يُهَاجِرْ فِي سَبِيلِ اللَّهِ يَجِدْ فِي الْأَرْضِ مُرَاغَمًا كَثِيرًا
وَسَعَةً ۚ وَمَن يَخْرُجْ مِن بَيْتِهِ مُهَاجِرًا إِلَى اللَّهِ وَرَسُولِهِ ثُمَّ يُدْرِكْهُ
الْمَوْتُ فَقَدْ وَقَعَ أَجْرُهُ عَلَى اللَّهِ ۗ وَكَانَ اللَّهُ غَفُورًا رَّحِيمًا

And whoever emigrates for the cause of Allāh will find
on the earth many [alternative] locations and abundance.
And whoever leaves his home as an emigrant to Allāh and
His Messenger and then death overtakes him - his reward
has already become incumbent upon Allāh. And Allāh is
The Ever Forgiving and Most Merciful. (Qur'an 4:100)

وَمَا أُمِرُوا إِلَّا لِيَعْبُدُوا اللَّهَ مُخْلِصِينَ لَهُ الدِّينَ حُنَفَاءَ وَيُقِيمُوا
الصَّلَاةَ وَيُؤْتُوا الزَّكَاةَ ۚ وَذَٰلِكَ دِينُ الْقَيِّمَةِ

And they were not commanded except to worship Allāh,
[being] sincere to Him in religion, inclining to truth,
and to establish prayer and to give zakah. And that is the
correct religion. (Qur'an 98:5)

وَمَن يُشَاقِقِ الرَّسُولَ مِن بَعْدِ مَا تَبَيَّنَ لَهُ الْهُدَىٰ وَيَتَّبِعْ غَيْرَ
سَبِيلِ الْمُؤْمِنِينَ نُوَلِّهِ مَا تَوَلَّىٰ وَنُصْلِهِ جَهَنَّمَ ۖ وَسَاءَتْ مَصِيرًا

And whoever opposes the Messenger after guidance has
become clear to him and follows other than the way of the
believers - We will give him what he has taken and drive
him into Hell, and evil it is as a destination. (Qur'an 4:115)

وَمَثَلُ الَّذِينَ يُنفِقُونَ أَمْوَالَهُمُ ابْتِغَاءَ مَرْضَاتِ اللَّهِ وَتَثْبِيتًا مِّنْ
أَنفُسِهِمْ كَمَثَلِ جَنَّةٍ بِرَبْوَةٍ أَصَابَهَا وَابِلٌ فَآتَتْ أُكُلَهَا ضِعْفَيْنِ فَإِن
لَّمْ يُصِبْهَا وَابِلٌ فَطَلٌّ ۗ وَاللَّهُ بِمَا تَعْمَلُونَ بَصِيرٌ

And the example of those who spend their wealth seeking means to the approval of Allāh and assuring [reward for] themselves is like a garden on high ground which is hit by a downpour - so it yields its fruits in double. And [even] if it is not hit by a downpour, then a drizzle [is sufficient]. And Allāh, of what you do, is Seeing. (Qur'an 2:265)

لَّا يُؤَاخِذُكُمُ اللَّهُ بِاللَّغْوِ فِي أَيْمَانِكُمْ وَلَٰكِن يُؤَاخِذُكُم بِمَا كَسَبَتْ قُلُوبُكُمْ ۗ وَاللَّهُ غَفُورٌ حَلِيمٌ

Allāh does not impose blame upon you for what is unintentional in your oaths, but He imposes blame upon you for what your hearts have earned. And Allāh is Forgiving and Forbearing. (Qur'an 2:225)

ادْعُوهُمْ لِآبَائِهِمْ هُوَ أَقْسَطُ عِندَ اللَّهِ ۚ فَإِن لَّمْ تَعْلَمُوا آبَاءَهُمْ فَإِخْوَانُكُمْ فِي الدِّينِ وَمَوَالِيكُمْ ۚ وَلَيْسَ عَلَيْكُمْ جُنَاحٌ فِيمَا أَخْطَأْتُم بِهِ وَلَٰكِن مَّا تَعَمَّدَتْ قُلُوبُكُمْ ۚ وَكَانَ اللَّهُ غَفُورًا رَّحِيمًا

Call them by [the names of] their fathers; it is more just in the sight of Allāh. But if you do not know their fathers —then they are [still] your brothers in religion and those entrusted to you. And there is no blame upon you for that in which you have erred but [only for] what your hearts intended. And ever is Allāh Forgiving and Merciful. (Qur'an 33:5)

Therefore, to benefit from one's actions, the intention must be good and solely to please Allāh, regardless of whether it is a matter of faith or worldly affairs.

What are some examples of the application of this principle?

a) Praying 'Asr Prayer with the intention of Dhuhr. One's prayer due to the incorrect intention must be redone with a renewed intention for the correct prayer.

b) When taking a shower after sexual relations with one's spouse or a wet dream, one must make it his intention to perform the ritual bath in order for the purification to be valid. One cannot take a shower with no intention and then convert his shower into a ritual bath.

Principle No. 2 المشقة تجلب التيسير
Al-Mashaqqatu tajlibut-taiseer
Hardship necessitates easiness.

This is also one of the great fiqhi principles that must never be ignored. Scholars have unanimously agreed to its importance in the application of the law because of the enormous textual proofs testifying to its validity. This is due to two reasons:

1. As humans, "weakness is part of us."
2. Situations may change, necessitating leeway or simplification of the ruling; in other words, "authorizing what was unauthorized."

Islām, therefore, accepts the fact that compromise may be necessary. Lifting a ruling temporarily has reached the level of *Qat'I*, or definitiveness, as eighth-century AH scholar, Imam Abu Ishāq Ibrahim Ash-Shatibi, one of the developers of Al-Maqāsid Ash-Sharī'ah (Goals of Sharī'ah), said.

This principle, however, explains that a ruling may be compromised because of necessity and *the reality* that Islāmic law does not

- command people to do that which they cannot afford;
- put them in difficulty; or
- command that which is contrary to their natural instinct.

As stated earlier, there are many textual evidences supporting this principle.

From the Qur'an

1. Regarding those who couldn't fast during the fasting month of Ramadān due to illness or hardship, Allāh said,

$$شَهْرُ رَمَضَانَ الَّذِي أُنزِلَ فِيهِ الْقُرْآنُ هُدًى لِّلنَّاسِ$$
$$وَبَيِّنَاتٍ مِّنَ الْهُدَىٰ وَالْفُرْقَانِ ۚ فَمَن شَهِدَ مِنكُمُ$$
$$الشَّهْرَ فَلْيَصُمْهُ ۖ وَمَن كَانَ مَرِيضًا أَوْ عَلَىٰ سَفَرٍ$$
$$فَعِدَّةٌ مِّنْ أَيَّامٍ أُخَرَ ۗ يُرِيدُ اللَّهُ بِكُمُ الْيُسْرَ وَلَا يُرِيدُ$$
$$بِكُمُ الْعُسْرَ وَلِتُكْمِلُوا الْعِدَّةَ وَلِتُكَبِّرُوا اللَّهَ عَلَىٰ مَا$$
$$هَدَاكُمْ وَلَعَلَّكُمْ تَشْكُرُونَ$$

The month of Ramadān [is that] in which was revealed the Qur'an, a guidance for the people and clear proofs of guidance and criterion. So whoever sights [the new moon of] the month, let him fast it; and whoever is ill or on a journey - then an equal number of other days. *Allāh intends for you ease and does not intend for you hardship* and [wants] for you to complete the period and to glorify Allāh for that [to] which He has guided you; and perhaps you will be grateful. (2:185)

2. Pertaining to forbidden food, Allāh said,

$$حُرِّمَتْ عَلَيْكُمُ الْمَيْتَةُ وَالدَّمُ وَلَحْمُ الْخِنزِيرِ وَمَا أُهِلَّ لِغَيْرِ اللَّهِ$$
$$بِهِ ... فَمَنِ اضْطُرَّ فِي مَخْمَصَةٍ غَيْرَ مُتَجَانِفٍ لِّإِثْمٍ ۙ فَإِنَّ اللَّهَ$$
$$غَفُورٌ رَّحِيمٌ$$

Forbidden to you are: dead animals, blood, the flesh of swine, and that on which Allāh's Name has not been mentioned while slaughtering ... *but as for him who is forced by severe hunger, with no inclination to sin then surely, Allāh is Oft-Forgiving, Most Merciful.* (5:3)

From the Sunnah

1. Abu Hurairah (may Allāh be pleased with him) narrated, that the
Prophet ﷺ said,

$$إِنَّ الدِّينَ يُسْرٌ، وَلَنْ يُشَادَّ الدِّينَ أَحَدٌ إِلاَّ غَلَبَهُ، فَسَدِّدُوا وَقَارِبُوا وَأَبْشِرُوا، وَاسْتَعِينُوا بِالْغَدْوَةِ وَالرَّوْحَةِ وَشَىْءٍ مِنَ الدُّلْجَةِ$$

*Religion is very easy and whoever overburdens himself in
his religion will not be able to continue in that way.* So you
should not be extremists, but try to be near to perfection
and receive the good tidings that you will be rewarded; and
gain strength by worshipping in the mornings, afternoons
and during the last hours of the nights.[13]

2. 'Aishah, may Allāh be pleased with her, narrated,

$$عَنْ عَائِشَةَ، أَنَّ النَّبِيَّ صلى الله عليه وسلم دَخَلَ عَلَيْهَا وَعِنْدَهَا امْرَأَةٌ قَالَ " مَنْ هَذِهِ ". قَالَتْ فُلاَنَةُ. تَذْكُرُ مِنْ صَلاَتِهَا. قَالَ مَهْ، عَلَيْكُمْ بِمَا تُطِيقُونَ، فَوَاللَّهِ لاَ يَمَلُّ اللَّهُ حَتَّى تَمَلُّوا . وَكَانَ أَحَبَّ الدِّينِ إِلَيْهِ مَا دَامَ عَلَيْهِ صَاحِبُهُ.$$

Once the Prophet came while a woman was sitting with
me. He said, "Who is she?" I replied, "She is so and
so," and I told him about *her excessive praying.* He said
disapprovingly, *"Do good deeds which is within your capacity
as Allāh does not get tired of giving rewards but surely you will
get tired and the best deed in the sight of Allāh is that which is
done regularly."*[14]

---

[13] Sahīh Al-Bukhāri, Hadīth #39.

[14] Sahīh Al-Bukhāri, Hadīth #43.

Eight reasons for granting *leeway*, as defined by scholars of fiqh:

1. Traveling (*safar*)
2. Sickness (*marad*)
3. Being forced (*ikrāh*)
4. Forgetfulness (*nisyān*)
5. Lack of knowledge (*jahl*)
6. Extreme difficulty (*kurh*)
7. Tribulation (*balā*)
8. Defect (*Naqs*)

In brief, Allāh, the Almighty, is all-Knowing and knows the challenges that man faces! Therefore, Allāh provides accommodation for His believers. This is a testament to Allāh's profound wisdom. Perhaps when we are too stringent and inflexible in areas where flexibility is possible, humankind feels pushed away and takes the path of abandonment. This is why the Messenger of God advised one of his best young companions, Muadh bin Jabal, may Allāh be pleased with him, when sending him off to lead the Muslim community in Yemen, to be easygoing and lenient. Because humankind benefits from gradualism and not imposition.

The main point regarding this principle is the "six rights of every human being, as explained by our predecessors as 'the necessities of life.'"

1. In some circumstances, where food is scarce, to protect one's life, one may be left no choice but to eat dead meat or other prohibited foods.

2. In many instances, such as with physical disabilities, one may not be able to pray in the way the Prophet generally instructed. Nevertheless, Allāh recognizes these circumstances and still expects Muslims to pray. Muslims are expected to pray as much as they can, even if they cannot perform ablution.

3. Alms giving, fasting, and pilgrimage to Makkah are all attached within the Qur'an "for those who can." Allāh said, "He has chosen you and has not placed upon you in the religion any difficulty" (22:78).

Principle No. 3 اليقين لا يزول بالشك
Al-Yaqeenu Laa Yazoolu bish-shakk
Certainty must never be erased with doubt.

This important basic principle covers most rulings of fiqh. It represents the importance of clarity in Islāmic law. Because Islām is the truth, everything must be made clear and unambiguous. An experience I had in an interfaith panel discussion comes to mind. Our world religions are diverse and followed by many. However, I have observed, when sitting next to respected experts of other faiths, that sometimes the explanation of the basic tenets of their faith seem to be ambiguous and theoretical. Yet when it was time for me to speak about Islām, the explanations were very straightforward, clear, and easy to understand. This is what Islām is all about, and this is what Allāh meant when He referred to the Qur'an as *Al-Bayān* (the clear proof). This principle's objective is to lift difficulty from the mind with a clear emphasis on certainty and the elimination of doubt. In our tradition, we believe that often these doubts are caused through satanic whispering (*waswās*). Common examples of these doubts caused by *waswās* is found in the fields of *tahārah* (purification) and *salah* (prayer). It is known that doubts from *waswās* could become chronic, causing emotional stress for a believer when executing these religious duties. Examples are as follows: "Did I miss raka'ah?" "Am I in wudu?" This principle is based on Islāmic law and sound reasoning to remedy the doubt that was caused by the satanic whispering.

Regarding the law, which is based on what the Prophet ﷺ dictated, in the Book of Ablution in Imam Al-Bukhāri's Sahīh collection, he titles one of the hadīth as "A doubtful person is not *required* to renew his/her ablution until being certain of its expiration".

Here is that hadīth, which is reported by Al-Hākim and narrated by 'Abbād bin Tamim, may Allāh be pleased with him, whose uncle said that a man complained to the Prophet about a person suspected to have invalidated his ablution during prayer. The Prophet ﷺ answered,

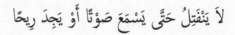

لَا يَنْفَتِلُ حَتَّى يَسْمَعَ صَوْتًا أَوْ يَجِدَ رِيحًا

"He must not suspend his prayer, *until he hears a sound or an odor.*"[15]

Explaining similar hadīth narrated by Abdullah bin Zaid, Imam An-Nawawi states, "All affairs are judged based on its original state until proven with certainty otherwise, the appearance of doubt on it cannot change its original status."[16] Certainty and doubt come in many words in the Arabic language. When analyzing them etymologically, we learn that these Arabic words are used in expressing how certain or doubtful the matter is.

Here are some examples:

1. *Al-Yaqīn* or certainty: 95–100 percent
2. *Az-Zann* or suspicious: 50–75 percent
3. *Ash-Shaqq* or doubt: 15–49 percent

Al-Yaqīn means certainty, to have full clarity on something and the disappearance of doubt, according to al-Jauhari. In other words, certainty is the opposite of doubt. It also means to last or to continue.

Az-Zann means suspicion, wrestling between two possibilities, one having more in its favor, without completely rejecting the possibility of the other, according to al-Hamawi.

Ash-Shaqq means doubt, an equal amount of hesitation between two possibilities. You may eventually have to lean toward one of the possibilities, but it is not based on certainty and is almost like a gamble; gambling is forbidden in Islām.

Principle No. 4 الضرر يزال
Ad-Duararu yuzaal
Harm must be eliminated.

---

[15] Sahīh Al-Bukhāri, Hadīth #176, graded *Sahīh.*

[16] Ibn Hajar Al-Asqalani, *Fat-hul Bāri*, vol. 1, 320.

This is one of the major principles and intersects with many branches in the field of fiqh, such as the goals of sharī'ah; in Arabic, *Maqāsidush-Sharī'ah*. The goals of sharī'ah come in six forms:

1. *Hifzud Dīn*—The Preservation of Religion
2. *Hifzun Nafs*—The Preservation of Life
3. *Hifzul 'Aql*—The Preservation of Intellect
4. *Hifzun Nasl*—The Preservation of Kinship
5. *Hifzul Māl*—The Preservation of Property
6. *Hifzul 'Ird*—The Preservation of Honor

This principle originates from the hadīth of the Prophet ﷺ when he said,

$$لَا ضَرَرَ وَلَا ضِرَارَ$$

"No harm nor reciprocating harm."[17]

The basic understanding of this principle is that in Islām, the main priority is to bring benefit and to avert evil. This principle guides scholars when analyzing whether matters are beneficial or harmful to humans. Therefore, choose the benefit, and always avoid the harm.

Allāh says in the Qur'an, in Surah Al-Baqarah,

$$وَأَحْسِنُوٓاْ إِنَّ اللَّهَ يُحِبُّ الْمُحْسِنِينَ$$

"Do good, for God loves the doers of good" (Qur'an 2:195).

Allāh said in Hadīthul Qudsi, regarding oppression,

$$يَا عِبَادِي! إِنِّي حَرَّمْتُ الظُّلْمَ عَلَى نَفْسِي، وَجَعَلْتُهُ بَيْنَكُمْ$$
$$مُحَرَّمًا، فَلَا تَظَالَمُوا$$

---

[17] Ibn Mājah, Book of Ahkām and An-Nawawi's Forty Hadīth. Graded *hasan* (good).

"O My servants, I have forbidden oppression for Myself and have made it forbidden amongst you, so do not oppress one another."[18]

In brief, elimination of harm is mandatory in Islām, and that should be done first through mutual agreement and peaceful means. If that is not possible, then the case should be raised to the leaders in the community and finally to the authorities. Vigilante justice is not encouraged in Islām.

People must not be made to suffer the oppressions of the oppressors; therefore, elimination of harm is either through peaceful means or legal action.

Here is the take-away message:

1. Harm or evil must not be eliminated with equal harm.
2. Severe harm must be eliminated with lesser harm.
3. When two harms clash, the lesser should be the alternative.
4. Avoidance of harms outweighs the securing of advantages.

From the marital perspective, in order to live in harmony, all kinds of harm between the couple must be eliminated. An abusive partner may lose his or her spouse. However, just as a toe or any severely infected part of the human body is amputated to save the life of the patient, the abusive partner must be amputated from the life of the abused. If a marital relationship is not working and symptoms are obvious, proper diagnosis must be observed and then work toward healing vigorously.

Principle No. 5 العادة محكمة
Al-'Aadatu Muhakkamah
Customs are visited during legislation.

This is a well-known and basic principle enshrined in the Qur'an and Sunnah. People's tradition has influence in observing Islāmic rulings and for its application.

---

[18] Sahīh Muslim, Hadīth #1957.

I will use two different verses that allude to this principle and the importance of custom and tradition:

1. Allāh said,

وَلَهُنَّ مِثْلُ الَّذِي عَلَيْهِنَّ بِالْمَعْرُوفِ

"Wives have rights similar to those which the husbands have, according to what is *recognized* to be fair" (Qur'an 2:228).

2. Allāh also said,

وَعَاشِرُوهُنَّ بِالْمَعْرُوفِ

"Live with them *in accordance with what is* fair and kind" (Qur'an 4:19).

According to Imam Al Qurtubi, the great commentator of the Qur'an, in his classic exegesis defining the word *Al-Maʿaruf, "Al-ʿUrf, Al-Maʿaruf and Al-ʾĀrifah:* Every noble quality accepted by both mind and reasoning."[19]

Maʿaruf comes from *'Urf,* which comes from *'arafa,* which means "known," "recognized," "good," "kindness," and "custom of the society."

Ali Ahmad An-Nadwi, in his thesis, wrote, "Based on the mentioned verses, Allāh guided couples in their intimate relationship and partnership to each deal with the other equitably *according to the norm accepted* by reasoning and mind. There is no doubt that this *differs from one country to another and also different situations and circumstances.*"[20]

Imam Ibn Taimiyyah, the great reformer of the seventh century, was asked, "How do we provide for our wives?" He answered, "It must be from goodness and based on *your tradition.*"[21]

In conclusion, Islām is a religion for all of humankind. Allāh does not forbid diversity, but diversity has its parameters, based on Qur'an and

---

[19] Al-Qurtubi, *Tafsīr Al-Qurtubi,* vol. 7, 346.

[20] Ali Ahmad An Nadwi, *Al-Qawāidul Fiqhiyyah,* 294.

[21] Ibn Taimiyyah, *Al-Fatāwa Al-Kubra,* vol. 3 (1987), 175.

Sunnah. This principle furthers that point by reminding us that we live in the world of diversity. Some parts of our world dress in a certain way, while another dresses in their traditional way. Islām did not come to change that. The code of dress, however, is what Islām dictates. Diversity is what makes our faith and community so great.

> Islām's respect and inclusion of beneficial customs worldwide is unique with regard to diversity. It's this very quality that stamps Islām as the final word of all divine religions.

The Five Pillars of Islām

Pillar No. 1 Ash-Shahādah
The Testification of Faith

The testification of faith is composed of two parts:

1. Testifying in uncompromising monotheism, translated as "There is no deity worthy of worship except Allāh." *Lā ilāha illal Lāh.*
2. Testifying in adherence to the seal of prophets, Prophet Muhammad, peace be with him, and that is translated as "Muhammad is the (Final) Messenger of God." *Muhammadur Rasoolul Lāh.*

Allāh is not confined by these worldly definitions and limits. *Tawhīd*, Islām's very fundamental pillar, is the belief in God's Oneness. This is the heart of Islām. Allāh has many Names and Attributes; they all confirm the reality of His Oneness. He is *the* One, *the* Gracious, and *the* Merciful. This *"the"* further proves the singularity and Oneness of Allāh, who is also referred to as Al-Ahad, which literally means *"the* One."

Muhammad, may peace be with him, is indeed a human and a Messenger. However, to claim that his humanness is similar to ours is blasphemous. We recognize him to be

- *Uswatul-Hasanah*, the best of examples;
- *Ashraful Anbiyā wal Mursalīn*, the noblest of prophets and messengers;

- *Khātamul Anbiyā*, the seal to all prophets; and
- *Rahmatun Lil ʿālamīn*, mercy to the worlds.

Pillar No. 2 As-Salah
The Establishing of Prayer

Salah is the offering of *five* obligatory prayers, with its conditions as prescribed by the Prophet. You would not be able to learn how to pray without looking at the traditional sources of the Prophet. Salah is the application of the Shahādah. Some things that are extremely important in Salah are your state of purification, the time frame, the direction in which you pray, and your *khushoo'*, which is clear focus in your worship. The following is one hadīth, where the Prophet ﷺ explains Salah and how it is performed properly.

قَالَ إِذَا قُمْتَ إِلَى الصَّلَاةِ فَأَسْبِغِ الْوُضُوءَ، ثُمَّ اسْتَقْبِلِ الْقِبْلَةَ فَكَبِّرْ، وَاقْرَأْ بِمَا تَيَسَّرَ مَعَكَ مِنَ الْقُرْآنِ، ثُمَّ ارْكَعْ حَتَّى تَطْمَئِنَّ رَاكِعًا، ثُمَّ ارْفَعْ رَأْسَكَ حَتَّى تَعْتَدِلَ قَائِمًا، ثُمَّ اسْجُدْ حَتَّى تَطْمَئِنَّ، سَاجِدًا ثُمَّ ارْفَعْ حَتَّى تَسْتَوِيَ وَتَطْمَئِنَّ جَالِسًا، ثُمَّ اسْجُدْ حَتَّى تَطْمَئِنَّ سَاجِدًا، ثُمَّ ارْفَعْ حَتَّى تَسْتَوِيَ قَائِمًا، ثُمَّ افْعَلْ ذَلِكَ فِي صَلَاتِكَ كُلِّهَا .

The Prophet ﷺ said as he was teaching one of his companions,

> When you get up for the prayer, perform the ablution properly and then face the Qibla and say Takbir (Allāhu Akbar), and then recite of what you know of the Qur'an, and then bow, and remain in this state till you feel at rest in bowing, and then raise your head and stand straight; and then prostrate till you feel at rest in prostration, and then sit up till you feel at rest while sitting; and then prostrate again till you feel at rest in prostration; and

then get up and stand straight, and do all this in all your prayers.[22]

Pillar No. 3 Az-Zakah
Almsgiving

Az-Zakah is often paired up with Salah in the Holy Qur'an. It was legislated in the second year of Hijra. Linguistically, it comes from the word zakā, which means *purification*. When analyzing it etymologically, you can derive the wisdom that to give is to purify the soul. Zakah is an annual giving that comes from 2.5 percent of one's savings with two conditions:

1. You must be able to afford the *nisāb,* which is the minimum prescribed limit. Scholars calculate nisāb based on the worth of gold and silver. If you were unable to save up that year for the nisāb, *you are exempt from giving zakah.* And if you do choose to give but it's below *nisāb,* it is recommended, but it is in another category known as *sadaqah* (basic charity).
2. This act of worship is to be completed on *annual* basis. And most Muslims prefer to complete their zakah obligation during the month of Ramadān. This is because during the holy month of Ramadān, good deeds are multiplied.

What Assets Can Be Given for Zakah?

1. Bank notes: gold and silver, etc.
2. Livestock: cattle, sheep/goats, camels, etc.
3. Agricultural produce: wheat, barleycorn, dates, grapes, etc.

---

[22] Sahīh Al-Bukhāri, Hadīth #6667.

Who Are the Recipients of Zakah?

According to Surah At-Tauba, Ayah 60,

$$إِنَّمَا الصَّدَقَاتُ لِلْفُقَرَاءِ وَالْمَسَاكِينِ وَالْعَامِلِينَ عَلَيْهَا وَالْمُؤَلَّفَةِ قُلُوبُهُمْ وَفِي الرِّقَابِ وَالْغَارِمِينَ وَفِي سَبِيلِ اللَّهِ وَابْنِ السَّبِيلِ فَرِيضَةً مِّنَ اللَّهِ وَاللَّهُ عَلِيمٌ حَكِيمٌ$$

> Alms are meant only for the poor, the needy, those who
> administer them, those whose hearts need winning over,
> to free slaves and help those in debt, for God's cause, and
> for travelers in need. This is ordained by God; God is all
> knowing and wise. (Qur'an 9:60)

I would like to explain these groups of recipients so that there are no misunderstandings. First, zakah is meant to assist those who are in need. Rich or poor, Allāh knows the circumstances. That is why Allāh targets the poor and needy primarily with the zakah, but He acknowledges even those who collect and then distribute the zakah! Allāh is the most Wise, and His wisdom is to allow the public servants to serve sincerely because they're being compensated for their service. Allāh knows about those who converted to Islām but have lost their families because of their conversion. Instead of isolating them, Allāh commands us to financially support those who have perhaps lost their social standing and homes for the new lifestyle they have chosen. This creates security in their hearts and demonstrates the justice of Islām—a demonstration that our community is a family willing to take care of those who are struggling. During the time of slavery, zakah was even used to help emancipate enslaved persons. Additionally, zakah is where people who are drowning in debt can find financial support to pay what they owe. When Allāh says "for God's cause," Allāh is generally permitting the usage of zakah on those who are not specified above, such as institutions of learning and hospitals, for example. And finally, Allāh knows the trials of travel. Perhaps, a foreigner is stranded in your community. You are allowed to give from zakah to those travelers, with the intention of assisting them to return to their destinations.

It should be emphasized that we are all created equal but not identical. Some have and some do not. Islām accepts the fact that in terms of wealth and material possessions, some of us are rich and others are poor. Those among the community members who have wealth must share and help the have-nots. This will help eradicate animosity and anger and simultaneously bring peace and security to all.

Pillar No. 4 Saum Ramadān
Fasting

Siyām is the establishing of fasting during the month of Ramadān, the ninth month of the Islāmic calendar. Etymologically, *saum* means "abstaining." We learned this for the first time in Surah Maryam regarding our Mother Maryam, the mother of Jesus, peace be with them, when she "fasted" from speaking while walking through her community with the baby Prophet 'Īsa (Jesus), who was miraculously born without the intervention of a man. Allāh informs with us in the Qur'an,

$$ فَكُلِي وَاشْرَبِي وَقَرِّي عَيْنًا ۖ فَإِمَّا تَرَيِنَّ مِنَ الْبَشَرِ أَحَدًا فَقُولِي
إِنِّي نَذَرْتُ لِلرَّحْمَٰنِ صَوْمًا فَلَنْ أُكَلِّمَ الْيَوْمَ إِنسِيًّا $$

"So eat and drink and be contented. And if you see from among humanity anyone, say, 'Indeed, I have vowed to the Most Merciful abstention, so I will not speak today to [any] man'" (Qur'an 19:26).

Islāmically, the context of *siyām* is the prohibition of eating, drinking, and sexual intercourse from dawn to sunset during the month of Ramadān, ranging from twenty-nine to thirty days. Allāh, being the most Wise and Merciful, exempts the sick and traveling from an obligatory fast. Additionally, menstruating women must never fast. However, they must make up the days missed after the fasting month. In scholarly discussion it is also argued that pregnant and breastfeeding women are exempt from fasting as well. The difference in this context is that there is scholarly disagreement on whether they have to make up their fasts. I take the opinion of some of our predecessors, like Ibn 'Abbas, who believed that pregnant and breastfeeding women do not have to make up the fasts that they missed during this period. Instead, what fiqh requires of them is the payment of *fidiya*, which means compensation by feeding the needy for twenty-nine to thirty days. This alternative is also granted to the terminally ill and elderly. It is based on the previously mentioned basic principle of fiqh that states that "difficulty necessitates for ease."

Pillar No. 5 Hajj Al-Bait
The Pilgrimage to Makkah

Hajj is the great pilgrimage to Makkah, perhaps one of the most popular and world-renowned pillars of Islām. We see images of the millions that circumambulate the Ka'abah, the holiest site for Muslims, located in Makkah, Saudi Arabia. This is the universal gathering of believers from all walks of life, meeting at a specific, prescribed time to perform certain specific rites, as prescribed by the Prophet.

The pilgrimage to Makkah is to achieve many goals, among which are the following:

- Spiritual nurturing
- Moral and ethical nurturing
- Material opportunity
- Equality of manhood
- Awareness of the certainty of death

Regardless of status, death is imminent, and all shall be buried with nothing but pieces of white cloth. The only things that matter are our deeds, not our status. Additionally, this pillar is an act of worship that commemorates the sacrifices and life of one of our greatest messengers, Prophet Ibrahim (Abraham), may peace be upon him. His sacrifices, which were the ultimate test of his undying devotion to Allāh 🕮, have given him one of most prestigious titles: the First Imam and the Friend of Allāh. Also, this great expression of worship commemorates the obedience of the son to his father, Isma'īl (Ishmael) to Ibrahim. And Isma'īl was blessed to be the father of the lineage that leads to the Final Prophet, Muhammad, peace be upon them all. Allāh says in the Qur'an, regarding the imamship of Abraham:

$$\text{وَإِذِ ابْتَلَىٰ إِبْرَاهِيمَ رَبُّهُ بِكَلِمَاتٍ فَأَتَمَّهُنَّ ۖ قَالَ إِنِّي جَاعِلُكَ لِلنَّاسِ إِمَامًا ۖ قَالَ وَمِن ذُرِّيَّتِي ۖ قَالَ لَا يَنَالُ عَهْدِي الظَّالِمِينَ}$$

And [mention, O Muhammad], when Abraham was tried by his Lord with commands and he fulfilled them. [Allāh] said, "Indeed, I will make you a leader for the people." [Abraham] said, "And of my descendants?" [Allāh] said, "My covenant does not include the wrongdoers." (Qur'an 2:124)

In brief, Hajj literally means "to intend for something." Islāmically, it means intending to the house of Allāh to perform certain rites at certain places in Makkah, based on certain times.

Three eligibility conditions of Hajj are outlined by our scholarship, based on analyzing a verse in Surah Al-Imran.

$$\text{وَلِلَّهِ عَلَى النَّاسِ حِجُّ الْبَيْتِ مَنِ اسْتَطَاعَ إِلَيْهِ سَبِيلًا ۚ وَمَن كَفَرَ فَإِنَّ اللَّهَ غَنِيٌّ عَنِ الْعَالَمِينَ}$$

"Pilgrimage to the House is a duty owed to God by people who are able to undertake it" (Qur'an 3:97).

Ability here means three things:

1. Good health
2. Provision
3. Security[23]

---

23 Sahīh Fiqh As-Sunnah, vol. 2, 164–165.

According to the majority viewpoint, there are four pillars of Hajj:

1. Ihrām—ceremonial duty to perform Umrah, or Hajj
2. 'Arafah—standing at the plain of 'Arafah
3. Tawāf Al-Ifādah—circling the Ka-'abah
4. Safa and Marwa—walking between Safa and Marwa

Hajj begins on the eighth day of the twelve month of the Islāmic calendar, Dhul Hijjah, and ends on the thirteenth of Dhul Hijjah.

It also is worth noting that women who are menstruating will perform all the rites except tawāf, the circling the Ka-'abah. If they can't wait to perform it after purification because of necessity or travel plans, they then are forced to perform Tawāf Al-Ifādah, which is one of the pillars of Hajj. The other two, however—Al-Qudoom and Al-Wadā'a—are suspended indefinitely. According to Ibn Taimiyyah, no sacrifice is necessary.[24]

> **Summary of the Five Pillars of Islām**
>
> 1. Both testifications—Oneness of Allāh ﷻ and the messengerhood of the Prophet ﷺ
> 2. Five obligatory prayers
> 3. Almsgiving—giving from zakah-able assets, like gold and silver, currency, livestock, or agricultural products
> 4. The holy month of Ramadān—the fasting for 29–30 days
> 5. Hajj: the pilgrimage to Makkah, to perform ritual at specific places

The Six Articles of Faith

1. Belief in Allāh
- He is One, the Creator, the Owner, and Maintainer of all affairs.
- He is the Originator of everything.

---

[24] Summarized from Fat-hul Bāri of Ibn Hajar Al-Asqalāni, in the book of Hajj, vol. 3, Fatāwa An-Nisa of Ibn Taimiyyah, 103–118 and Abu Malik, in his book, *Sahīh Fiqh As-Sunnah*, in the chapter of Hajj, vol. 2.

- He alone deserves to be worshipped.
- He alone is the Giver and Taker.
- He alone is Perfect, and all are His creation and are imperfect.
- None equal Him.
- His Names and Attributes are perfect.

2. **Belief in Allāh's Angels**
   - Angels are innumerable, and some have specific roles.
   - They are sinless creatures with no free will.
   - They belong to the realm known as *Al-Ghaib* (the unseen).
   - They are created from divine light.
   - Jibrīl, also known as Gabriel, was entrusted with the divine revelation, sending it from the heavens to the prophets on earth, may peace be with them all.

3. **Belief in Allāh's Books** (which serve as a guide and light to humankind)
   - Torah to Prophet Musa (Moses)
   - Gospel to Prophet 'Isa (Jesus)
   - Qur'an to Prophet Muhammad, may peace and blessings be upon them all.

Please understand that, although Islām mandates all Muslims to believe in these books, we also are taught in the Qur'an that some of these books have been tampered with.

4. **Belief in Allāh's Messengers**
   - Messengers are all-human and possess no godly characteristics.
   - Messengers are *not* divine, nor do they possess divine characteristics.
   - They were sent with the same message: "Worship none but God; you have no god but Him."
   - They may have different sharī'ah (law), based on time and space. As previously shared from Surah Al-Maidah:
     And We have revealed to you, [O Muhammad], the Book in truth, confirming that which preceded it of the Scripture and as a criterion over it. So judge between them by what Allāh has revealed and do not follow their inclinations away from what has come to you of the truth. *To each of you We prescribed a law and a method.* Had Allāh willed,

He would have made you one nation [united in religion], but [He intended] to test you in what He has given you; so race to [all that is] good. To Allāh is your return all together, and He will [then] inform you concerning that over which you used to differ. (Qur'an 5:48)

- There were many prophets and messengers; Qur'an only mentioned twenty-five of them.
- They were infallible and protected from sin.
- According to the majority of Muslim scholarship, all messengers are prophets, but not all prophets are messengers.
- They are not themselves the message but conveyers of the message.
- Most, if not all, of them suffered persecution at the hands of their people. Some even were killed. Jesus was not one of those killed, but Yahya (John the Baptist) was.
- Five are "men of firm will," or *Olul Azm minar Rusul:* Nuh (Noah), Ibrahim (Abraham), Musa (Moses), 'Īsa (Jesus) and Muhammad, may peace be with them all.
- Adam is the first prophet, and Muhammad is the last and the seal to the lineage of prophets.
- Muslims believe in all the divine prophets and revelations that were given to them by Allāh, as is written in Surah Al-Baqarah:

قُولُوا آمَنَّا بِاللَّهِ وَمَا أُنزِلَ إِلَيْنَا وَمَا أُنزِلَ إِلَى إِبْرَاهِيمَ وَإِسْمَاعِيلَ وَإِسْحَاقَ وَيَعْقُوبَ وَالْأَسْبَاطِ وَمَا أُوتِيَ مُوسَىٰ وَعِيسَىٰ وَمَا أُوتِيَ النَّبِيُّونَ مِن رَّبِّهِمْ لَا نُفَرِّقُ بَيْنَ أَحَدٍ مِّنْهُمْ وَنَحْنُ لَهُ مُسْلِمُونَ

Say, [O believers], "We have believed in Allāh and what has been revealed to us *and what has been revealed to Abraham and Ishmael and Isaac and Jacob and the Descendants and what was given to Moses and Jesus and what was given to the prophets from their Lord. We make no distinction between any of them*, and we are Muslims [in submission] to Him." (Qur'an 2:136)

- None is a `believer if he rejects Moses or Jesus as "the great Messengers of God." Peace and blessings of Allāh be with them.

5. Belief in the Hereafter
- Muslims all believe that this worldly life shall come to an end and that everything will perish except Allāh.
- Everyone will be resurrected and held accountable by God for the life they lived.
  a. All shall be rewarded for their deeds, either with paradise, the reward for the righteous; or hellfire, the abode for the wicked.

6. Belief in the Divine Decree
- God knows everything—past, present, and future.
- All matters are preordained and written in the divine tablet known as *Lauhul Mahfooz.*
- No one is forced to be evil; it is one's own free will.

In conclusion, I cite the beginning of the second chapter of the Qur'an for reflection:

ذَٰلِكَ الْكِتَابُ لَا رَيْبَ ۛ فِيهِ ۛ هُدًى لِّلْمُتَّقِينَ - الَّذِينَ يُؤْمِنُونَ بِالْغَيْبِ وَيُقِيمُونَ
الصَّلَاةَ وَمِمَّا رَزَقْنَاهُمْ يُنفِقُونَ - وَالَّذِينَ يُؤْمِنُونَ بِمَا أُنزِلَ إِلَيْكَ وَمَا أُنزِلَ مِن
قَبْلِكَ وَبِالْآخِرَةِ هُمْ يُوقِنُونَ - أُولَٰئِكَ عَلَىٰ هُدًى مِّن رَّبِّهِمْ ۖ وَأُولَٰئِكَ هُمُ الْمُفْلِحُونَ

This is the Book about which *there is no doubt*, a guidance for those conscious of Allāh—Who *believe in the unseen, establish prayer, and spend out of what We have provided for them,* And *who believe in what has been revealed to you,* [O Muhammad], and *what was revealed before you,* and of *the Hereafter they are certain [in faith].* Those are upon [right] guidance from their Lord, and it is *those who are the successful.* (Qur'an 2:2–5)

Summary of Six Articles of Faith
1. Belief in the Oneness of Allāh
2. Belief in His Angels
3. Belief in His Books
4. Belief in His Messengers
5. Belief in the Hereafter
6. Belief in the Divine Decree

Conclusion of the Islāmic Perspective

Now that we have finished our humble crash course on Islām's main sources, the science of understanding them, and the two basic pillar systems that comprise Islām, I would like to provide you with a takeaway message:

1. Qur'an is the Word of Allāh.
2. Sunnah is His word being applied through the sayings, actions, and approval of the Prophet.
3. Fiqh is the science of understanding the former two.
4. Fiqh, although governed by many principles, has five main principles. They are what scholars use in this very comprehensive Islāmic science.
5. Islām is the clearest faith and also the natural lifestyle that guided the first human being.
6. Islām consists of the five pillars of Islām and the six pillars of īman (faith). The former is about the actions of worship, while the latter is about matters of faith.
7. If someone does not abide by these two pillars systems, that person cannot identity as a Muslim.

May Allāh increase us all in beneficial knowledge and grant us His blessings. Amīn.

CHAPTER 2

An Introduction to Counseling

Counseling is the process of actively listening to another human being who is sharing significant verbal and nonverbal information, feelings, emotions, and beliefs. Counselors also engage with counselees[25] by suggesting methods where the counselee can arrive at his/her own appropriate conclusions and solutions. Counselors assist counselees in comprehending the cause of their problems and guide them in resolving the issues. Counseling, as a practice, is a complex process, one where right or wrong is not always visible, where sacrifices must be made, and where scrutiny may occur.

The word *counseling* comes from the old Latin word *consilium*, which roughly translates to "consultation" or "advice". This root definition is embedded within the modern term, but in a contemporary definition, counseling is associated with professional advice giving. When counseling as a Muslim, it is important to give advice[26] not only from a professional perspective but from an Islāmic perspective as well.

In Islām, counseling must not violate the rules of divine-revealed laws that are enshrined in the Qur'an and Sunnah. Although counseling inherently focuses on bettering a person mentally, Islāmic counseling incorporates

---

[25] In counseling, the words *counselee* and *client* are interchangeable.

[26] In the professional field of counseling, instead of using the word *advice*, professional counselors prefer the term *goal insight*.

the spiritual well-being of an individual as well. Solutions to problems are found in the Qur'an and Sunnah, as well as by the prioritizing of the idea of remaining true to Allāh, the Almighty.

Counseling is a serious concept with many varying aspects. Counselors must be reliable, trustworthy, and have personalities that make others comfortable. Furthermore, they must also be knowledgeable in both counseling methods and in Islām.

It is important to remember that each counselee and each case is unique. No two situations will be identical, and many resolutions will be influenced by the judgment of the counselor. Four subtopics to be discussed in this regard are (1) what is counseling, (2) qualities of a counselor, (3) what to do as a counselor, and (4) what to know as a counselor.

Counseling as a Profession

Counseling is a serious responsibility, and we are required to take ownership of our actions. Proper knowledge of the Islāmic faith is a necessity and a core responsibility with regard to counseling. This refers to attending school or being taught the dīn in a systematic and reputable way. Professional guidance is also necessary in this profession. Counselors must understand clearly the ethics of being a counselor and their perspectives as counselors. Guidance on personal responsibility derives from the Qur'an and Sunnah. Only when they follow the Qur'an and Sunnah to the best of their abilities are they deserving of becoming a counselor in an Islāmic environment.

It is crucial that counselors refrain from performing actions that may put their status in question. As people who advise others, they are held to a standard above others and must do their absolute best to live up to those expectations. Additionally, going to school and getting a formal education is a must for any serious counselor. Knowledge of the field of counseling is just as important as knowledge of Islām with regard to professionally assisting. This formal education, however, should not be segregated from Islām; instead, it should be incorporated and utilized with Islām to better those in need.

Counseling is a *collaborative process* that involves the counselor and the counselee finding a lasting solution to the existing problem. Therefore, a genuine dialogue is necessary. *Genuine dialogue* means that every word or nonverbal act of communication is important and relevant to the matter at hand. Counselors cannot assume that they already know what is needed; they must actively pursue all information in order to make accurate assessments. Counselors must share with the counselees what they feel is needed for counseling to be successful. Counselees need help, and their seeking a counselor means they have admitted there is an issue that needs to be resolved. This is a positive mind-set that can be rewarded with the counselee's getting the benefit.

The only way a counselor can come to a legitimate conclusion and suggest proper solutions is by obtaining all relevant information and predicting consequences for the counselee. The counselor must develop the habit of listening more than talking. The relationship between counselor and counselee is symbiotic; both parties work together to overcome the obstacles in front of them.

Although counseling is a collaborative process, the counselor remains in charge and does not shift his role to others or allow those involved to take over or question the counselee and counselor. This scenario can happen if one of the counselees realizes the counselor's weaknesses. He will try to suppress the other participant and dictate the outcome of the process.

Qualities of a Good Counselor

It is important to establish a safe environment for effective communication. There must be a mutual sense of privacy, and the counselee must be comfortable in the setting. The fewer participants involved in a counseling session, the better the session will turn out. People tend to cooperate in a more meaningful way when they are comfortable. When dealing with matters that are private, it is better to keep it between the people who are involved or people who can help. If people feel threatened or attacked, they tend to refuse sharing vital information and ignore the help they need.

Demonstrating encouragement and modeling positive qualities—caring, honesty, and sensitivity—are essential to the therapeutic process. It is important that the counselor not only demonstrate these values but also encourage the counselees to practice them as well. This will better the counseling process and improve the individual.

Caring

Caring is a vital part of the process. Any stable relationship, whether intimate or professional, requires each party to show a realistic amount of care for the other party and the relationship in general. The counselor must emphasize to the parties that they care for the matter. The counselees must be able to see this and reciprocate a certain level of interest as well. Theodore Roosevelt once said, "People do not care how much you know until they know how much you care."

Honesty

All divine religions agree upon the importance of honesty. Honesty is the promise and practice of telling the truth; it is a justice and is never compromised. Compromising justice results in the dismantling of a relationship. Honesty is the foundation of any relationship, and overcoming an obstacle requires trust from both sides. A counselee needs to trust that the counselor has his or her best interests in mind and must believe in the counseling process. The Prophet was well known as as-Sādiq al-Amin, the honest and the trustworthy; this is the counselor's model.

Sensitivity

Sensitivity must not be ignored. Sensitivity is to have the emotional intelligence to assess a situation and solve it effectively. Although problems are hidden, a sensitive counselor's eagle vision will sense it right away and approach it with precise measure. The issue being presented often is severe, and the emotions of people and their well-being are at risk. A counselor must be sensitive to the issues and try to see what is going on from the counselee's perspective. In doing so, a counselor will better understand the situation, and the counseling process will benefit from the counselor's shifting his paradigm through the eyes of the counselee. Some situations may not make sense, no matter how the counselor views them, but the counselor still needs to be sensitive to whatever the counselee relays. Compassion increases the chance of positive thinking and, consequently, positive behavior. Compassion is the water for the social plant.

According to two of the Messenger of God's students, Anas ibn Mālik and Abu Huraira (may Allāh be pleased with them both), a Muslim Bedouin entered the *masjid* (place of worship for Muslims) and proceeded to urinate in the sacred sanctuary. The companions around the Prophet severely scolded the man, but the Prophet told them, "Do not put a halt to his urinating but instead, leave him." After he was done, he ordered that water be poured over the affected area, as the Prophet told the Bedouin man, "Any kind of urine or filth is not suitable for the masjid. Instead they are only [appropriate] for the remembrance of Allāh, the Prayer, and the recitation of the Qur'an."[27] The Prophet was merciful, but he was also able to properly assess the situation and execute the appropriate method of guidance to effectively benefit the community.

The Prophet was sensitive to the man's unintentionally disrespecting the masjid, an act to which that many of us would react quickly and harshly. By being patient, however, he not only prevented the action from becoming worse but was able to calmly inform and correct the actions of the man in an effective and efficient manner. People do things for many reasons. Counselors need to take their time to learn, in a respectful, meaningful manner, the concerns of the counselees in order to help them. Sensitivity also dictates that we must be mindful of our diversity and avoid inappropriate name-calling or discriminatory words and actions. We must respect all boundaries.

Counselors must remind themselves that while working in the profession, they are both *humans* and *students*. Of course, they may take various other roles in society, but remembering that they are humans and students is critical to helping others.

---

[27] Sahīh Al-Bukhāri, Hadīth #220; Sahīh Muslim, Hadīth #284.

As humans, we must remember the following two innate qualities that define us: Man is weak, and man makes mistakes.

Man Is Weak

Man is weak and needs help. Allāh, in Surah An-Nisā, says,

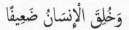

"And man was created weak" (Qur'an 4:28).

Man cannot survive alone. This is why we help one another through divine guidance so that we can live in peace and harmony. We must never forget this.

Man Makes Mistakes

A counselor is not a perfect being and, therefore, mistakes will be made. Owning up to shortcomings and accepting errors is essential. People appreciate others who take responsibility for their mistakes, as opposed to those who insist that they are right when they are wrong or those who make excuses and shift the blame to others. Unfortunately, many today have become great blamers. This is because they refuse to take responsibility for their actions.

As a student of the field of counseling, it is important that learning is continual and persistent. The Prophet ﷺ once said, "Seek knowledge from the day you are born to the day you die." Regardless of your age, credentials, or any other factor that may cause you to believe you know so much, effective counselors are always learning. Counselors must be humble; this trait will cause the counselor to be consciously aware of new information and absorb it. A student of counseling has intellect and reasoning and is willing and eager to increase his knowledge. A student in the field of counseling must have the proper resources, such as reliable textbooks and another educated counselor for critical clinical dialogue and assistance.

Self-improvement is a must in this profession; pretending to know it all is unrealistic. As humans, we are imperfect, but as students, we must strive to be as perfect as we can be. A counselor must never believe he or she has completed learning and can stop taking in information. As an imam who completed his bachelor's degree from an Islāmic university and came to the United States for his master's degree, I continue to learn to this day. I enrolled in Sage University to complete basic counseling courses. I continue to purchase books; I continue to research; and I continue to discuss with my colleagues and other professionals to better serve my community and the community at large. Pretending to know everything is foolish and unrealistic. We achieve positive results in our everyday lives when we learn from other people's experiences. People make mistakes, and we must learn how to avoid those mistakes. People also achieve excellence, and we must learn how to replicate and achieve our own sense of accomplishment. We must do all of this learning and self-improvement while relying on Allāh. An effective therapeutic relationship cannot be isolated from human qualities; keep learning and keep improving.

Some might declare that studying at Western educational institutions is wrong and that only the study at Islāmic institutions is valid. What, however, makes Western educational institutions un-Islāmic? Muslims take beneficial knowledge from all sources. Moreover, many Western sciences are greatly influenced by the accomplishments of Muslim scientists in medieval times. More than half a century ago, Professor Bernard Myers of the City College of New York wrote,

> The intellectual and economic accomplishments of the Moslem (Mohammedan) world reached their height between 800 and 1300, a height which the West was not even to approach until after 1500 ... The Moslem Empire therefore meant more than another new state and a new religion; it created the most advanced form of civilization in the Western world between the ninth and thirteenth centuries and made outstanding scientific, commercial, and administrative achievement. In the realm of ideas, of religious and other areas of tolerance, and in everyday products the Moslems surpassed many of the accomplishments of their Christian contemporaries ...

> Together with the expansion of Europe itself and the rise of the middle class, the impact of *Moslem learning* was among the most important forces in the subsequent growth of Western civilization.[28]

If what we are learning poses no harm, we should not exclude ourselves from it. Muslim or non-Muslim, knowledge is valuable. It is imperative that we open our minds and broaden our horizons by engaging in the sciences.

Recognized credentials are important for counselors to be accepted as reliable, but more important is the mind-set of *tawakkul*, an intrinsic reliance on Allāh. This mentality should humble the counselor. *Tawakkul* is the understanding that while we may have the greatest counseling approaches and the highest success rates in resolving conflicts, all our victories come from Allāh. All the positive results on our records are due to His grace. To conclude this point, I cite a hadīth from Jami' At-Tirmidhi, where Anas bin Mālik (may Allāh be pleased with him) narrated that a man asked the Prophet,

قَالَ رَجُلٌ يَا رَسُولَ اللَّهِ أَعْقِلُهَا وَأَتَوَكَّلُ أَوْ أُطْلِقُهَا وَأَتَوَكَّلُ
قَالَ "اعْقِلْهَا وَتَوَكَّلْ"

"O Messenger of Allāh! Shall I tie it [my camel] and rely (upon Allāh), or leave it [the camel] loose and rely (upon Allāh)?" He said, "Tie it [the camel] and rely (upon Allāh)."[29]

An effective counselor must avoid stereotyping, which is generalizing or oversimplifying a static belief of a person or idea. Avoiding stereotyping is not as easy it may seem. Stereotyping is a form of recognizing patterns, which is an innate, natural skill all animals possess and use in survival. Humans are especially adept at recognizing patterns. Although this skill can aid our intellects, it can be deadly as well.

---

[28] Bernard S. Myers, *Art and Civilization* (1957), 281–297.

[29] Ibn Mājah, Hadīth #2707.

46

Apophenia is the phenomenon of recognizing false patterns. A famous example of this may be where a face seems to appear on the moon, but it's actually just rock formations that, when clearly displayed, resembled nothing of a face. Another example may be when individuals attempt to create shapes out of clouds. These examples may seem harmless, but there are some more extreme scenarios of false patterns.

Although stereotyping is no different from recognizing patterns, certain factors are harmful to both counselor and counselee. Counselors who stereotype may hinder themselves from fully grasping the specific cases they are working on. Their views of the counselees may be obstructed and detrimental to the well-being of the counselees. It is up to counselors to clear their minds of stereotypes and be open to the individuals being assessed.

According to African American intellectual Glenn C. Loury, in his book *The Anatomy of Racial Inequality*, stereotypes are generalizations of a group of people that cannot be easily proven right or wrong due to their general nature. He argues that the problem with stereotyping is that it causes the generalization to be "self-confirming." This means that with such a judgmental mind-set, the individual will experience everything in a way that validates the generalized worldview.[30]

Furthermore, any information given must be analyzed and processed as it is. A counselor must refrain from making negative interpretations of what the counselee is saying. As mentioned, the counselee deserves the benefit of objective and professional treatment.

Additionally, Allāh, in Surah Al-Kahf, powerfully asks a question:

$$\text{قُلْ هَلْ نُنَبِّئُكُم بِالْأَخْسَرِينَ أَعْمَالًا - الَّذِينَ ضَلَّ سَعْيُهُمْ فِي الْحَيَاةِ الدُّنْيَا وَهُمْ يَحْسَبُونَ أَنَّهُمْ يُحْسِنُونَ صُنْعًا}$$

Say, [O Muhammad], "Shall We inform you of the greatest losers as to [their] deeds? [They are] those whose

---

[30] Glen C. Loury, *The Anatomy of Racial Inequality* (2003), 20–21.

---

effort is lost in worldly life, while they think that they are doing well in work." (Qur'an 18:103–104)

The counselor must be a role model in his or her actions and speech. Being honest and sincere in the therapeutic relationship with the counselee will create a favorable environment, where the counselee may talk freely because there is trust. To be an effective leader in any platform, always aim to be a sincere role model. In Islām, our role model is none other than the Prophet. We hail him as our guide and hold him as the ideal man. The counselor is someone who holds power and whose voice matters. The saying "Do as I say, not as I do" is not applicable to counselors. They must practice what they preach and be examples of their words; only then will others be willing to seek their guidance and advice and take what they say seriously. The counselor needs to be a trustworthy leader, and this is no easy task. Trust is the rope that binds together a leader and his people. A trustworthy leader is composed of a strong knot, while a dishonest leader is a rope fraying away. It takes an incredible amount of effort, time, and energy to be trustworthy. The counselor needs to be dedicated to being reliable and someone counselees can look to in their time of need. Relationships need trust; this goes beyond a counselor and counselee. This can be translated to a husband and wife, a parent and child, or a teacher and a student. Wherever there is trust, there is hope. To be an effective leader, a counselor must be a role model. And to be a role model, counselors have to embody good qualities, not just preach them. The Prophet was the best example of a role model. How did the mother of the believers and his beloved wife A'isha (may Allāh be pleased with her) describe him? A living, walking embodiment of the Qur'an.[31] May Allāh send His peace and blessings upon His beloved Prophet.

Positive Features of a Counselor

The counselor's features can make or break a positive counseling relationship. As a counselor, legitimizing and making sure you possess the following positive features is critical:

---

[31] Sahīh Muslim, Hadīth #139.

- Have an identity, which in this context refers to both your professional and personal sides. You must have established credentials, follow the principles you value, and govern your life through them. Your identity should be a priority, and you should refuse to compromise it. Moreover, in order to help others, you must have a strong understanding of who you are. Only when you have a strong knowledge of self can you help others know themselves.

- Be honest and sincere. Without these two vital qualities, counseling is rendered useless. Your counselees will distrust you, and your reliability will be at stake as a result.

- Have a sense of humor or be lighthearted; it allows for smoother counseling. Although the process of counseling is a serious one, there may be times when laughter and smiling will go a long way. It shows optimism and belief that there is hope. If counselees are worried when they enter the session, let them leave hopeful.

- Learn from others, including those who do not share your beliefs as a Muslim. Remember, as a student, there are always different perspectives and new information to explore. Serving humanity and pursuing broad and various sources will improve you, specifically, and society in general. Sheikh Ibn Taimiyah mastered Hebrew, Aramaic, and Greek in order to translate and wrote works on their literature from the Islāmic perspective.[32] Another notable scholar is Imam Al-Ghazali, may Allāh have mercy on them all.

- Take responsibility for your actions and always be willing to improve relations with others, without compromising core values.

- Be mindful of the multicultural setting of society, and be sensitive in dealing with cultural issues. There may be issues or topics that are considered taboo in some cultures, so these should be discussed in a careful and precise way. Being sensitive to other cultures shows respect to and understanding of the counselee and will further establish a strong relationship.

- Avoid overgeneralizations and being judgmental. Avoid creating a scenario where the counselee feels it is "me against you" or that one party is good and another is bad. These thoughts are a plague to the counseling process and to the greater community. It is

---

[32] Ibn Taimiyah, *The Relief from Distress*, trans. Abu Rumaysah (2002), 13.

important to show respect and compassion and to remember first that the counselee is human.

• Avoid perfectionism. Counselors are human and make mistakes. You can atone for your mistakes if you admit them. Counselors are not perfect. Perfection belongs to Allāh alone.

There is a hadīth found in *Sahīh Muslim*, in which Abu Huraira (may Allāh be pleased with him) reported Allāh's Messenger (ﷺ) as saying,

مَنْ نَفَّسَ عَنْ مُؤْمِنٍ كُرْبَةً مِنْ كُرَبِ الدُّنْيَا نَفَّسَ اللَّهُ عَنْهُ كُرْبَةً مِنْ كُرَبِ يَوْمِ الْقِيَامَةِ وَمَنْ يَسَّرَ عَلَى مُعْسِرٍ يَسَّرَ اللَّهُ عَلَيْهِ فِي الدُّنْيَا وَالآخِرَةِ وَمَنْ سَتَرَ مُسْلِمًا سَتَرَهُ اللَّهُ فِي الدُّنْيَا وَالآخِرَةِ

He who alleviates the suffering of a brother out of the sufferings of the world, Allāh would alleviate his suffering from the sufferings of the Day of Resurrection, and he who finds relief for one who is hard-pressed, Allāh would make things easy for him in the Hereafter, and he who conceals (the faults) of a Muslim, Allāh would conceal his faults in the world and in the Hereafter.[33]

What to Do as a Counselor

Precautions before Interview

Two issues must be analyzed that affect most relationships, as well as sometimes, because of their nature, affecting the therapeutic process negatively. These are (1) clear issues versus unclear issues, and (2) new versus unresolved issues.

Incomplete information from the counselees will surely lead to erroneous conclusions. Therefore, it is essential that the counselor be given correct and uncorrupt information, and the only person who could lead that

---

[33] Sahīh Muslim, Hadīth #2699.

discussion is the counselee. The counselee must trust the system and be confident about confidentialities; this, coupled with a safer environment, enables him or her to participate fully.

On most occasions, however, counselees maintain that they are the victims and will share only the information that supports their argument, while not offering that which may be critical in understanding the situation. In order to avoid making serious mistakes, which may arise through incomplete information, a counselor should take a three-part approach. First, ask questions that will obtain as much critical information as possible. Second, investigate the matter, either through witnesses or by hearing the views of the counselee's antagonist. Third, if necessary, consult with a trustworthy team of colleagues.

It is very important not to rush into accepting a person's argument or jump to conclusions, especially when dealing with victims or functionaries. Everyone will portray his or her own story. The counselor's job is to extract the truth and follow personal instinct from there. It is necessary in this profession to be mindful of conclusions. As a counselor, after relying on Allāh, rely on your God-given gift, the intellect, especially with the information that reaches you. Information must always be properly scrutinized. Unclear issues become clearer when you try to ascertain what, why, how, where, and when. There is no shame in asking the same question twice or even more.

Sometimes it takes more questions, phrased differently, to understand the why. Don't be intimidated when people react emotionally to direct and tough questions; it is a normal process. Consulting a chosen clinical team cannot be overemphasized. They come from different backgrounds, and their diversity of thinking along with their expertise, can be essential in helping counselees. Remember what Allāh said:

$$ وَمَا أُوتِيتُم مِّنَ الْعِلْمِ إِلَّا قَلِيلًا $$

"You [humankind] have only been given a little knowledge" (Qur'an 17:85).

51

An incident happened in one of the Islāmic centers I led as imam. I had a very vibrant youth program that the community all loved and appreciated, but young adults are challenged with regard to controlling themselves; it is a difficult time in life. One of the youths in the program made a mistake that caused me to be restless for a week. Because I was stressed, I felt compelled to call my respected friend and scholar, Hajj Bawa, thousands of miles away from my home in Clifton Park, New York, to his home, Kejebi, Volta Region, Ghana. Just as I expected, he provided me with a beautiful solution that not only helped the young offender but also the rest of the group and those involved in the program

He suggested that I speak with the parents of the youth, initially at different times, to clearly explain what had happened and then to allow the parents to contribute to a solution together that would fit everyone. It helped greatly because one of the parents of the young adult, after accepting the truth, agreed that it was unacceptable behavior. The parent then suggested that if he was in a position of authority, he would surely suspend this young person. I found the parent's conclusion reasonable and decided to take the parent's suggestion. I suspended the young adult from the program. It ended very well, with all being appreciative of the system. The youth apologized for his actions, and the parents were appreciative of the decision. Additionally, I, as the imam of the community, was relieved of this great burden. Although the situation was indeed stressful, I found myself very proud of both the youth and his victim for their cooperation in this lasting solution of peace. As a Muslim, I must give thanks to Allāh first, but appreciation also goes to my friend Hajj Bawa, who was a great teammate for an excellent conclusion.

Hajj Bawa is an intellectual who resided for a while in Washington, DC. Hajj Bawa was a businessman who owned a traditional clothing store, known as KOBOS. He returned to his home of Ghana to help in the rebuilding process of the nation's young and fragile economy. After returning to Ghana, he focused on livestock and agricultural produce. Sometimes when we had discussions, he would tease me, claiming to be enjoying fresh, organic coconut. God bless you, Bawa!

Although we are from different intellectual backgrounds and disciplines, this did not hinder our cooperation for the benefit of humanity. Together, with our collective and diverse backgrounds, we were able to produce what one person or specialty could not. Teamwork is indeed a unique tool for an effective result. Finding effective colleagues is not an easy task because of the lack of competence today. If you happen to find such a colleague, count yourself blessed.

Also, such teamwork reminds me of the late doctor Niaz, may Allāh shower him with His mercy. When I became imam at Islāmic Center of the Capital District, he was not only a friend but a companion. When asked by some concerned Muslims to share an Islāmic view regarding organ transplantation, I consulted Dr. Niaz to clearly understand the procedure from the medical point of view. We both produced an effective and intellectual article that many appreciated. We need a team to succeed in our endeavors, and we should never think of ourselves as self-sufficient; someone who can answer all questions. This is the sign of ignorance and academic immaturity.

During the Initial Interview

Creating the Collaborative Mind-set in Your Office

As counselors, it is indeed important to meet all the people involved in the conflict. There may be a time when you choose to meet and work with individuals within the family or relationship. To help understand the problem and its proposed solution, all those involved are given *equal* opportunity to share their versions of the issue, without interruption, fear of retaliation, or humiliation.

They should be guaranteed those three components. After sharing sensitive information, they should not be labeled negatively in any way, especially regarding culturally sensitive matters, in-laws, or intimacy.

Everyone must feel safe and protected in preserving basic human rights and must feel safe from all danger, real or imagined. When vulnerable or injured, people avoid that which will result in their destruction. Everyone wants to survive! As humans, our basic survival system permits us to completely withdraw from those things and actions that threaten our existence or social status. For this reason, someone may give incomplete information in order to survive, which causes continual abuse that may negatively affect everyone. For instance, an abuser may accuse his/her spouse of lack of discipline and moral values and may continue to threaten and demonize that spouse. If this persists, it can escalate. When the abused person is told that his/her parents were undisciplined, his/her children or future children may live under no discipline at all.

During interviews, all those involved should avoid personal questions directed to opponents that demand immediate answers. This leads to a counter-reaction that creates an unhealthy environment of a highly emotional state, where no one is willing to listen.

The counselor must make it known to all that the target is the issues that lead to lack of connectedness, and the goal is to learn and relearn how to connect through meaningful dialogue and understanding.

When the target becomes a person instead of an issue, no one is safe. To open the door of meaningful communication and cooperation, there must be a favorable environment, where all feel safe and respected, although they may be told respectfully that their current actions are not helping the family to connect successfully. Therefore, change is necessary to bring connectedness in the relationship. No one can do this for them; they must do it themselves, or they may later regret it.

Regarding interruption, there may be a time when *clarification* of an issue is warranted to achieve a clear understanding. Even so, interruption should be minimal and should only come from the counselor and not from any of the counselees.

There will be times when, as a counselor, you will need to make some tough ethical decisions regarding a counselee. During these instances, it is important to stay personally grounded and to follow these steps:

- **Identify the problem.** What is the actual problem at hand? The answer to this question may not always be on the surface and may require digging deeper into the matter. Questions and a cooperative search are needed to reach an effective conclusion, based on evidence. Moreover, Islām is a religion of investigation and clear understanding before judgment. That is the proper method for deriving justice. Allāh says,

$$ يَا أَيُّهَا الَّذِينَ آمَنُوا إِن جَاءَكُمْ فَاسِقٌ بِنَبَإٍ فَتَبَيَّنُوا أَن تُصِيبُوا قَوْمًا بِجَهَالَةٍ فَتُصْبِحُوا عَلَىٰ مَا فَعَلْتُمْ نَادِمِينَ $$

"Believers, if a troublemaker brings you news, check it first, in case you wrong others unwittingly and later regret what you have done" (Qur'an 49:6).

For those who understand classical Arabic, Allāh refers to the one who brings unverified information as a fasiq, which is an individual who defies the commandments of Allāh ﷻ. Don't overgeneralize all those who spread false information; the role of the arbitrator is a just one role. The just always hear both sources of information, distinguish between the two, and extract the truth from both arguments using reasoning. Additionally, Imam Al-Bukhāri names a chapter:

$$ الْعِلْمُ قَبْلَ الْقَوْلِ وَالْعَمَلِ $$

"The Book of Knowledge: It is essential to know a thing first before speaking or acting upon it." I think the title explains itself beautifully and can be lesson for all.

- **Pinpoint the source of the problem.** Once the counselor has clearly established what the problem is, it is necessary to investigate the source of the problem. Focusing on the source can help determine what actions need to be taken for the issue to be resolved.
- **Remind the counselees of their rights.** There should transparent communication between the counselor and the counselee. Expectations, rights, and other important matters must be discussed clearly. Having a relationship between the counselor and the counselee means the counselor must serve the counselee

by providing time and attention; and due to the counselor's service, compensation is required.

- **Maintain confidentiality.** This is a concern for every individual; no one wants private and personal information to be shared. As a counselor, your credibility and respect will be tarnished if you allow private matters to become public. Keeping certain information private is the bare minimum of the counselor's duty. Even if you cannot provide a direct solution for the problem, a respect for privacy is established.

There will be times when you, as the counselor, would like to seek advice or share the wisdom derived from a story. When conferencing with colleagues with the sole intention of seeking advice, respect privacy by not sharing names; use pseudonyms when giving details of the case. Keep it as general as possible without transgressing from the code of confidentiality.

To develop a trusting collaborative relationship, counselors must respect and protect the privacy of their counselees. Anonymity is a must. It is an ethical responsibility of the counselor not to reveal or discuss any information regarding his or her counselee except what will help solve his/her problem.

Caution must be taken in discussing your counselee's problems publicly, when addressing social issues that resemble those of your counselees. It requires the following:

- **Anonymity.** This entails prioritizing the privacy of the counselee. Names of counselees should only be revealed under the rarest of circumstances.
- **Avoid indirect publication.** Information may get out in an indirect way. As a counselor, speaking about the case must be done carefully and only in the presence of reliable associates. An effective way to educate the masses while preserving the counselee's privacy is to add/subtract from the counselee's story enough that it takes away the counselee's ownership of the story. That way, the public can learn from the experience without anyone knowing whose experience is being discussed.

- **Move beyond criticism**. Embrace constructive solutions because that is the main purpose of counseling. Criticism and judging are useless and don't have any relation to counseling. Even when discussing how to improve, criticism can be structured in a constructive way.

Counseling is a collaborative process, but during the interview, the counselor must be in charge and not shift his responsibility or allow any of those involved in the crisis to take over and begin asking questions of the others involved or the counselor—this happens all the time. If one of the counselees realizes the counselor's weaknesses, he or she will try to suppress the other counselee and dictate the outcome of the process. Such a counselee knows that the only way to get what he or she wants is by threatening or overpowering the other. This make it impossible for anyone to detect his or her mischievous attitudes and wrong-doings. Clinical psychotherapist Ronald Potter-Efron calls it *deliberate anger*, saying, "Power and control are what people gain from deliberate anger."

Similarly, others may use *shame-based anger*. "People with this anger style get rid of their shame by blaming, criticizing, and ridiculing others. Their anger helps them get revenge against anybody they think shamed them. They avoid their own feelings of inadequacy by shaming others ... [and sometimes] end up attacking the people they love."[34]

Therefore, as a counselor, watch out for these two anger styles:

1. Deliberate anger
2. Shame-based anger

Referral to another imam counselor with the appropriate credentials may be necessary if one believes he is facing someone who may be in charge, positively or negatively; for example, one's teacher or one's leader.

---

[34] Ronald and Patricia Potter-Efron, *Letting Go of Anger* (1995), 9–10.

Lack of Full Participation

There have been instances when a member of a family argues that many issues are hurting the relationship, but the member is unwilling to share or will say, "All that has been said is not true. I know the truth, but I will not share it." This indeed is nonsensical and unreasonable. It's impossible to attain the complete and necessary information without everyone's involvement. The lack of full participation is an unacceptable behavior, and as a counselor, you must never allow such an attitude. Instead, counsel your counselees on a one-to-one basis, but if that does not work, seek the assistance of family who know the counselees well. Don't feel threatened, however, by their involvement. If this circumstance does not work, referral may be necessary.

Anyone involved in the counseling process who knows helpful information must share it. Perhaps with that information, you may reach a lasting solution. Those with helpful information who refuse to share are, in most cases, part of the problem and are indeed dangerous. Unwillingness to share is synonymous to an uncured disease that eventually affects the entire body and may consequently lead to one's demise. Similarly, if an unhealthy relationship is not healed, the once-happy family could very well become a dead one.

Functional and Dysfunctional

There are two types of counselees: functional members and dysfunctional members. The functional members want to cooperate and genuinely solve the problem by engaging with the counselor. Dysfunctional members, however, have trouble cooperating for many reasons. The counselor must be able to assess the level of cooperation among the persons involved. Keep in mind that it is not the counselor's job to castigate the dysfunctional but rather to work wholeheartedly with the healthier counselee to come an understanding as to why the other is not willing to cooperate. When counselees will not cooperate, make your best effort as a counselor to connect with the counselees and to learn the root cause of their lack of cooperation. It that's not possible, referral may be necessary.

In Summary

1. Taking notes is essential in this profession for the purpose of recording the details; these must be kept confidential.

2. The compilation period, when the counselor gets multiple sides of the story, must be on an individual basis.

3. For the assessment period, when the counselor assesses all stories to derive what really happened, the parties need to be interviewed on a mainly collective basis (a "Q&A").

4. Before the interview begins, the counselor must explain the ground rules to all the participants. (Example: There is no tolerance for intimidation, character assassination, or invalidation in the office.) A positive environment can be achieved only by maintaining total protection for all participating counselees. This is maintained through sincere and honest communication to achieve connectedness in the relationship.

The Power of Emotions

I would like to share a story to help visualize the concept of the power of emotions:

It was a Saturday evening. The news program I was watching showed a police chase that brought an armed robber to a halt when he was surrounded. He abandoned the stolen vehicle and ran toward traffic, grabbing at as many car doors as possible, probably trying to hijack another vehicle. Eventually, he managed to open the door of a car driven by a woman, who he dragged out of the vehicle. This woman immediately started to run away, but then, to my surprise, she stopped and quickly ran back to the car. I immediately viewed this woman as foolish and reckless with her life, only to find out later that she ran back to the vehicle to rescue her child in the back seat. It was her human instinct for survival that caused her to run away immediately. Once she remembered her child was in the car, however, regardless of the danger, she returned to save her child. Similarly, due to my intense emotions while watching the scene, I assumed this woman was foolish for returning. Once I realized the full context behind her actions, however, I understood her duty as a mother.

Carl Pacifico, in his book *Think Better, Feel Better*, discusses that the human brain works in moments of intense pressure as follows:

1. The emotional response may be so strong that it ignores the intellectual instructions.
2. The intellectual instructions may modify the emotional response.
3. The intellectual instructions always arrive too late to prevent the start of the emotional motor response.[35]

The human brain is indeed a wondrous instrument. When used well, we all can live and feel better. This is the meaning in the title of Pacifico's book. He argues that anyone who puts in the effort to understand the thinking process will improve his or her quality of thinking significantly. That person will be more successful and will improve his or her social relations with family. Most important, the person will feel better as an individual.[36]

Pacifico divides most emotions into two categories: those that are pleasant (joy, love) and those that are unpleasant (anger, fear). These two emotion types exert a great contextual influence on the counselor with regard to how to approach the counselee, as well as what to avoid. He argues clearly that intense emotions can seriously "impair the processes that control organized behavior." Moreover, he says that "low levels of emotional arousal improve performance at a task, but intense arousal is usually disruptive. The state of heightened arousal that results can take its toll of the individual's ability to function efficiently."

Did you know that your emotional state can manifest through your physical health? Scholars of psychology teach that "psychophysiological disorders (also called psychosomatic illnesses) are physical illnesses in which psychological factors play a major role." Examples of real illnesses that manifest from negative emotional states are asthma, skin rashes, ulcers, high blood pressure, and migraine headaches. In brief, studies prove that your psychological state truly affects your physical health.[37]

---

[35] Carl Pacifico, *Think Better, Feel Better* (1990), 27.

[36] Carl Pacifico, *Think Better, Feel Better* (1990). xiii.

[37] Ernest R. Hilgard, Richard & Rita Atkinson, *Introduction to Psychology* (1975), 345, 357, 359, & 456.

For this reason, an effective counselor must always understand through verbal and nonverbal communication when the environment is right for effective counseling to take place. Moreover, when emotions are high, there will be no existing environment for a productive counseling session. The counseled parties will be unwilling to listen or cooperate with the counselor in finding the lasting solution to their problems. Although these parties likely will change, due to their highly emotional state that causes their reasoning to be suspended, no productive discussion, let alone effective change, will occur.

Why? The whisperer is whispering, and none is willing to listen or cooperate. Satan has used that state of mind to cause injury to many people and many relationships. The prophetic solution to this problem is enshrined in Surah Al-A-'arāf, where Allāh says, "And if an evil suggestion comes to you from Satan, then seek refuge in Allāh. Indeed, He is Hearing and Knowing. Indeed, those who fear Allāh - when an impulse touches them from Satan, they remember [Him] and at once they have insight" (Qur'an 7:200–201).

These verses offer the following two vital messages from God to His creation: (1) to be aware of the trap set by Satan, and (2) human beings must have a willingness in their hearts to be saved through patience and piety. As Allāh reminds us in Surah Fatir:

$$ \text{إِنَّ الشَّيْطَانَ لَكُمْ عَدُوٌّ فَاتَّخِذُوهُ عَدُوًّا ۚ إِنَّمَا يَدْعُو حِزْبَهُ} $$

$$ \text{لِيَكُونُوا مِنْ أَصْحَابِ السَّعِيرِ} $$

"Indeed, Satan is an *enemy* to you; so take him as an *enemy*. He only invites his party to be among the companions of the Blazing Fire" (Qur'an 35:6).

A high emotional state is a conducive environment for accusations, escalations, and invalidations. Perhaps during this time it might be better to first meet with principals individually to calm things down before the actual meeting. If someone realizes that demonstrating these "high emotions" are only temporary and that the emotions could be contained, a great breakthrough could be made. However, without that realization, a postponement of the interview will be the best option. It's important to be cautious about allowing counselees to override your judgment and use your platform for character assassination. The effective counselor must be firm but colored with kindness. The Prophet was *nadheerun* (one who warned the people), but he also was *basheerun* (one who gives glad tidings).

Emotional expressions are innate; humans throughout the world laugh when happy and cry when hurt. In most cases, with a few exceptions, people come to counselors seeking help but at the same time try to influence the process. The most effective way to do this is through crying. The reason is that it is an innate feeling to sympathize with the victim against the victimizer. Therefore, being influenced by one of the counselees because of emotional expressions could hurt the effectiveness of the process. Yes, you could sympathize with the emotional expression of one of the parties, but be mindful not to make assumptions against the other before hearing that side of the story. As a counselor, you may say, "If what I am hearing from you is the truth, you have a point and therefore have a right to grieve. However, we need to also hear from the other to help motivate connectedness." Never promise to advocate for one against the other because that could hurt the process in the long run.

As a counselor, never be influenced by emotional attitude, as some emotions may be deceptive and misleading. The reality is that humans are emotional beings; nevertheless, the human being must have both emotional intelligence and reasoning. When we, as humans, incorporate both aspects of our human nature, we stand the chance of helping others to see realistically the problem that hinders the progress to an effective change and healing.

In brief, the counselor must do the following:

1. Listen carefully.
2. Ask gracefully.
3. Attend and focus fully.
4. Assess completely and accurately. This will help the counselor to produce not only a cooperative environment for meaningful discussions but also an appreciative ending.

A continual highly emotional state is unhealthy to the survival of all relationships and to the survival of the human body. A Harvard Medical School study of 1,623 heart attack survivors concluded that anger brought on by emotional conflicts doubled the risk of subsequent heart attacks.[38]

Avoid, as much as possible, making statements, coming to conclusions, or making promises based on pure emotion, which may cost both *Dīn* and honor. Allāh says in Surah Al-Hujurat:

$$ يَا أَيُّهَا الَّذِينَ آمَنُوا إِن جَاءَكُمْ فَاسِقٌ بِنَبَإٍ فَتَبَيَّنُوا أَن تُصِيبُوا قَوْمًا بِجَهَالَةٍ فَتُصْبِحُوا عَلَىٰ مَا فَعَلْتُمْ نَادِمِينَ $$

> O you who have believed, if there comes to you a
> disobedient one with information, investigate, lest you
> harm a people out of ignorance and become, over what
> you have done, regretful. (Qur'an 49:6)

Here Qur'an emphasizes the scrutiny of information that comes to us, especially that which involves the honor of the other. It is a fact that our physical actions are based on our emotions because of the link between mind and body. When the mind is convinced that it is hurt or someone is hurt, the body reacts, sometimes negatively. Think! Think! And think! Before it is too late. The counselor is not representing one person against the other but representing all and trying to find a lasting solution to the existing problem so that all can improve their lives, and all can feel appreciative and appreciated. A counselor is not an attorney. Nevertheless, great attorneys fight fair and never violate the basic principle of justice. Similarly, a counselor must never compromise his or her role as an unbiased problem-solver. Resist the emotional pressures that come from counseling. Be diligent in the quest for truth and fact, and always remain a professional of reason.

---

[38] Don Colbert, MD, *Deadly Emotions* (1995), 9.

63

In Summary
1. When emotions are high, no one is willing to listen, and productive counseling cannot take place.
2. Be mindful. Do not come to a conclusion until you have all the facts.

The Counselor as a Community Leader

The ummah is the number-one priority of any leader. The counselor is the group leader and must have the group's best interests in mind in every decision. The collective well-being of the ummah is above all else and is not ignored in counseling. If an incident pressures a counselee and the ummah, it is the counselor's obligation to put the ummah before the counselee. The rights of the majority matter. This does not mean that the rights of the individual should be neglected, but the collective benefit is top priority.

As a counselor, protecting a counselee's revelations generally is your primary duty. Even when disclosing information, be discreet, and reveal as little as possible—only that which is necessary. However, there are times when authorities or other important figures must be notified; for instance, when a counselee indicates, either directly or indirectly, that destructive and/ or threatening behavior or action is taking place or will take place. These actions include the following:

- Self-harm. If a counselee is intentionally harming himself or discussing suicide, he needs immediate help. The life of this individual is at stake, and this delicate situation must be approached and handled carefully but directly.
- Harming others. Harming others branches off into two kinds of "harming" and two kinds of "others." Abuse can be both physical and mental, and they are equally serious to one's health. The abuser may be someone within or outside of the victim's family.

  Domestic violence is a difficult topic to manage. Although it is very much a prevalent issue, there is no clear, precise way to resolve it. Domestic violence brings into play culture and environmental upbringing, both of which must be respected when counseling.

However, if a spouse, child, or any other family member is being abused, actions must be taken to prevent the abuse, physical or nonphysical.

If a counselee confesses to a crime involving the harming of a person or makes clear an intent of harming an individual, is the counselor is legally required to notify the proper authorities immediately.

• Harming property. This pertains to the destruction of property such as a spouse's car or someone's office. This horrific behavior must not be encouraged or tolerated. Nothing positive will come of temporarily releasing emotions in an irrational way. The counselor must do what is necessary to prevent and discourage this kind of action.

If a counselee displays self-destructive or environmentally destructive motives ("acting out"), the ethical law of confidentially is suspended, and proper authorities should be informed. These actions may be performed in front of the counselor. An example is a man who beats his wife during the counseling session or a woman who attempts to harm herself. It could be communicated verbally, such as a man confessing he want to harm someone, or it could be alluded to indirectly. If these situations ever occur, the counselor's is required to put the safety of the ummah first. Notify the authorities.

Boundaries

There are boundaries that a counselor must avoid. The gist of it is avoiding multiple relationships with counselees. The phrase "multiple relationships" means adding, either intentionally or unintentionally, another level of relationship between a counselor and a counselee. These relationships could be sexual, platonic, or financial, all of which could potentially benefit the counselor. These personal interests cannot be allowed to interfere with the counseling process. The additional layer of relationship creates a conflict of interest between the counselor and counselee, and the counseling process is put into jeopardy. Loyalty to the process is nullified, and resolutions will be impossible.

Although these multiple relationships may be Islāmically correct, they are professionally and ethically incorrect. They go against the morality of a counselor and the values a counselor must represent. A multiple relationship is having a professional duty with a person while at the same time having another role with the same person or with those very close to the counselee.

- Sexual. Avoid promises of entering into multiple relationships. For example, do not promise a woman, "If your relationship that we are currently counseling ends, I will be there for you." This has become counseling with ulterior motives and is an injustice to the counselee, regardless of the reaction.
- Platonic. Intimacy is not limited to those with sexual interests. When counseling, you may become fond of person, as a friend. This can be detrimental to the counseling process due to the potential of a bias occurring. The counselor may treat the friend in a special way, and that may affect the case tremendously.
- Financial. A financial relationship may occur when a counselor are working with a wealthy counselee. The counselor may be tempted to dismiss his or her values for financial assistance or a bribe and essentially compromise the legitimacy of the counseling session.

Such relationships could undermine effectiveness and future trust. As a counselor, if you are unable to refrain from such multiple relationships because its merit outweighs its defects, honesty and integrity must be applied. You may need to consider referring the counselee to another counselor. Even when you are unable to directly help a counselee, you still can guide them to the right help. That is putting the ummah first, and that is the duty of a counselor.

Referral

Referring a counselee to another counselor is nothing to be ashamed of. It is not a defeat. There will be cases where there is little a counselor can do, or when the effort put in is yielding little to no positive results. Instances where a counselor may need to refer a counselee include the following:

1. When a counselor suspects a counselee has a form of mental illness, it is the counselor's obligation to direct the counselee to a professional doctor. The counselee needs to be assessed, monitored, and treated by someone proficient in the field of mental health.

2. If counselees exert warning signs or obvious symptoms of their health being in jeopardy, then they need proper medical attention that is outside of the field of counseling.

3. If counselors come to the conclusion that their efforts have not made any substantial improvement, it may be time for them to refer their counselees to a colleague. This lack of progress or lack of effectiveness in no way reflects negatively on the counselor's competence; it is simply the understanding that he or she may need another approach or professional opinion. This actually demonstrates a professional maturity because not everyone has the leadership to know when it is time to transfer the responsibility.

4. When justice may be compromised, either through biases or personal interests, then it is time for counselors to admit that they can no longer work with their counselees, and it is in their best interests and the best interest of the ummah for them to see another counselor.

5. A counselor may want to get clarification or reassurance from another counselor. It is helpful to reintroduce the case to another professional in order to get a different perspective to ultimately resolve the issue.

6. Sometimes when we, as counselors, are occupied with other responsibilities and may not be able to give our time and minds to a situation, referral may be an ideal solution, rather than making a serious mistake that may lead to lack of connectedness.

It is the counselor's duty to develop a protective mechanism aimed at reducing potential consequences. The best protective mechanism is self-monitoring. Always maintain clear boundaries and ask yourself, "Am I being honest in my professional relationship with others? Am I doing what I am asking others to do?" Counselors need to prioritize their duties and know exactly what needs to be done.

There are many ways to reassure yourself of your main responsibilities. You can practice a few skills in order to properly assist counselees in solving their problems. These methods include but are not limited to the following:

1. Effectively listen to what is being shared. There is pain and struggle in the voices of the counselees, and they yearn for their counselor's help. Pay close attention to the minute details. You must listen not only with your ears but with your heart and mind as well. Show compassion at all times. If you don't understand, ask questions! It is important to pay attention to nonverbal behavior during interviews, such as facial expressions, tone of voice, and gestures. As authors Derald Wing Sue and David Sue expressed, "What a person says can either be enhanced or negated by his/her nonverbals."[39] Sometimes, asking these questions and provoking thoughts can assist a counselee tremendously.

2. Encourage the involvement of both the mind and the soul in the therapeutic process. Stay focused and be attentive to whatever goes on in front of you.

3. Replace negative thinking with the positive thinking. Denounce the evilness of Satan and remind your counselees that only through the will of Allāh will they overcome their hard times. Be optimistic and hopeful, and they will follow. Avoid being pessimistic.

4. Understand that the process of counseling is gradual. The remedy to issues is tough and complex. It requires time; behavior does not change instantly. Show appreciation when progress is made, and encourage similar behavior from the counselees.

5. Do not shy away from the idea of follow-up sessions. This not only shows your dedication and willingness to improve the issues, but it's also a great way to motivate your counselees to show effort.

6. Create realistic goals cooperatively and link them with follow-up sessions. These goals are what counselees should expect and what they hope to achieve from counseling. Work alongside counselees to create detailed steps on how to achieve the established goal.

7. As a counselor, you sometimes may need to take a step back and reevaluate what is occurring. Encouraging counselees to do the same is an effective strategy. A reality check is beneficial to properly summarize a session and break it down to its core. In doing this, you

---

[39] Derald Wing Sue and David Sue, *Counseling the Cultural Diverse* (1990), 52.

will understand what the problem is and what can be done to prevent/ solve the issue. Ask the counselees these three questions:

What do you want from this relationship?
What is the expectation of the relationship, and what do they want to achieve as a couple? How does their current relationship compare to their image of an ideal relationship?

Does this make sense to you?
Is this something you want to work out? Is it worth it to you? If not, could you envision it ever being something you want?

How can you want positive when you put in negative?
What are you doing to aid, prevent, or assist?

As counselors, what do we do when counselees need serious psychological or psychiatric attention? Do we prescribe medications, or do we provide behavior modifications strategies?

Remember: Counselors are not doctors. We give advice, and sometimes that advice may include seeing doctors to seek certain help. Counselors are not certified to treat physical or psychiatric issues that may require pharmaceutical drugs or medicine. So what do we do? We provide suggestions for behavior modification strategies. It is not up to us; the counselees have to change. Their thinking, if optimistic, will replace a negative situation.

What to Know as a Counselor

External conditions cannot be isolated in this profession as they contribute to the larger context of our thinking and behavior, positively or negatively. Therefore, positive counseling cannot be achieved in a vacuum. We must understand and recognize the influences of the five external conditions that affect humans: (1) social influences, (2) political beliefs, (3) environmental background, (4) cultural upbringing, and (5) biological makeup.

Social influences. This factor relates to the society the counselee comes from. Understanding social influences when attempting to understand the counselees' struggle and while trying to advise them is a necessity. Recognize what is acceptable in their society and what is taboo. From an Islāmic point of view, Allāh instructed Prophet Yunus (Jonah) to go back to his people to show them the truth after he abandoned them. Involving oneself with one's society and community is important. Moreover, it is an act of jihad. Islām is all about interactions with one's community and society. This is something substantiated by the *fiqhi* principle known as العادة محكمة ("Customs (cultural context) are considered during legislation"). There are both positive and negative aspects of culture. As a counselor, help highlight the positive while getting rid of the negative to prevent harm of the self, the other, and the larger community.

Political beliefs. While social influences address how a counselee interacts with other humans, the political beliefs of a person pertain to how a counselee interacts with the government and government-related organizations. More specifically, this is how a person views certain topics in society. In some parts of the world, due to injustices perpetrated by politicians or law enforcement agencies, people simply accept bribery as common practice. As a result of the corruption in some legal systems, victims may refrain from reporting incidents, such as domestic abuse. Furthermore, some may not trust certain forms of counseling and may consider suggestions from a counselor to be ludicrous. An example is a person who grew up in an impoverished area and thus has negative views of the police and does not entirely trust them. When dealing with a case where the boundary of the law is being pushed, prematurely involving the police potentially could harm the case. A counselor must consider the political belief of a counselee when devising a plan for a counselee.

Environmental background. The environment an individual comes from entails both the social influences and political beliefs of a person. It is a larger, broader aspect of society and creates a grand mixture of various influences that affect a person. Environment also includes habitat, which is the hometown of a counselee. A person coming from West Africa may require different strategies when counseling than a person from Subcontinental Asia. Different environments, no matter where on earth, cause counselees to act and react differently, and this must be taken into account.

Cultural Upbringing. Cultural upbringing is the notion that culture varies in size. The environment a person comes from can be classified as a culture, but a culture of an individual could also be his private life at home. These influences may have the strongest impact on individuals, considering it defines how they were raised. This is the nurture aspect of the famous psychological debate of "nature versus nurture." Many of a person's behavioral aspects or intellectual perspectives can be traced back to cultural upbringing.

Biological makeup. The "nature" side of the "nature versus nurture" debate is found in the biological makeup of a person—his or her genetic makeup, the hereditary factors, and anything involving the person's health. The health of a person is also broken down to physical health (conditions that may affect counseling, such as difficulty hearing) and mental health (conditions that may affect counseling, such as ADHD). Attention deficit/hyperactivity disorder is a collection of traits the reflect a person's inborn neurologically based temperament.[40]

Family Networks and Their Influence on Marriage

The counselor should pay heed to the influence of family. To help achieve family peace and functionality, the counselor must understand about *family systems*.

There has been a change in family dynamics in most cultures around the world. The two main family types are the extended family and the nuclear family. In an extended family, grandparents, parents, uncles, aunts, cousins, siblings, and others (including community members) are involved in the nurturing of the family. When a child's parents are at work, grandparents, uncles, aunts, and the rest of the family are involved in the child's upbringing. A nuclear family is a more modern family concept. The family consists of simply the parents and their children. We live in an

---

[40] William Sears and Lynda Thompson, *The ADD Book* (1998), 3.

environment where it is forbidden for the village to raise the child. This prohibition is due to the twenty-first century's popularizing the nuclear family framework.

In analyzing the extended family network, we see a range of advantages and benefits. For example, there seems to be better health, happier attitudes, and great family stability. The virtue of the extended family network is its multigenerational household. The couple does not have to depend so heavily on each other alone for emotional, social, disciplinary, and even financial needs. Their children are exposed to a diversity of adult behavior and not just the behavior of their parents. Another virtue is that the elders of the family are not left alone; they can be taken care of by the children, as well as the children being exposed to the wisdom of their elders.[41] Extended family surely is a supportive system, where every member of the family, male or female, young and old, contributes to the totality of the family, a strong unit that is impenetrable. However, the extended family is *not* ideal for all situations because in every family is an Abu Lahab.

Abu Lahab was the Prophet's uncle, who, when informed of the birth of the Prophet, freed the slave that shared with him this glad tiding of the birth of his nephew. However, he became one of the most aggressive and arguably the worst enemy of Muhammad's message and died as a staunch enemy of Islām. His blood relations and his ties with the Prophet did not stop him from attacking his nephew, along with his message. He was so infamous with his ruthless behavior that even Allāh wrote him down in history with a chapter dedicated to cursing him. Allāh says,

$$\text{تَبَّتْ يَدَا أَبِي لَهَبٍ وَتَبَّ - مَا أَغْنَىٰ عَنْهُ مَالُهُ وَمَا كَسَبَ - سَيَصْلَىٰ نَارًا ذَاتَ لَهَبٍ - وَامْرَأَتُهُ حَمَّالَةَ الْحَطَبِ - فِي جِيدِهَا حَبْلٌ مِّن مَّسَدٍ.}$$

May the hands of Abu Lahab be ruined, and ruined is he.
His wealth will not avail him or that which he gained. He
will [enter to] burn in a Fire of [blazing] flame. And his

---

41 Ronald. C. Federico, *Sociology* (1979), 376.

wife [as well] - the carrier of firewood. Around her neck is a rope of [twisted] fiber. (Qur'an 111:1–5)

Some siblings, uncles, and cousins could be as ugly as Abu Lahab. How many times do we see a person prejudged and sentenced to life in prison without the possibility of parole, based on circumstantial evidence juried by his own family. Why? Mainly because of envy and self-centeredness. For this reason, when dealing with the extended family system, although it is a support unit, you must understand that such a system may be misleading, or it may be unhelpful and unhealthy in terms of helping to solve certain problems.

Qābil, the murderer, was the brother of his victim, Hābil. Envy was the motive for killing his brother. I am not suggesting that all families are like that, but as a counselor, when dealing with extended family, it's wise to be cautious and mindful that things could be complicated, especially with the dysfunctional members, because a lot of people may be involved. Moreover, the solution may not be in the hands of the couple but with the leader of the family, such as a grandfather or an elderly uncle. It's difficult to deal with such circumstances because the grandfather or the uncle may control everything and won't like being castigated by his own family. They may be forced to adopt or accept a position that they are not comfortable with, but they abide by it for the sake of protecting the larger family. In this family system, the goal is not the individual interest but the larger collective family; therefore, they believe that one must sacrifice the individual mind-set for a collective happiness.

Communication must be the key in helping the family cope with its marital problems. This is a very dangerous edge of a cliff to be on because of triangulation. Involving elders may not be helpful, except in a very few occasions. Complaining every time to elders means, on most occasions, every member of that family knows what goes on in the other's apartment within the family. Unfortunately, sometimes even the children know every detail of others' problems, which is transmitted to them, knowingly or unknowingly, through the adults of the family, mostly their own parents. It is one of the reasons why, on most occasions, it becomes so complicated and sometimes impossible to resolve an issue in which uncles and cousins are involved. It is said, "When the conversation seems to be irrational and beyond understanding, there are always more than two people involved." Therefore, we must do whatever we can to minimize complicating the issue by reducing the number of people involved. Don't underestimate the positive effect of the extended family, but realize that many within an extended family may not be helpful. Be mindful of who knows what. In dealing with couples in this family system, the counselor must ask:

1. Who among the family members knows about the problem?
2. How much information is known?
3. What was done previously to solve the problem?
4. When did that happen?
5. Where did it happen?

If nobody knows about the issue in an extended family, the problem may be solved with less pain and less hostility—the less family involvement, the fewer contaminations. However, it depends on the level of development of that extended family network. In a healthy extended family, the leadership is responsible and works hard to limit the escalations and the spread of the problem. In an unhealthy dysfunctional family, everybody knows everything. Accusation and escalation dominates this camp. Those who live under this intense and unhealthy situation should limit the spread of the immediate family's information, and seek help outwardly because at home there is only chaos. There are responsible and disciplined extended families, and those who live in them should count themselves blessed. With a strong extended family comes a strong defense mechanism against outside intruders.

In a nuclear family, which in most cases involves only parents and their children, all are vulnerable to internal and external influences. This is especially true if the couple is of the working class. The pressure and the stress of the working environment, coupled with the pressure at home, may be too much for the family to handle alone. However, things may seem to be much easier to a certain degree when counseling the nuclear family unit because it involves fewer people. The fewer the people, the less the escalation. However, sometimes the protection guaranteed for an extended family may be missing for the nuclear family in terms of early involvement of family support. Fewer does not necessarily mean better; things could be very intense in such an environment. It is therefore necessary that all the members are involved:

1. Avoid isolationism; it is a killer.
2. Shop around for a support unit in the community so that you are not depressed or harmed, but be careful not to be trapped by the toxins.
3. Communicate wisely when sharing the problems with others. Be mindful not to overshare. Oversharing means showing too much emotion and less reasoning.

Scare tactics are a deceptive strategy used by some members of the nuclear family, where the weaker is threatened with severe consequences if he or she reveals information about the family. Therefore, the person remains oppressed out of fear of retaliation. This is rampant in mostly immigrant families due to their loneliness in their new country. In this situation, all support systems have been disconnected on false pretenses by demonizing every institution in society and glamorizing isolationism.

Many immigrant families have been destroyed and continue to be destroyed because of isolation. The reason for the imminent disaster is that the new couple is accustomed to the extended family network, but due to their relocation, they have no family available to provide support. In many cases this contributes to depression and the deterioration of relationships. Sometimes when they seek help, it is poorly handled due to the language barrier.

Parents and guardians who give their daughters into marriage must understand their continued responsibilities. Children are entrusted to their parents, and it is the parents' duty to continue to protect them, even though they are married in a foreign land. They are not commodities to be sold; these are priceless children and grandchildren who need continual protection. They should be treated with respect and kindness. Some may understand, but others may not, not because of extreme poverty but because of extreme ignorance. In some third-world countries, when someone from the United States or Europe proposes to marry their daughters, the family cannot resist the temptation of the "mighty dollar." No questions are asked; there is a total surrendering to a stranger, who may be a danger to the welfare of the innocent child. In most cases these innocent girls have lovers locally, but the power of the dollar and the euro outweighs the power of love. This is because materialism has dominated the lives of many guardians who were supposed to protect their children. Instead, they complied with the societal crime known as the commercialization of the innocent daughter.

I may be speaking in general terms, but I don't believe in overgeneralization. Some people are great parents, but I want to address a serious and common problem that has engulfed most Muslim communities. And Allāh knows best.

A solution to this serious problem that has occupied the minds of leaders and concerned parents is this:

1. As parents, we must first put our intrinsic trust and reliance in Allāh.
2. We must inquire from authentic sources who this future spouse is. It is very important to do our homework.
3. We must venture out and find a support system overseas for our child if she chooses to relocate.

Avoid being the cause of your daughter's hopelessness. Here is a case study: A girl came to me, informing me that after rejecting her parents' proposal for marriage, she was forced into it anyway—she faced the ultimatum of marriage or being cursed. Obviously, this is completely antithetical to Islāmic values, but this is the culture of many. She was left to choose marriage to please her parents, despite already having a man in mind since high school. However, her husband, who was a drug dealer, was eventually caught and sentenced to years in prison, while the man she was previously loved was blessed later with high status and financial independence through a good work ethic. This is a classic story of families that only understand the language of currency and are willing to get it at the expense of their own honor. As Shakespeare said, "All that glitters is not gold."

Goal

The well-being of the individual and the family must be a priority. That could be achieved through meaningful cooperation and communication, accepting responsibility, and a willingness to change

When parties involved are willing to communicate meaningfully and share important information without accusations, there is the chance that all will be appreciative. As humans we are bound to make mistakes, directly and indirectly, intentionally and unintentionally. However, as the Prophet mentioned, "The best among us are those when they make mistakes ask for forgiveness."[42] It is therefore better to accept responsibility by acknowledging our mistakes and working toward asking those we have harmed to forgive us. People tend to forgive those who accept responsibility over those who are buried in ignorance and arrogance. There is a lesson in humility. When a person is open to new ideas and able to learn from others, he or she flourishes in life.

Willingness to change is the fruit of effective knowledge, but change is always difficult and requires a lot of patience and sacrifice. How can we change without the proper knowledge? At the beginning, it may seem impossible and even hopeless, especially, when some friends and family members try to criticize and belittle our change in behavior. Change begins as a blueprint; then the construction begins and later becomes a reality—a building. It is also important to mention that it is never too late, and we are never too old to begin. This is because to learn and to change is indeed a lifelong process. As Sheikh Ibn Taimiyah said, "What matters is not the flawed beginning but a good ending."

I would like to categorize people into three groups:

1. Those who not only believe in change but will sacrifice for it (the reformers). This group contains few people.
2. Those who rebel against change because they are the beneficiaries of its lack (the greedy). This group is interested in maintaining the status quo.

---

[42] At-Tirmidhi, Hadīth #2499.

3. Those who believe change is necessary but are scared to follow up with action (the cowards). This group contains most of humanity.

Unconditional change must be a priority for those who wish for a better future. We must be convinced that our lives will be better with change. We therefore believe in changing, not to please others but for the betterment of ourselves.

Here are some reasons why people avoid change:

1. State of denial (the people who say, "I don't have a problem")
2. Shifting responsibilities (the great blamers)
3. Inconsistency (the lack of a plan)
4. Isolationism (the people who say, "Leave me alone")
5. Conditional (the people who say, "If you change, *then* I will change")
6. Antiposition (always desire to be the opposition)

Change could be achieved with the following:

1. Keep it simple. (Be clear and easy to understand.)
2. Take one step at a time. (The prophetic tradition is gradualism.)
3. Be patient. (Change doesn't happen overnight.)
4. Be consistent. (Don't shirk from responsibility.)
5. Evaluate improvement. (Follow up.)
6. Have a reality check. (Have accountability.)
7. Have a protective unit or network. (Use the buddy system.)
8. Congratulate yourself for improvement. (Reward yourself.)
9. Rely on Allāh. ("Worry about the effort, not the result.")

Toxicity

The Prophet once said, "A man follows the religion of his friend; so each one should consider whom he makes his friend."[43] In life, we have good and bad influences. In the counseling world, when counselors analyze

---

[43] Sunan Abi Dawūd, Hadīth #4833, graded *hasan*.

problems, there are two kinds of people: (1) the positive and beneficial, and (2) the toxic and problematic.

Lillian Glass, one of America's top interpersonal communication and body language experts, defines a toxic person as "anyone who has poisoned your life, who is not supportive, who is not happy to see you grow, to see you succeed, who does not wish you well. He or she sabotages your efforts to lead a happy and productive life."[44]

Toxic Issues

Based on the above definition by Glass, any issue that affects one's life negatively—be it power, prestige, or profit—is poisonous and must be rooted out or else the consequences will be enormous and its result cataclysmic.

Money could be toxic, when the goal becomes accumulation of wealth, regardless of its source. Many people, in their quest for wealth, indulge in questionable business practices. They cheat, they harm, and they destroy anything that stands in their way of making a dirty profit. Their religion is money at the expense of their honor and other people's lives. They may be Muslims by noun but are materialists by verb. Greed dominates such lives, and they care not how many lives they destroy to achieve a worldly profit. It is all about the "I-ness," and all others must be sacrificed to please them. Such lives are heading toward failure and destruction. Ours is not abandoning the pleasures of this life[45] but in enjoying *halālicly*, with moderation and avoiding harm to others to please the self.

Sexual desire is toxic. *Halāl* (lawful) sexual desire is a reality, but when people try to satisfy themselves through illegal sexual means—through cheating, coercion, or other kinds of perversion—the desire is tainted by toxicity. Those who have programmed their minds to believe that a naked woman is better than a protected wife are bound to fail tremendously. Those who believe that pornography is the way to go are harming and

---

[44] Lillian Glass, *Toxic People* (1995), 12.

[45] Surah 7:32.

weakening themselves. It is a commonly known fact that satisfying one's sexual desire through deviant and perverted means weakens one's sexual performance with his spouse. In brief, one's means to achieve perhaps a short-term satisfaction will lead to a long-term loss.

Toxic Partners

Humankind is gregarious in nature, and we surround ourselves with people we view as friends and helpers to lead us toward a prosperous lifestyle. We surround ourselves with those who care for our interests and defend our rights in times of need. However, there are times when people that we regard as helpers lead a double life with regard to how they view us. Their outer look is in favor, but their inner being is the opposite. And who has the right to judge? The only criterion is judging according to what people say or do. However, relying on the apparent realities could be misleading. Yes, they will show you all the care that you need, and they will advise you, but it's with deception and treachery. They may try to misguide you. Your downfall is their goal. They wish you would fail. They wish you would lose. You never could win with them as advisers, and they never will give you an opportunity to know their sinister intentions because they do not want to be exposed.

Families could be toxic to a relationship. There are many family members who could help their unhealthier other and have the means to do so but will not. These include the following:

- Parents who are overly involved in the lives and are controlling of their adult children.
- Children who are rarely involved in the lives of their aging parents (Negligent children who do not repay their parents for nurturing them)
- Siblings who believe in their divine right and that they are entitled
- Uncles and cousins who are extremely envious (causing extended family rivalry)
- Untrustworthy friends in sheep's clothing who inwardly are ravenous wolves

Toxic Attitude

Attitude is so important in our relationship with others, especially during conflicts. Being too serious could mean it's too dangerous. However, having a calm and respectful demeanor could create a favorable environment so that even the dysfunctional person may be willing to cooperate in the process. Watch your attitude toward others; people will always judge you according to your approach to issues and how you handle problems. We should show the attitude of an even-tempered person who is quick to forgive. That will help us all in the long run. Moreover, this is the tradition of the Prophet. He increased his forbearance in the face of ignorance, yet he was a man who was disciplined.

It is not the counselor's job to generalize and label all family and friends as toxic. With my more than a decade of experience in counseling, I use my reasoning and prayers to understand and to detect who or what is helpful and not harmful. Do not hurt any member of the family. Even in dealing with toxic people, never compromise your patience and justice. Toxic people are most certainly not our teachers.

Toxic Environment

Not all environments are safe; likewise, not all times are good for effective counseling. Examples of a toxic environment include an environment where individual rights are abused, where prejudices and discrimination are the norm, and where privacy is not practiced. Such places are to be abandoned immediately and completely because they will add more poison to the existing poison. Discrimination is wrong and all abuse should not be tolerated, especially within circles of counselors. Injustice anywhere is indeed injustice everywhere. When there is an evidence that counseling will not lead to establishing justice and kindness, avoiding such an environment may be the smartest move. Just the same, keep looking, keep trying, and remain open to learning; the best time and place shall soon come.

Toxic Counselors

To counsel is to listen and advise sincerely for a positive change. However, there are those who may have the knowledge and the skills to conduct effective counseling but choose not to do so. Why? Because of personal interests and the abuse of power. They have a bad reputation and ugly attitude; they spread the disease of corruption and immorality through every level of our community. They disguise themselves as saviors, but they are the most dangerous predators. They will only add fire to the existing blaze. Toxicity is not just actions but a mentality. A counselor with a toxic mentality is harmful to those he serves and would be unwilling to take accountability for the catastrophes he causes. Therefore, my humble advice is the same advice as that of author John C. Maxwell: "People do not care about how much you know until they know how much you care."[46] Give people some of your time, and many of them will be appreciative; likewise, be sincere during your care. Sincerity brings trust, and trust wins the hearts of the counselees.

A question of ethics regarding counseling is: Are they good or bad people? The answer is to always assume the best of counselees. There is good present in every man and woman. When counseling, remember that behavior does not define a person. As counselors, we must separate the action and the person. It is okay to disapprove of a behavior, but it is unacceptable to disapprove of an individual. The target, when counseling, is the negative behavior. People change; some great people have ugly pasts. As counselors, our job is to encourage our counselees toward progress. When we attack our counselees for their mistakes, we further push them away from the main goal of guidance.

Stress is behind many issues in relationships. The root causes of stress are typically economic issues, cultural dilemmas, and personal problems. As counselors, it is our job to find the cause of the stress and help alleviate it in our counselees. We may not be able to actually root out all the causes of the stress, but we must do whatever we can with the tools that we have to minimize the negative effects.

---

[46] John C. Maxwell, *The 21 Irrefutable Laws of Leadership* (1998), 122.

Examples of stress with regard to economic issues are struggling financially to survive or enjoy lives; unemployment; or constantly being burdened by others (usually in the extended family) to help support them financially. Examples of cultural dilemmas, on the other hand, include culturally based expectations from one's spouse; the clash of two cultures in a mixed marriage; and the role in-laws play in a marriage. Examples of personal problems includes the death of a loved one; parental responsibilities; and extended family conditions. These examples are huge root causes to stress and can even ruin a marriage, if not addressed.

Expectations can sometimes bring serious problems to the relationship. Go easy with the expectations and understand that we are all human. There are expectations in all relationships, including marriage. The husband is expected to fulfill certain conditions, such as taking care of the family, providing, and protecting the family from any danger. The wife is expected to fulfill certain conditions, such as taking care of the home. If either one neglects the responsibilities and what is expected, stress begins to build up. Therefore, as counselors we need to understand the expectations of our counselees and help mediate things to the best of our ability. Part of our job as counselors is to convince our counselees to learn the art of negotiation through compromise. Know what to compromise and which values that are non-negotiable. One of the world's best negotiators of his time, Herb Cohen, wrote, "To get to the Promised Land you have to negotiate your way through the wilderness."[47]

---

[47] Herb Cohen, *You Can Negotiate Anything* (1980), 15.

CHAPTER 3

Counseling from an Islāmic Perspective

Nasīhah

Etymologically, *nasīhah* is "purity" and "genuineness." Islāmically, it is an act of "sincere advice" or earnest counseling. The root with its above form *Nasaha-Yansahu-Nasīhah*.

Prophet Hud (peace be upon him) said to his people,

أُبَلِّغُكُمْ رِسَالَاتِ رَبِّي وَأَنَا لَكُمْ نَاصِحٌ أَمِينٌ

"I am a Messenger from the Lord of the universe conveying unto you the messages of my Lord, and I am your sincere and honest adviser" (Qur'an 7:68).

Our predecessors define the word as being compassionate, loving, and caring to all Muslims and striving for that which brings good to them and working to avoid harm against them.[48] *Nasīhah*, therefore, is a comprehensive word of being truthful and honest with words.

---

[48] Ibn Hajar Al-Asqalāni, *Fat-hul Bāri*, The Book of Īmān #42, vol. 1, 187–188.

Counseling is *An-Nasīhah* (sincere advice). Counseling is Ar-Rahmah, showing compassion. Likewise, counseling is Al-'Adl, being just. Counseling is *Al-Birr* (an act of goodness). Here are key words, defined etymologically and Islāmically, that comprehensively explain counseling from the Islāmic perspective.

Birr

Imam Ar Rāghib, compiler of one of the oldest Arabic dictionaries, defined *birr* as *At-Tawassu' fee fielil khair*, extensive in the act of goodness; acting well toward all.[49]

The root with its above form *barra-yabirru*.

Allāh said,

$$وَتَعَاوَنُوا عَلَى الْبِرِّ وَالتَّقْوَىٰ ۖ وَلَا تَعَاوَنُوا عَلَى الْإِثْمِ وَالْعُدْوَانِ ۚ وَاتَّقُوا اللَّهَ ۖ إِنَّ اللَّهَ شَدِيدُ الْعِقَابِ$$

"Help one another in goodness and in piety. Do not help one another in sin and transgression. Fear God! He is severe in punishment" (Qur'an 5:2).

Rahmah

Rahmah (root word: rahima, yarhamu, rahmah), when defined, means to show mercy or goodness.

Allāh is Ar Rahmān Ar Raheem, which shows His continuous giving of mercy to the righteous and unrighteous; to the young and the old, and to all His creation, regardless. His forgiveness, however, is only to those who seek it.

---

[49] Ar Rāghib Al Isfahāni, *Mufradātul Alfāzzil Qur'an*, 19.

وَمَا أَرْسَلْنَاكَ إِلَّا رَحْمَةً لِّلْعَالَمِينَ

"We have not sent you but as a Mercy to Humanity" (Qur'an 21:107).

Therefore, the "why-ness" of Islām is to bring mercy to every home, regardless. And the methodology of spreading Islām cannot be isolated from soft-heartedness and compassion. Harsh-heartedness, on the other hand, is not only abhorred but detested, even by animals. Mercy and kindness are the unique characteristics of a sincere believer.

Abu Hurairah (may Allāh be pleased with him) narrated that he heard the Prophet saying, "Allāh created one-hundred mercies. He kept with Him ninety-nine mercies and released one to the world; and that mercy alone encompasses the entire creation including a horse that raises it hooves for the fear of hurting its baby." And in another version, it added in the hereafter that Allāh, with *all* the one hundred parts of mercy, shall judge His creation.

Ibn Hajar Al-Asqalani (may Allāh have mercy on him) wrote, "This Hadīth has different versions but they all convey the same message, His mercy is unimaginable to all His creations." In Imam Muslim's version, the Prophet concluded, "Had a disbeliever known what is with Allāh of His mercy, he will still be optimistic of entering paradise."[50]

There will be no order without mercy, and surely the world would not exist without it. A merciless heart is a dangerous one. Treat others compassionately, and you will receive in return more appreciation from the recipients of your generosity and—most important—from the most Generous and the most Merciful, Allāh the Almighty.

Since counseling involves *communication*, the Prophet advised, "Good word is an act of giving."[51]

Do not underestimate your reward when you sincerely counsel those in need of advice. Your words could save relationships or even lives.

---

[50] Sahīh Al-Bukhāri, Hadīth #6000.

[51] Sahīh Al-Bukhāri, Hadīth #6023.

'Adl

The word 'adl means to act equitably. According to Ar-Rāghib, 'adl means to be fair and to establish justice. Allāh (SWT) says in the Qur'an,

$$إِنَّ اللَّهَ يَأْمُرُ بِالْعَدْلِ وَالْإِحْسَانِ$$

"God commands justice and good" (Qur'an 16:90).

The Prophet ﷺ said,

$$إِنَّ الْمُقْسِطِينَ عِنْدَ اللَّهِ عَلَى مَنَابِرَ مِنْ نُورٍ عَنْ يَمِينِ الرَّحْمَنِ
عَزَّ وَجَلَّ وَكِلْتَا يَدَيْهِ يَمِينٌ الَّذِينَ يَعْدِلُونَ فِي حُكْمِهِمْ وَأَهْلِيهِمْ
وَمَا وَلُوا$$

Verily, those who were just will be in the presence of Allāh upon pulpits of light, near the right hand of the Merciful, the Exalted, and both of His sides are honorable. They are those who practiced justice in their judgments and with their families and in all that they did.[52]

Justice Can't Be Compromised

The Qur'an, which we know is the Word of God, commands us to be truthful and just in all our situations and with all people, regardless of whether we are dealing with friend or foe. Even if telling the truth is against us, Islām teaches us to say what we mean and to mean what we say. There may be occasions when the message is difficult or emotional because of kinship or hostility, but Islām mandates that justice must prevail.

---

[52] Sahīh Muslim, Hadīth #1827.

What the Qur'an Says about ...

1. Kinship

يَا أَيُّهَا الَّذِينَ آمَنُوا كُونُوا قَوَّامِينَ بِالْقِسْطِ شُهَدَاءَ لِلَّهِ وَلَوْ عَلَىٰ أَنفُسِكُمْ أَوِ الْوَالِدَيْنِ وَالْأَقْرَبِينَ ۚ إِن يَكُنْ غَنِيًّا أَوْ فَقِيرًا فَاللَّهُ أَوْلَىٰ بِهِمَا ۖ فَلَا تَتَّبِعُوا الْهَوَىٰ أَن تَعْدِلُوا ۚ وَإِن تَلْوُوا أَوْ تُعْرِضُوا فَإِنَّ اللَّهَ كَانَ بِمَا تَعْمَلُونَ خَبِيرًا

O you believe! Stand out firmly for justice, as witnesses to Allāh; even though it is against yourselves, or your parents, or your kin, be it rich or poor, Allāh is a better Protector to both (than you). So, follow not the lusts (of your hearts), lest you avoid justice; and if you distort your witness or refuse to give it, verily, Allāh is Ever Well-Acquainted with what you do. (Qur'an 4:135)

2. Hostility

يَا أَيُّهَا الَّذِينَ آمَنُوا كُونُوا قَوَّامِينَ لِلَّهِ شُهَدَاءَ بِالْقِسْطِ ۖ وَلَا يَجْرِمَنَّكُمْ شَنَآنُ قَوْمٍ عَلَىٰ أَلَّا تَعْدِلُوا ۚ اعْدِلُوا هُوَ أَقْرَبُ لِلتَّقْوَىٰ ۖ وَاتَّقُوا اللَّهَ ۚ إِنَّ اللَّهَ خَبِيرٌ بِمَا تَعْمَلُونَ

O you who believe! Stand out firmly for Allāh as just witness; and let not the enmity and hatred of others make you avoid justice. Be just' that is nearer to piety; and fear Allāh. Verily, Allāh is Well-Acquainted with what you do. (Qur'an 5:8)

The Prophet as a Family Man

Let us reflect upon this hadīth, narrated by Al-Aswad:

عَنِ الأَسْوَدِ، قَالَ سَأَلْتُ عَائِشَةَ مَا كَانَ النَّبِيُّ صلى الله عليه
وسلم يَصْنَعُ فِي أَهْلِهِ قَالَتْ كَانَ فِي مِهْنَةِ أَهْلِهِ، فَإِذَا حَضَرَتِ
الصَّلَاةُ قَامَ إِلَى الصَّلَاةِ.

Al Aswad asked the mother of believers, 'Aishah, "How was the life of the Prophet with his family?" She answered, "He is working for his family and when it is time for the prayer, he leaves to pray."[53] This highlights the Prophet ﷺ's ability to establish justice in the context of fulfilling the rights that his family have upon him, as well as God's.

Ibn Hajar cites the narration found in At-Tirmidhi. "He was the most gentle, flexible and generous. Surely, he's a human like you except that he is the most smiling person."[54]

The Sanctity of People's Honor

The Prophet warned in his last sermon,

قَالَ " فَإِنَّ اللَّهَ حَرَّمَ عَلَيْكُمْ دِمَاءَكُمْ وَأَمْوَالَكُمْ وَأَعْرَاضَكُمْ،
كَحُرْمَةِ يَوْمِكُمْ هَذَا فِي شَهْرِكُمْ هَذَا فِي بَلَدِكُمْ هَذَا ".

"[From this day on] Your blood, properties and honor are sacred as the sanctity of this day, in this month and in this sacred place."[55] This hadīth

---

[53] Sahīh Al-Bukhāri, Hadīth #6039.

[54] Al-Asqalāni, *Fat-hul Bāri*, vol. 12, 78.

[55] Sahīh Al-Bukhāri, Hadīth #6043.

highlights the Prophet ﷺ's emphasis on establishing justice in the context of preserving one another's honor.

> The Prophet's methodology in advising his ummah is as follows:
>
> 1. Show sincerity in advice.
> 2. Show optimism.
> 3. Be fair, but also be mindful of people's sensitivities.
> 4. Avoid completely attacking and exposing the fault of others.
> 5. When and how to give advice are as important as to what to say during advice.
> 6. Have calmness in words and deeds.
> 7. Gradualness may be required.
> 8. Offer Islāmic alternatives.
> 9. Avoid provocation and invalidation.
> 10. Remind the person of the consequences of his/her actions.
> 11. Target the action.
> 12. Emotions and feelings are not the problem, but the "how-ness" of it must be checked.
> 13. Help, and don't hurt.

CHAPTER 4

Introduction to Premarital Counseling

Half the worry in the world is caused by people trying to
make decisions before they have sufficient knowledge on
which to base a decision. If a man will devote his time
to securing knowledge in an impartial, objective way, his
worries will usually evaporate in the light of knowledge.
—Professor Herbert Hawkes[56]
Columbia University

A Professor Thomas and his colleagues at St. Louis University once stated, "The best and the wisest decision you have ever made was carefully and intelligently choosing a mate who cares about you and the relationship." That is why when two people come to me, seeking my assistance in marrying them, I remind them that my role is not solely to officiate their marriage but to plant the seeds of guidance for their marriage. Premarital counseling is all about helping single men and women make the transition to marriage. They come to me as people with carefree mind-sets, and I guide them in developing mind-sets that are ready for marriage and equipped for the responsibilities ahead. For my young men and women, their most important decision, after faith, is the choice of a marriage partner who will help and care for the relationship. It would be better to never marry than to

---

[56] M. R. Kopmeyer, *Thoughts to Build On* (1970), 18.

rush into marriage with a disastrous partner, one who will lead the other away from Allāh and into a life of sin and condemnation. Marriage is all about helping, encouraging, and comforting one another. Marriage is the art of loving and caring for one another.

Marriage Is about Caring

This is proven in the most-used ayah in the Qur'an with regard to marriage, in which Allāh says,

وَمِنْ آيَاتِهِ أَنْ خَلَقَ لَكُم مِّنْ أَنفُسِكُمْ أَزْوَاجًا لِّتَسْكُنُوا إِلَيْهَا وَجَعَلَ بَيْنَكُم مَّوَدَّةً وَرَحْمَةً ۚ إِنَّ فِي ذَٰلِكَ لَآيَاتٍ لِّقَوْمٍ يَتَفَكَّرُونَ

> And of His signs is that He created for you from yourselves
> mates that you may find tranquility in them; and He
> placed between you affection and mercy. Indeed, in that
> are signs for a people who give thought. (Qur'an 30:21)

Do you want to get married? This is a beautiful desire to pursue, but slow down for a second. As a counselor, I have to advise you and equip you with some knowledge that, if learned early, will save you from a future filled with pain. First, when you are on the journey of choosing a mate, the process will get very stressful at times. Society has determined fictitious standards of success, beauty, and so forth. I advise you to know what you are and are not willing to compromise. This will help you navigate through this process with less stress. The wisest and noblest among you will prioritize faith and character first, as the Prophet ﷺ encouraged.

Congratulations! You've chosen your mate and have gotten married. When navigating the journey of marriage, *care* is the key. Be the water to your spouse's fire, and let your spouse be the water to your fire as well. Complement one another, and always communicate with one another through the virtues of care and mercy. There will be fights, disagreements, and conflict, but long-lasting relationships will use care, compassion, and mercy to handle their problems.

You are married now, and you have come to realize that the movies deceived you. Marital problems are bound to happen. It's human to have expectations, and problems often stem from these expectations. Expectations are one of the main causes of the destruction of marriages and families. As people come into a relationship, each one of them has a set of expectations—financial, social, emotional, religious, and many more. These come from society, family, and personal experiences. For example, an American bride has a totally different set of expectations than a bride from Africa. Likewise, a European has a different set of expectations than an Asian. I see these issues all the time in the office. It manifests in the level of extravagance of the wedding or in personal things, such as how to express oneself in a relationship. This is exactly why interracial marriages can be difficult at times. Additionally, this is why marriages between people of different socioeconomic status are so difficult as well. Expectations are not always bad, but compromise is essential to the success of a relationship.

Even worse than having over-the-top expectations is creating false expectations through deception. Men may foolishly pretend to be something they are not to impress women they want to marry, but in the end, the truth always prevails. To the men driving their uncles' Mercedes-Benz and Land Cruisers; to my brothers—did you happen to think about the look on her face when she finds out that you are financially struggling? Fear Allāh, and be who you are. Whoever accepts you that way is the one who is a blessing for you. Exaggeration never has worked for anybody. To the sisters who bleach their skin and apply artificial beauty products to look whiter and more European—fear Allāh. Not only will your skin suffer, but again, the truth will always prevail. Embrace your natural beauty. The man who accepts you that way is truly who is best for you. I'm not telling our women not to "beautify" themselves; I'm arguing for authenticity, for beautifying yourself without the expense of altering your original physical appearance. And Allāh knows best.

Are you a father or a mother? Here is my advice on children: They need the presence and guidance of their parents. Parents need to provide them with proper nurturing, a balance between discipline and mercy.

Realistic Expectations vs. False Expectations

This is perhaps the toughest part to discuss when it comes to marriage, but as the counselor, it is my duty to advise sincerely, but Allāh judges! There will be cases when spouses fight and have already tried to communicate their differences with compassion. They tried to compromise and minimize their expectations. Nevertheless, there seems to be no way for the marriage to be of benefit to either spouse. In this circumstance, divorce is the last resort. When going about this journey, remember that divorce is not the end of the world, but it must be done with harmlessness. Slandering and involving the family and community in your conflict with your future ex is not only immature but unbeneficial to the relationship. Ours is to always end things with grace and not to burn bridges.

Premarital counseling's main goal and purpose is the same as the law:

1. **To prevent harm**. Through premarital counseling, the prevention of harm is seen by averting serious marital problems. Counselors help avert these challenges through making young single men and women aware of themselves as individuals and aware of the challenges that come from marriage.
2. **To bring benefit**. Premarital counseling brings benefit by strengthening the family structure and equipping future spouses with the necessary tools to make their marriage last.

Most marriages are conducted in the masājid (Islāmic places of worship), so it only makes sense that our imams consider it a high priority to be trained counselors in the field of premarital counseling. Imams should be well informed on what makes marriages work and what causes marriages to fail. Imams are the leaders of the community, and successful marriages reflect the success of the community. Here are a few guidelines for imams to share with future couples:

Respecting Biological Differences

Allāh created us male and female. This is how humankind continues to procreate and exist on this planet. Future couples need to understand one another, emotionally, spiritually, physically, and biologically. This is targeted more toward the men in the relationship. Men need to support their wives during their times of change, such as menstruation, pregnancy, breastfeeding, and other matters concerning women's health. For too long, men have not concerned themselves with these matters, and it has had a profoundly negative impact on relationships. We are a society and a people of self-improvement, and this problem needs amending.

Respecting Different Roles

In marriage, Allāh made us husband and wife. Each one of us has something to contribute for the relationship to succeed. The husband is the breadwinner. He is to provide generously, to the best of his abilities, for the family. That position should never be compromised, unless he is disabled. This is indeed not an easy task, but Allāh does not overburden the soul with more than it can handle.

$$\text{لِيُنفِقْ ذُو سَعَةٍ مِّن سَعَتِهِ ۖ وَمَن قُدِرَ عَلَيْهِ رِزْقُهُ فَلْيُنفِقْ مِمَّا}$$

$$\text{آتَاهُ اللَّهُ ۚ لَا يُكَلِّفُ اللَّهُ نَفْسًا إِلَّا مَا آتَاهَا ۚ سَيَجْعَلُ اللَّهُ بَعْدَ}$$

$$\text{عُسْرٍ يُسْرًا}$$

> Let a man of wealth spend from his wealth, and he whose provision is restricted - let him spend from what Allāh has given him. Allāh does not charge a soul except [according to] what He has given it. Allāh will bring about, after hardship, ease. (Qur'an 65:7)

Lessons derived from this powerful ayah are as follows:

1. **When you have the wealth, spend it.** It came from Allāh anyway. Where else should you spend your wealth if not on your family, your wife, and your children? Remember, the husband will be blamed if the family is financially suffering.
2. **When you do not have the wealth, spend it.** Allāh knows what's in your bank account. "I don't have it" is not the correct answer. One of

two pillars of marriage is the ability to provide for your family. If you are seeking marriage, you should be able to provide. If you are suffering financially, that is a reality that many face. You have to work out your entire soul as sacrifice for the welfare of your family. If you would like the respect of your family, your wife, and your children, spend. This is the only option.

This verse teaches us *that spending is not an option but a mandatory command from Allāh upon husbands.* How many marriages have crumbled because the man could not provide? How many husbands complain to their counselors that respect is absent at home, when their participation in the duties of husband and breadwinner is absent as well? These are tough realities, but counselors have to speak truth to injustice.

Not only do our Islāmic texts endorse this understanding but also secular works, such as Derrick Sherwin Bailey's *The Mystery of Love and Marriage*, in which he writes, "Male and female are thus shown to have a common origin; they are not independent but complementary, and individually incomplete until they have achieved the union in which each integrates and is integrated by the other."[57]

For our women who have become wives, it is extremely important to be cooperative with the husband. Abu Hurairah narrated the Prophet's answer when asked, "Which woman is the best?" The Prophet replied, "The one who makes him happy when he looks at her, obeys him when he commands her, and she does not go against his wishes with regard to herself nor her wealth."[58] Let me be very clear: Obedience has its limits. As human beings, our unfailing and uncompromising obedience is for Allāh alone. If the husband encourages unlawful behavior, the wife is required to disobey him. Obedience, however, is a very important role for the wife in the marital relationship. We live in a world of feminism, and some critics may argue, "Why does the man have to be obeyed, and why does the man lead the woman?" These are real questions that should never be ridiculed. If Islām is the truth, it can confront these questions with

---

[57] Lyle B Gangsei, *Manual for Group Premarital Counseling* (1997), 44.

[58] Sunan An-Nasāi, Hadīth #3231.

clarity and concise speech. To answer that question, one must revisit the role of the husband. Allāh obliges, commands, and mandates the husband to provide. The man's entire earnings are completely purposed for the consumption of the family. Shouldn't that individual, in whom is placed such a responsibility, be deserving of respect and obedience? Obedience should not come from the attitude of "I have to" but because of a genuine appreciation for the role that that husband has taken on. A conscious and genuine wife will immediately understand that her obedience toward the responsible husband is necessary for the very success of that relationship. And Allāh knows best.

A reminder to husbands is to respect the role of wives. They also have distinct responsibilities that are deserving of acknowledgement and immense appreciation. Although the man is to be obeyed, communication between the spouses is extremely important. Men who act like dictators and tyrants do not benefit anyone. The Messenger of Allāh ﷺ once said,

$$\text{لاَ طَاعَةَ فِي مَعْصِيَةِ اللَّهِ إِنَّمَا الطَّاعَةُ فِي الْمَعْرُوفِ}$$

"There is no obedience in matters involving disobedience to Allāh. Obedience is in matters which are good and universally recognized."[59]

Although Islām instructs traditional roles for husband and wife, do not doubt that Allāh means well for society. These roles, although abused by some scholars, husbands, and men in general, were never meant to suppress the other. The purpose of marriage, as mentioned in Surah Ar-Rum, is to live in an environment of *mawaddah* (affection) and *rahmah* (mercy). For the logical mind, how can Islām then be supportive of the abuses done by many in the name of "obedience"? This is inconceivable and cannot be substantiated. May Allāh bring ease to our world and to our relationships. Amīn.

In Summary
Both spouses must be responsible, respectful, and reasonable. That is the essence of obedience.

---

[59] Sunan Abi Dawūd, Hadīth #2625.

The Awareness of the Three Marital Organizations

In the world of business, there are three major types of organizations. Counselors, however, have adopted the same terms for marriage. They are as follows:

Proprietorship: This is the relationship dynamic where one of the spouses is in total control of the couple's relationship. Often this is a relationship that abusive men establish in their perverted understanding of "obedience" to the husband.

Corporation: This is the relationship dynamic where, like businesses, many individuals have a sense of ownership to the couple's relationship. This is one of the most common problems in our world, especially in the Muslim world, due to our environment's embracing the worldview known as collectivism. Our family networks are extended, and therefore, many people, including parents, siblings, cousins, uncles, aunts, and community elders, feel free to simply tamper with the couple's relationship. This can be a major issue and is very unproductive when the spouses have conflict with one another. The extended family network, however, can be useful with advice from the experienced elderly and the knowledge that in-laws have on the spouses. However, triangulation occurs when two individual spouses look to solve their differences, and then others, who are unrelated to the issue, involve themselves. This creates distraction and can even further escalate the conflict.

Partnership: This is the relationship dynamic where the couple views one another as partners in the relationship. The investment and participation in the well-being of the relationship is equal and fairly distributed. Choose this dynamic, and your relationship will be on the safer side, by the will of Allāh. This is Islāmically the encouraged and ideal relationship, as Allāh stated in Surah Al-Baqarah.

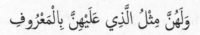

"And for the wives is similar to what is expected of them, according to what is reasonable" (Qur'an 2:228).

The Philosophy of Marriage and the Hollywoodization of Marriage

To reiterate, our minds have been contaminated by the romantic love fallacy that stems from Hollywood and other sources of popular culture. When women enter marriage, some have the assumption that husbands will be extremely mature, responsible, handsome, wealthy, well known in the community, and perfect when in his relationship with Allāh. Men have the assumption that their wives will be extremely mature, responsible, beautiful, obedient, talented cooks, and perfect in her relationship with Allāh. As your beloved imam and counselor, I request that you wake up! Marriage is a collaborative effort between man and woman, one in which they grow together as they guide themselves and their family to their Promised Land in this life and, most importantly, the hereafter. However, the roadblock to the road of righteousness and guidance is unrealistic expectations. When husbands expect their wives to consistently provide them with a warm home-cooked breakfast in bed, and when wives expect their husband to consistently buy them expensive gifts, the relationship's expiration date is soon. When we are unforgiving and very rude when our spouse errs, we destroy the marital relationship and the family structure. Do we expect to be forgiven by Allāh when we cannot forgive one another?

Expectations, feelings, and challenges in the relationship often stem from five main things:

1. work or employment
2. money
3. sex
4. in-laws
5. children

One of the most difficult things to talk about with your future spouse is finances. Questions like "How much do you make?" or "What is your monthly budget?" are tough but crucial questions in order to understand the type of relationship you will have. However, there are expectations that are unreasonable with regard to work and money. Many women seem to expect to marry a millionaire or a neurosurgeon or politician.

Let's visit the hadīth of Fatimah Bintu Qais when she went to the Prophet, seeking his advice on two marriage prospects. The Prophet frankly advised her to accept neither one by stating, "Mu'awiyah is destitute and he has no property, and Abul-Jahm is very hard on women."[60] [Al-Bukhāri and Muslim]. A lesson from this hadīth is that after understanding the context of who Muawiyah Ibn Abi Sufyan was, the son of one of the wealthiest Makkans at that time, you would wonder why the Prophet told Bintu Qais not to pursue Muawiyah. However, here is the wisdom of the Messenger of God, and Allāh knows best. The Prophet acknowledged that the wealth was the wealth of his father Abu Sufyan and not the wealth of Muawiyah. The Prophet looked at the work ethic of the man and not the family money. He matched his female followers with men of hard work, and even if they earned little, it was the effort that made them men. Therefore, he advised Bintu Qais to avoid both men who sought her hand.

I encourage our women to not limit themselves to only wealthy men, but I also encourage our women to be selective. Set your standards high. You should view yourself highly but learn to compromise. Two things to never compromise on, however, are your faith and your honor. In most cases, those who go for billionaires are deceived. Most of these men with such wealth are so immersed in their business that they neglect their marital affairs and the fathering of the children.

The marital relationship is also influenced by sex. Astaghfirul-Laah (I seek refuge in Allāh), Imam! How can you say such disgusting words? A reminder to the reader is a saying of our beloved Prophet:

$$ إِنَّ اللَّهَ لاَ يَسْتَحِي مِنَ الْحَقِّ $$

"Verily, Allāh does not feel shy to tell the truth."[61]

The Prophet taught us something when mentioning that hadīth. So yes, may Allāh forgive me and forgive us all. Now, back to the topic of sex, which is a natural instinct. If not regulated, however, it will destroy individuals,

---

[60] Sahīh Muslim, Hadīth #1480; Sunan Abi Dawūd, Hadīth #2284.

[61] Sahīh Al-Bukhāri, Hadīth #6121.

as well as their communities at large. It was through Allāh's infinite wisdom that the creation of the ancient institution known as marriage came to fruition. How can sex manifest as an expectation? Each of us has a desire, men along with women, and therefore, if either spouse cannot sexually satisfy his or her partner physically, emotionally, or spiritually, it will cause great tension between the spouses. Hence, the second of the two pillars of marriage is *al-wat-u*, the ability to consummate the marriage. Many times I have counseled couples, and when speaking with each one alone, they have informed me that their expectation of their spouses' sexual performance was unsatisfactory. This is a very serious problem and can stem from many things.

Sometimes, sexual health has deteriorated, but also, what we barely talk about as counselors are the dangers of pornography and masturbation, which sometimes contributes to the weakening of sexual performance. Since this is premarital counseling, I advise young single men and women to enter a relationship with the understanding that sex is a very important aspect of marriage. The fact that Muslim scholars have divided marriage into two pillars expresses that point profoundly. To young men and women looking for their future spouse, when reaching that point of finding the potential partner, I humbly advise taking the appropriate tests with medical experts in order to understand each other's health needs. It will prove very helpful in the future. A common example is getting blood tests. These tests disclose potential genetic disorders of which future spouses should be made aware.

More than two decades ago, my wife and I had tests. Now, we still reap the benefits of knowing our health conditions and learning how to navigate through them. Another example are the tests that check sexual health. It's important to take tests that detect STDs and sexual deficiencies before you commit to your partner for the rest of your life. I share this information with the intent of spreading awareness because knowledge is power.

My favorite topic to discuss is the infamous problem known as the in-laws. By Allāh, may they be blessed because it's through their blessing that couples get married to begin with. However, what follows after the marriage is disaster for some couples. May Allāh bless them again, for we must understand the context of this problem. In-laws are parents and are experienced in marriage, and therefore, they are very aware of the challenges that come from marriage. It is the parents' instinct to protect their children from harm, regardless of how old they are. This is why some parents are so involved in their children's marriages. Sometimes their intentions are noble; they want to protect their loved one from abuse and harm.

However, when in-laws are so involved in the couple's affairs that they get carried away and start dictating to the couple, they have gone too far. In addition, sometimes wives have been mistreated by in-laws because they say the husband "will always be my baby," regardless of his age. They should fear Allāh and let the husband run his marriage. They have already enjoyed their relationship with their son, so they should let the husband and wife enjoy their relationship and grow together. They may advise them and encourage them, but dictating to them means the in-laws have transgressed from their roles.

When triangulation is mentioned the first thing that comes to mind is involving the extended family with marital conflict—mothers-in-law, siblings, and stepfamilies. While the wife is there, some mothers will cook for their sons, asking, "Honey, what would you eat today?" without consulting their daughters-in-law—the wife. This oversteps the boundaries of the in-law and creates marital conflict. If the wife cannot cook for her husband, that is when her in-law, through grace and compassion, should teach the wife how to cook. It is not the job of the righteous in-law, however, to walk into the homes of their married children and dictate to them. This is an injustice to the institution of marriage.

Brothers- and sisters-in-law, fear Allāh as well. Focus on your marriages, and do not interfere in the marriages of your siblings. You may advise but never impose. So many siblings-in-law have caused tremendous amounts of pain and agony to marriages, all for the sake of stroking their egos. This is evil, and if we truly believe that the family structure is a sacred one, we will be humble and not impose our understanding upon others. Those siblings who live at their married siblings' homes should understand that they are living there, Islāmically, under the mercy of their in-laws. This means that just because the person is the brother or sister of one of the spouses in the relationship, that does not give the in-law any role or ownership in the affairs of that home. Live there with humility and respect; that is all Islām encourages. This is the opinion of some of our predecessors, like Umar ibn Khattab.

Dr. Thomas Fogarty, a physician and professor for the Center of Family Learning, affirmed all that I have said when he stated that if we want to avoid serious problems, we should "avoid *all* triangles ... Triangles are avoidance processes that people use to avoid dealing on a one-to-one basis with each other ... every time there is a problem there will be tendency to triangle."[62] Triangles *need* to be deferred.

Finally, *children*—raising the future generation is an important task. Children are a blessing, but they could be a curse and liability if not disciplined properly. Many children have gone to jail in their teenage years due to the lack of discipline and proper nurturing in their childhood. Remember that whatever they see us adults doing is exactly what they will be doing when they grow up. If you are a religious family, be a family of action and not just words. I have seen many kids get sent to Islāmic schools with the intention of training them to be devout Muslims, but due to the lack of devotion in the home, these children only pray Dhuhr (noon prayer) because it is in school. Children often neglect reading the Qur'an because they have never seen their parents do so. In order to raise competent children, the parents need to be competent nurturers and leaders for their families. And Allāh knows best.

In conclusion, to substantiate my claims with evidence, the 1992 *Statistical Handbook on American Family* notes that marital disagreements are mostly centered on money, sex, and in-laws, given the supporting evidence and rationale already described.[63]

---

[62] Thomas F. Fogarty, *Operating Principles* (1983), 25–27.

[63] Bruce A. Chadwick and Tim B. Heaton, eds., *Statistical Handbook on the American Family* (1992), 53.

Predominant Faults

Premarital counseling, as mentioned earlier, is meant to bring benefit and to avert harm in marriage. One way to bring benefit through premarital counseling is by helping young couples to learn about themselves as individuals. Throughout the lengthy premarital counseling sessions, counselors engage the couple with questions that help them reflect on their personalities, their compatibility as a couple, and—most important—the predominant fault that each future spouse has. Awareness of the self is instrumental to the success of a couple that follows the partnership model of marriage.

In order to complement your spouse, you must know exactly who you are and how you act. Once there is a state of awareness, then there can be a state of willingness to change. Moreover, you cannot marry someone blindly. It is absolutely necessary that you know the critical flaws of the partner with whom you plan to live your entire life. In my premarital counseling sessions, I ask couples to write a one-page reflection on their predominant fault and discuss how to remedy that fault when it exposes itself. Examples of predominant faults are as follows:

Rage

A major predominant fault is anger. When a partner is in disagreement with the other, he or she is consumed by emotional immaturity and becomes unjustifiably and intensely angry. This can cause some to physically harm their spouses, a major cause for domestic abuse. This can cause spouses to leave the house for certain periods, which lures the in-laws into intervening. Generally, it is a problem that requires immediate remedy if the relationship is to succeed. Always look at the consequences of your rage and anger. When your anger intensifies and continues to worsen, you join the camp of Shaytan.

Awareness of the Self

Let us look at this extremely powerful hadīth, narrated by Abu Hurairah:

أَنَّ رَجُلاً، قَالَ لِلنَّبِيِّ صلى الله عليه وسلم أَوْصِنِي.
قَالَ " لاَ تَغْضَبْ ". فَرَدَّدَ مِرَارًا، قَالَ " لاَ تَغْضَبْ "

> A man said to the Prophet "Advise me!" The Prophet
> (ﷺ) said, "Do not become angry and furious." The man
> asked (the same) again and again, and the Prophet said in
> each case, "Do not become angry and furious."[64]

By Allāh, when the Prophet repeats something, there is even greater weight in the warning he is giving us. A perfect follow-up hadīth is found in Al-Bukhāri's *Adab Al-Mufrad* (not to be confused with Sahīh Al-Bukhāri; this is a separate book on everyday etiquette by Imam Al-Bukhāri). This hadīth is narrated by Ibn Abbas:

قَالَ رَسُولُ اللهِ صلى الله عليه وسلم:
عَلِّمُوا وَيَسِّرُوا، عَلِّمُوا وَيَسِّرُوا، ثَلَاثَ مَرَّاتٍ، وَإِذَا
غَضِبْتَ فَاسْكُتْ، مَرَّتَيْنِ.

> The Messenger of Allāh, may Allāh bless him and grant
> him peace, said, "Teach and make it easy. Teach and make
> it easy." three times. He went on, "When you are angry,
> be silent" twice.[65]

Glory be to Allāh, notice that the Prophet in both hadīths repeats himself on the concept of controlling one's anger. This is no coincidence but rather is a wisdom that our beloved Prophet is sharing with us. I once taught my students that the one who acts on anger is the one who regrets later. Anger

---

[64] Sahīh Al-Bukhāri, Hadīth #6116.

[65] Al-Bukhāri, *Al-Adab Al-Mufrad*, Hadīth #1320.

takes your reasoning away and causes the human to be equal to the animal. A reminder to all is that Allāh's favor on the children of Adam is the brain, and anger takes that away from us. People have destroyed their lives due to their inability to tame their anger, and marriages have been destroyed due to one spouse acting preemptively, based on anger. As well, relationships have burned to the ground due to the emotional immaturity of some when dealing with anger. I suspect that many people are in prison right now, due to their lack of anger management. Anger is, without disagreement, a major cause of self-destruction, but there are positive forms of anger. Anger, after all, is a natural human emotion for survival, but it's all about balance and self-control. When anger is needed, because the law has been violated, the expression of anger is appropriate. A reminder from Allāh in the Qur'an is to never allow anger to affect our ability to execute justice. (Read Surah Al-Maidah 5:2 and 5:8.)

Laziness

When entering a relationship as important as marriage, understand that responsibilities will multiply. Husbands, you are no longer a carefree man; you are now in charge of the financial and security needs of your household. You are to pay the bills and feed and clothe the wife and kids, while maintaining a roof over their heads. This is not the life of the lazy. Wives, you are no longer a carefree woman; you are now in charge of taking care of the house, cooperating with your husband when he needs you, and raising competent children. This is not the life of the lazy.

I have a student, who mā shā Allāh (it has been willed by Allāh), is affiliated with much good work in the community. However, this young man takes on so many responsibilities that he ends up doing none, due to being unorganized and lazy. One day I was so frustrated with him that I asked him, "If this is how you are as a single man, how disastrous will it be if you found yourself a wife?" Although I was being lighthearted with him, this indeed is a very serious problem that he and many others need to solve.

The first step to solving the problem is to be aware of it. From there, honesty is a major key in the improvement process. Being able to say no to what you cannot handle and being able to commit your personal responsibilities to memory while taking them seriously is the next step. This is a common yet critical and predominant flaw. As a people, we should combat it aggressively. This is why the Prophet specifically sought, in Allāh, refuge from laziness in this hadīth found in Al-Bukhāri, where Anas bin Mālik narrated the Prophet, saying,

$$ اللَّهُمَّ إِنِّي أَعُوذُ بِكَ مِنَ الْعَجْزِ وَالْكَسَلِ $$

"O Allāh! I seek refuge with You from helplessness and laziness."[66]

Amīn to this prayer, and may Allāh protect us all from it. As we grow older, may we also mature and take our responsibilities seriously. What is the general solution to predominant faults? To resolve differences, the general answer would be to manage our anger and to communicate positively. If we are truly invested and concerned with the well-being of the relationship, we will not allow our predominant faults to ruin the relationship. Yes, it will be difficult, especially if it is a very serious fault. However, both must work together. In the face of impatience, be patient. In the face of anger, be calm. In the face of laziness, actively and respectfully hold the spouse at fault accountable for it. Always communicate positively. We tend to treat strangers with positivity, but we often treat our loved ones with negativity. If you love your spouse, then reason would argue that you would treat him or her with love and compassion. It would be naive, however, to state that this is the answer to every marriage's issues. There are some problems that are simply irreparable or not worth the pain one has to endure. As previously mentioned, in such times, divorce may be the only way—that is, divorce with the attitude of harmlessness. Burning bridges will not benefit anyone. And Allāh knows best.

Cross-Cultural Characteristics

Prominent theologian David Augsburger, in his work, *Pastoral Counseling across Cultures*, states, "In some cultures, marriage is expected to fulfill virtually all basic human needs; in others, the expectations are much more modest. No one relationship can fulfill all the needs of a person. Expecting

---

[66] Sahīh Al-Bukhāri, Hadīth #2823.

one person to provide so much is asking the impossible from marriage, so the stress on the contemporary nuclear family and on marriage as the central coalition is increasingly heavy."

It seems that whatever we cover in terms of premarital counseling, the underlying theme is always expectations. This topic, specifically, is concerned with the expectations that arise from intercultural or interracial marriages. When two families that come from different geographical regions, cultural understandings, and social lifestyles merge, challenges are to be expected. Here are some things that Augsburger believes everyone shares, regardless of the culture to: which they belong:

1. Cross-culturally, marriage is frequently a relationship between groups, rather than just a relationship between two individuals.
2. Marriage is not only a sexual relationship; it is a form of exchange involving the transfer of rights and obligations between the contracting parties.
3. All societies have restrictions, taboos, and exogamous boundaries.
4. Comparatively few societies limit their numbers to one spouse.[67]

Group Premarital Counseling

James Alfred Peterson, in his work *Education for Marriage*, wrote that "one of the most promising movements to aid young people to prepare more adequately for marriage" is group premarital counseling.[68] Furthermore, as psychologist Ruth Strang argues in her *Group Work in Education*, "Co-operation is strengthened when a group tries to attain both group goals and the 'hidden agenda' of individual goals."[69] Group premarital counseling is a unique approach of increasing awareness for young future spouses. This is where counselors give education and increase young future spouses' awareness collectively in group settings, where future spouses are assigned tasks and engage with them interactively. Imams who conduct group premarital counseling should understand that this environment should

---

[67] David W. Augsburger, *Pastoral Counseling across Cultures* (1986), 177.

[68] James Peterson, *Education for Marriage* (1964), 221.

[69] Ruth Strang, *Group Work in Education* (1958), 30–31.

be made a safe space for individuals in the group to express their opinions and feelings, without castigation or judgment. The imam should create an environment filled with love, respect, and tolerance.

Premarital counseling is an approach dedicated to the protection of our future marital relationships. As such, we imams need to make the participants feel important, not worthless. Let those couples in the group premarital counseling sessions know that there is no such thing as a bad question. With an unequipped counselor, however, unfortunately there can be bad answers. Counselors, a conducive environment is essential to achieve your counseling objective. Your approach and mannerisms are crucial to achieving your objective's success. Four things will help couples think about the big question of who they are going to marry: faith, values, standards, and goals.

Faith

Faith should always be the guiding principle to all our relationships because when the vertical relationship (between humans and God) is connected with the horizontal one (between humans and creation), all is safe. Before going about your life and social interactions, make sure your relationship with God is outstanding. This will affect your relationship positively. Abu Hurairah once narrated that the Prophet stated,

لَا يَشْكُرُ اللَّهَ مَنْ لَا يَشْكُرُ النَّاسَ

"He who does not thank the people is not thankful to Allāh."[70]

Our relationship with others is a reflection of our relationship with Allāh. When searching for a spouse, understand his or her spirituality and knowledge of his or her faith. It will have a tremendous impact in the relationship, so equip yourself.

---

[70] Sunan Abi Dawūd, Hadīth #4811.

Values

After faith, your values should be your guiding principle in the relationship. There is a great connection between our values and our faith. Some examples of values are honesty, trustworthiness, patience, appreciation, compassion, hard work, determination, and even a sense of humor. When entering a relationship, prioritize which values are more important to you than others because you will not be able to find a partner who has mastered each value. You do have a right to seek someone who values the same values that you place in high priority. In essence, values are important because they are the building blocks to your relationship's culture.

Standards

What constitutes beauty? What are the things that you, the future spouse, want in a relationship? Once again, the theme of expectation returns. Always be ready to compromise your basic standard when you see something genuinely good available for you. Perhaps the potential spouse is not as beautiful as you had dreamed. However, does she fear Allāh? Is he hardworking? Is he or she committed to pleasing you and caring for the relationship? As a counselor, I know these are far more important than appearances. Poets say that looks fade, but character always stays. Allāh says in Surah An-Nisā,

$$\text{وَعَاشِرُوهُنَّ بِالْمَعْرُوفِ ۚ فَإِن كَرِهْتُمُوهُنَّ فَعَسَىٰ}$$
$$\text{أَن تَكْرَهُوا شَيْئًا وَيَجْعَلَ اللَّهُ فِيهِ خَيْرًا كَثِيرًا}$$

"And live with them in kindness. For if you dislike them - perhaps you dislike a thing and Allāh makes therein much good" (Qur'an 4:19).

Allāh addresses the realities within our hearts and knows the end result of our lives. So be patient; perhaps Allāh will finally guide you to seeing the benefit that He intends for you. Perhaps your impatience will cause you to lose in the long run. For those who are waiting to marry angels—human beings who are perfect inside and outside—why are you not an angel?

Do not let your unreasonable standards, which are influenced by outside sources, such as the media, misguide you into a life of misery, unhappiness, and dissatisfaction. Like the faces you see in the magazines, your standards are nonexistent in this world. Be humble in your standard. Allāh will choose what is best for you in this life and the hereafter.

Goal

What do you intend to get from this relationship? The foolish will simply seek worldly desires, separated completely from divine guidance. This, however, is a very dangerous route, which has misguided many women into marrying criminals, simply because of their financial prowess. There is a new trend in our world today known as *li-mālihā*, which is when men marry women based on the women's wealth. In such situations, when those women go bankrupt, the relationship crumbles. Why is that? Because the goal is in something temporary, something worldly and completely separated from the fear of Allāh. Abu Hurairah narrates that the Prophet ﷺ taught us:

$$ \text{تُنْكَحُ النِّسَاءُ لِأَرْبَعٍ لِمَالِهَا وَلِحَسَبِهَا وَلِجَمَالِهَا وَلِدِينِهَا فَاظْفَرْ} $$

$$ \text{بِذَاتِ الدِّينِ تَرِبَتْ يَدَاكَ} $$

"Women may be married for four reasons: for her property, her status, her beauty and her religiosity. So get the one who is religious and prosper."[71]

In this hadīth, the Prophet teaches us that there is nothing wrong with seeking these kinds of reasons when marrying a woman, but when it becomes solely for those material reasons, completely divorced from Allāh, there is the danger—all these matters are temporary, and the fear of Allāh should be eternal. Prioritizing eternal matters cleanses and beautifies the temporary ones. Focus on the one who will help you both enter the gates of Jannah, for indeed Jannah is for those who seek to prosper as our Prophet said. With all this in mind, never abandon what you are attracted to. To sacrifice your preferences in terms of sexual attraction for the sake

---

71 Sunan Abi Dawūd, Hadīth #2047.

of religiosity may also cause you to fall into conflict. Islām is the faith of moderation and balance. Marriage is all about living with the one to whom you are attracted, not just emotionally but absolutely in the physical sense as well.

In brief, when you begin pursuing marriage, ask yourself four major questions:

1. Am I using faith as my primary lens in this journey of life? Indeed, being without faith is to be without Allāh's blessing. To be without Allāh's blessing is indeed imminent failure.
2. What are the values I hold to the highest standard? What are values I cannot tolerate abandoning in a marriage? Be principled and cautious when seeking a mate. Human rights activist Malcolm X once said, "A man who stands for nothing, will fall for everything." Your values will keep you morally grounded in the relationship. This is absolutely crucial.
3. Are my standards realistic? If not, what can I compromise? Media programming of standards of beauty and wealth has plagued the younger generation as well as some of our older generations. Let Islām help us unlearn some of these restrictions and guide us to choose the right spouse, not the right celebrity.
4. What are my intentions when pursuing marriage? If they are not connected to the closeness of Allāh and the betterment of society, you have truly failed yourself. This life is only a blink, while the next life is ongoing and never-ending. What will be your legacy? When I think about the Prophet, I think about the centuries upon centuries that have been influenced by his message of compassion and harmlessness. When I give counseling to couples, I model everything on his example of his marital life.

If we can simply contribute one benefit to the future generations, we can pass on victoriously. I ask again: What is your goal when entering marriage? If you are not ambitious with your goal, ask yourself why you are not. Indeed, if you seek Allāh's assistance, He will make whatever is your goal a reality. As is said in the famous hadīth, "All deeds are rewarded by their intention." Victorious and clever spouses frame their goals with the same goals on which sharī'ah is set; that is, the bringing of good and the averting of evil. May Allāh guide us all. Amīn.

Recommended Qualities

Marriageability Traits

MEN	WOMEN
Jamaaluddīn (Spiritual Attractiveness)	*Jamaaluddīn* (Spiritual Attractiveness)
Jamaalul Khulq (Moral Attractiveness)	*Jamaalul Khulq* (Moral Attractiveness)
Jamaalul Khalq (Physical Attractiveness)	*Jamaalul Khalq* (Physical Attractiveness)
Jamaalul Mu`aasharah (Good provision also specific for men.)	*Jamaalut Tua`ah* (Obedience within boundaries of Islam.)

Marriage and family therapist H. Norman Wright wrote in his work, *The Premarital Counseling Handbook*, "As most people eventually get married, it is important to be aware of the traits that make an individual a better partner and give him/her more potential to make a marriage work. Eight basic factors have been called marriageability traits."[72] Here are those traits:

1. **Adaptability and flexibility.** Remember that compromise is the classic tool to solving problems in the relationship. There are times where things should not slide in a relationship, but there are also times where the attitude of water instead of fire is best. One example of adaptability or flexibility is in scheduling time for romantic dinners. Perhaps your spouse has late-night work shifts. Are you to punish him for working

---

[72] H. Norman Wright, *The Premarital Counseling Handbook* (1992), 47.

hard to provide for the family? Of course not. In that situation, the best policy is to work around the schedule instead of complaining to and fighting with your spouse, which will hurt everybody, and neither of you will enjoy the nice steak at the restaurant.

2. **Empathy.** Be the water to your spouse's fire. You know what your spouse is going through better than anyone else. Perhaps your wife is dealing with a lot of stress from friends or children. As the husband, it is your job to mother the mother of your children. You understand what she is going through and know what makes her happy. When she feels low or extremely frustrated, surprise her with what she loves. Acts of kindness keep the relationship strong in the hardest of the times. Acts of kindness will help your spouse to forgive you when you mess up—and indeed you will.

3. **Ability to work through problems.** A common phrase we hear is "Stop complaining, and find the solution." Our lives are full of challenges, and no relationship is without problems. Who is mature enough to get his or her hands dirty and work toward the solution instead of settling into perpetual bickering? A major tool in solving problems is positive communication. Communication, in general, is very important. How can we identify the problem if we do not talk about it? Context is the most important thing to keep in mind. Wisdom is acting during the right time, the right place, and with the right words. Be wise, and know when it's time to speak and when it's time to shut up. He/she who is blessed with communication skills is surely destined to solve problems. Great leaders are great communicators.

4. **Ability to give and receive love.** The importance of reciprocity is generally understood. To receive, you have to give. In order to expect thoughtfulness from your spouse, you have to *do* thoughtful things for your spouse. The Prophet, even after his beloved wife, Khadijah, passed away, would visit her friends with food because of how emotionally connected and appreciative he was of his wife. In order to receive that kind of love, you have to give it. Khadijah, may Allāh be pleased with her, was his number-one supporter from the very first day of his prophethood. How could he ever forget that? There was no way.

5. **Emotional stability.** Controlling your emotions is very important to a productive and positive relationship. When you are emotionally immature or unstable, your reasoning is diminished, and you are bound to act regretfully. I will never forget a story that my beloved Sheikh Umar Ibrahim Imam shared with me after seeing me angry one day during his visit to the United States in 2016.

This incident occurred back in his student days in Madinah, Kingdom of Saudi Arabia. His room had a window that gave him the unflattering view of an alleyway, where scorpions would congregate. He soon learned that cats loved to eat scorpions. There is a wisdom in the way the cat approaches the highly poisonous, predatory arachnid. First, it finds a way to separate the scorpion *jama'ah* (Arabic word for community) to attack on a one-on-one basis. *Pow!* The cat then strikes the scorpion precisely one time, causing the flustered scorpion to pull out its highly fatal arsenal and strike its stinger tail aimlessly. The cat calmly stands by, waiting for the blindly enraged scorpion to finish its strike, and then levels another precise strike to the scorpion. Once again, the scorpion attacks viciously, with no sense of direction or aim, only to get a third strike from the cat. The scorpion, being tired and out of poison, is devoured by the feline.

After telling me this story, my teacher looked me in my eyes and said, "Son, you are acting like the scorpion! It is not good for you. You will be eaten easily!" God bless you, Sheikh Umar Ibrahim Imam, for your priceless and unforgettable lessons. And because of this lesson, when there is a disagreement, my wife Ummu Ubaidah will ask patiently, "Who is the cat, and who is the scorpion?"

6. **Similar family backgrounds.** One of the reasons noninterracial marriages work smoothly in most cases is due to the similarities of culture and family structure, although this should not be generalized. Indeed, *al-kafā-a*, or compatibility, is a very helpful tool to the survival of a relationship. Often in the United States, young future spouses come to me from extremely different backgrounds. Although I am a proponent for diversity, I also try to be an honest counselor. So, I equip them with the awareness of the challenges that come when their backgrounds are extremely different. When your family backgrounds

share similar economic status, language, and cuisine, the transition and merging of families will be smoother. Not long ago a couple had a problem about cuisine. The bride came from a tradition of very spicy foods, while the groom had low tolerance for spices. I was able to help them compromise by advising them to go spicy *in moderation*; Islām is moderation, and the basic principle requires us to eliminate harm wherever we happen to be. Especially for spouses in the United States, things can be problematic when exiting a comfort zone through intercultural marriage. Likewise, in Ghanaian society, it can be very dangerous to marry interculturally, due to ethnocentrism. Therefore, although Islām encourages us to not allow our cultures and status to limit us from marrying one another, these ethnic and cultural similarities do ease the process.

7. **Similarities between couples themselves.** The similarities can be things such as youthfulness, level of education, careers, political views, hobbies, likes and dislikes, and so forth. It is basically impossible to have everything in common or to agree on everything, so that is when the classic tool of compromise comes in. It is always a plus when your spouse shares your joys and sorrows with you.

8. **Communication.** "Nothing is more essential to success in any area of your life than the ability to communicate well."[73] As previously said, one of the greatest blessings in a relationship is to be great in communication. Perhaps your partner is not as good as you are in communicating. Due to your impressive communication skills, you can help him or her come to conclusions and solutions with you. Lack of communication has always destroyed relationships. We are to do whatever we can to communicate positively. Many times couples come to me, complaining, "I am communicating!" But communication is not just words; it's body language, choice of words, and much more. Communication is verbal and nonverbal, and perhaps it is an art and science that needs mastery from both spouses. The relationships that are destined to last are those in which the couple can communicate effectively.

---

[73] Paul W. Swets, *The Art of Talking So That People Will Listen* (New York: Simon and Schuster, 1992), 4.

Crisis resolution consultant and author Dudley Weeks, PhD, has written on many topics in the humanities field. In his book *Conflict Resolution*, he explains there are eight essential steps to resolving conflict:

1. Create an effective atmosphere.
2. Clarify perceptions.
3. Focus on individual and shared needs.
4. Build shared positive powers.
5. Look to the future; then learn from the past.
6. Generate options.
7. Develop "doables," stepping stones to action.
8. Make a mutually beneficial agreement.[74]

Regarding communication, it is extremely important to understand the power of negotiating. You are not always right, nor is your spouse. Therefore, enter the relationship with an open mind and humility. Be ready to compromise. American negotiation expert Herb Cohen teaches that how we handle moments of disagreement determines not only whether we prosper but also whether we can "enjoy a full, pleasurable, satisfying life." He advises that negotiations should focus on mutual satisfaction. To accomplish that, three necessary activities are needed. Those activities are as follows:

1. Building trust.
2. Gaining commitment.
3. Managing opposition.[75]

In summary, we go back to H. Norman Wright, who says, "If those elements are present, there is a greater likelihood of marital satisfaction and stability. As the counseling proceeds, one should be evaluating the couple in light of those factors."[76]

As a father of many daughters, I have some thoughts to share. Often we warn our women against marrying someone with the intention of

---

[74] Dudley Weeks, *Conflict Resolution*.

[75] Herb Cohen, *You Can Negotiate Anything* (1980), 163.

[76] H. Norman Wright, *The Premarital Counseling Handbook* (1992). 47.

"reforming" him. Why? Because addiction is a very expensive problem to treat, and an adult is harder to change than a child. Die-hard habits are extremely difficult to eradicate, and our daughters should not have to marry projects. Let us return to the hadīth of Fatimah Bintu Qais and reflect. When she mentioned the proposals of Muawiyah and Abul Jaham, the Prophet could have said, "If you love Abu Jaham, we will pray for him." He was aware, however, of his abusive qualities toward women, which could not be treated. The Prophet is our example, so we should not sacrifice our daughters by marrying them to individuals who are sick and in need of psychological or other assistance. Why is it that so many of our women pursue this immature desire of being with a "bad boy"? Do they not understand that "bad boys" hit women and will continue to do so unless Allāh intervenes? Let us wise up and make better choices. Psychiatrist Gerald Stein noted there are six qualities to look for in a potential spouse. We have already addressed most of them, but I'll reiterate that the qualities to look for are as follows:

1. Similarity of religion
2. High moral character
3. Affection
4. Compatibility
5. Compromise
6. Health[77]

With all these marriageable traits to consider, the process of finding a spouse can get uncertain and stressful. Professor Thomas and his colleagues at Saint Louis University advised two things:

1. Use common sense. In a world where common sense is not so common, this advice comes in handy!
2. Consider the experiences of others. This means to seek the advice of experienced couples. Who is a better qualified for this task than your parents? Of course, there are some toxic parents who care less about their children than their own needs. Those parents do not even deserve to be parents. The majority of parents love and care

---

[77] Gerald Stein, *Emotional Maturity*, 1948.

for their children, however, and their experiences and guidance are priceless.

If I could add a more spiritual and Islāmic perspective, I also have two pieces of advices. First, seek the guidance of righteous men and women in your community, those you can approach and trust. These people will give you genuine and sincere advice with your interests in mind at all times. Keep those groups of people close, for they will benefit you enormously. Second, remember that no matter what, everyone can only help you by what Allāh allows them to do. Your reliance and dependence should be strictly and solely toward Him. When making the decision of choosing your future husband or wife, my advice and the advice of our predecessors is *Salāt Al-Istikhārah*.

CHAPTER 5

Salātul Istikhārah

I teach my students to always define a word in order to explain it. I always begin by etymologically explaining the word and then providing the Islāmic definition. When seeking *istikhārah* in its etymological form, the great scholar Ibn Hajar Al-Asqalani defines it in his Fat-hul Bāri as coming from two root words: *al-khair* or *al-khiyarah*. *Al-Khair* means favorable, preferable, good, or agreeable. I think you get the picture. *Al-Khiyarah* means choice, selection, the best choice, etc. When we merge the two meanings, we can see that, linguistically, *al-istikhārah* is related to choosing the best, most preferred, and most favorable decision. From the Islāmic perspective, *al-istikhārah* is searching for the best choice between two or more things, while leaving it in the Hands of Allāh, due to our understanding of *tawakkul*, intrinsic reliance upon Allāh. Furthermore, *al-istikhārah* is a prayer with its set of rituals.

People pray *Salātul Istikhārah* for situations where they need to choose between job offers or choose between areas of relocation or other stressful choices where they truly do not know what the right move is. Can people pray this prayer for minor matters as well? Of course! However, since this book's focus is marital counseling, we will discuss *Al-istikhārah* from the perspective of the future spouse and seeking Allāh's clarity when deciding whether the potential partner is the right one. Both future spouses, along with their families, must pray and ask Allāh to choose what is best. They should be sincere in their supplication and humble enough to accept Allāh's will. How many times do people make *Al-istikhārah* prayer after already settling on one outcome and being unwilling to accept another? When entering the mind-set of *Al-istikhāra*, we must remember our fallibility as human beings and the all-Knowingness of Allāh.

There are many misconceptions of *Salātul Istikhārah*. Many people think *istikhārah* comes to you like a dream, but dreams can be misleading! Others think it manifests as a sign in their day-to-day interactions. We must remember, however, the concept of self-fulfilling prophecy. When we set our minds on something already, we will find everything as a sign to justify our decisions.

Oh, children of Adam, use your God-given gift of intellect—not superstition—when it comes to making your decisions! In some parts of the world, people go to sheikhs, asking them to pray *istikhārah* for them. This is a form of *bid'ah*, or innovation. Only you can seek clarity on your issue from Allāh. Yes, you may ask people to pray for you, but to make people pray *istikhārah*, as if they are an intermediary or agent, is nonsensical. *Al-Istikhārah* indeed works, and eventually, how you should decide will become apparent to you. It becomes apparent, when you start to see the opportunities present or hide themselves. When it becomes clear that what you wanted to do would not be in your best interest, avoid acting on it, or you will face the consequences. Often Allāh's will may go contrary to your desire, but the glad tiding is that Allāh knows what's best for you better than you do. Follow Allāh, for you worship Him, and avoid your desires. Allāh says in Surah Al-Baqarah,

وَعَسَىٰ أَن تَكْرَهُوا شَيْئًا وَهُوَ خَيْرٌ لَّكُمْ وَعَسَىٰ أَن تُحِبُّوا شَيْئًا وَهُوَ شَرٌّ لَّكُمْ وَاللَّهُ يَعْلَمُ وَأَنتُمْ لَا تَعْلَمُونَ

"But perhaps you hate a thing and it is good for you; and perhaps you love a thing and it is bad for you. And Allāh Knows, while you know not" (Qur'an 2:216).

How to Perform Salātul Istikhārah

Istikharah is performed by praying two units (rak'ahs) of supererogatory (nāfila) prayer. Then, after the prayer, supplicate the du'a of istikhārah, which is taught by the beloved Prophet, as reported in Al-Bukhāri:

إِذَا هَمَّ أَحَدُكُمْ بِالْأَمْرِ فَلْيَرْكَعْ رَكْعَتَيْنِ مِنْ غَيْرِ الْفَرِيضَةِ ثُمَّ لِيَقُلِ: اللَّهُمَّ إِنِّي أَسْتَخِيرُكَ بِعِلْمِكَ وَأَسْتَقْدِرُكَ بِقُدْرَتِكَ، وَأَسْأَلُكَ مِنْ فَضْلِكَ الْعَظِيمِ، فَإِنَّكَ تَقْدِرُ وَلَا أَقْدِرُ وَتَعْلَمُ وَلَا أَعْلَمُ وَأَنْتَ عَلَّامُ الْغُيُوبِ، اللَّهُمَّ إِنْ كُنْتَ تَعْلَمُ أَنَّ هَذَا الْأَمْرَ خَيْرٌ لِي فِي دِينِي وَمَعَاشِي وَعَاقِبَةِ أَمْرِي ـ أَوْ قَالَ عَاجِلِ أَمْرِي وَآجِلِهِ ـ فَاقْدُرْهُ لِي وَيَسِّرْهُ لِي ثُمَّ بَارِكْ لِي فِيهِ، وَإِنْ كُنْتَ تَعْلَمُ أَنَّ هَذَا الْأَمْرَ شَرٌّ لِي فِي دِينِي وَمَعَاشِي وَعَاقِبَةِ أَمْرِي ـ أَوْ قَالَ فِي عَاجِلِ أَمْرِي وَآجِلِهِ ـ فَاصْرِفْهُ عَنِّي وَاصْرِفْنِي عَنْهُ، وَاقْدُرْ لِي الْخَيْرَ حَيْثُ كَانَ ثُمَّ أَرْضِنِي بِهِ ـ قَالَ ـ وَيُسَمِّي حَاجَتَهُ.

He said, "If anyone is distressed by an important matter, he should offer a two rak`at prayer other than the compulsory ones and say (after the prayer): -- O Allāh! I ask guidance from Your knowledge, And Power from Your Might and I ask for Your great blessings. You are capable and I am not. You know and I do not and You know the unseen. O Allāh! If You know that this job is good for my religion and my subsistence and in my Hereafter --Then You ordain it for me and make it easy for me to get, And then bless me in it, and if You know that this job is harmful to me In my religion and subsistence and in the Hereafter- -Then keep it away from me and let me be away from it. And ordain for me whatever is good for me, And make

me satisfied with it." The Prophet (ﷺ) added that then
the person should name (mention) his need.[78]

Let's break this down:

1. The Prophet instructs us to pray two units of prayers. The wisdom
   behind this is to connect whatever we seek in this life to Allāh. This
   is similar to addressing our personal goals when pursuing marriage.
   The Prophet wants us to connect our desires to God because prosperity
   comes from Him. When we make those two rak'ah of nāfila prayer,
   we submit to Allāh and ask for His blessing and protection.

2. The Prophet then taught us the *du'a* (supplication), which begins with
   invoking Allāh's Names and Attributes. This is the prophetic etiquette
   of Du'a. Think about it like this: Your parents have done everything
   for you. They love you unconditionally. You need fifty dollars for
   something. How will you approach them? The most successful way
   is to go to them with humility and respect, such as saying to them,
   "Mom, Dad, you have done everything you can to take care of me."
   Showing this kind of appreciation will put a smile on their faces and
   fifty dollars in your pocket. To be clear, no being can be compared to
   Allāh. Perfection belongs to Allāh alone. However, this is a beneficial
   example for us to better understand the wisdom behind invoking His
   many Perfect Names and Attributes. We all know the ayah in Surah
   Ibrahim, where Allāh says,

$$\text{وَإِذْ تَأَذَّنَ رَبُّكُمْ لَئِن شَكَرْتُمْ لَأَزِيدَنَّكُمْ}$$

"And [remember] when your Lord proclaimed, 'If you are grateful, I
will surely increase you [in favor]'" (Qur'an 14:7).

The more sincere you are in your prayer and the more glorification
you send to Allāh, the more likely it is that Allāh will put even more
blessing in your du'a than the other. Put quality in your *istikhārah*, and
you will get quality in your result.

---

[78] Sahīh Al-Bukhāri, Hadīth #1162.

3. The third aspect of *istikhārah* is the reminder that "I do not know." How many times in the du'a do supplicants remind themselves of their limited sight and knowledge, while reminding themselves of how infinite Allāh's sight and knowledge is? This is because *Istikhārah* is all about asking Allāh to choose, not us. This is because we are weak, and we can be misled by the short-term rather than the long-term benefit. This is why we ask Allāh to choose what is best for us, and we must prepare ourselves to accept His will, for it is infinitely superior than what we want for ourselves. And Allāh never harms His believers.

If Allāh willed what is contrary to what you wanted, understand that it is what's best for you. A story comes to mind about Hudaibiyyah. The Prophet had a dream of the Muslims making *tawāf*, circumambulating the *Ka'bah*. This was during a time of multiple military victories for the Muslims in Madinah. Despite that, the Muslims walked all the way to Makkah unarmed, eager to fulfill this sacred pilgrimage and then return to their home. However, when arriving in Hudaibiyyah, the Prophet realized that Allāh had a different plan for the Muslims. The disbelievers of Makkah were not going to allow the Muslims to make Hajj that year. Great companions, such as Umar bin Al-Khattab, were unable to fathom that the Prophet would accept the restrictions of the disbelievers of Makkah. By numbers and strength, along with the support of Allāh, they were easily capable of imposing their will upon the people of Makkah. The Prophet, however, was fully confident and reliant on Allāh's will and signed the Treaty of Hudaibiyyah, causing the Muslims to return home when they were so close to the holy city of Makkah.

History teaches us later how decisive and brilliant the Prophet was for being patient. It was shortly after the signing of this treaty that the Muslims were justifiably able to liberate Makkah and make Hajj whenever they wanted to do so after that. Umar Ibn Al-Khattab, may Allāh be pleased with him, struggled with this reality because he is a human being with much pride for the Prophet and the ummah. Just the same, the Prophet knew better and is always prepared to humble himself before the will of Allāh, no matter what he wants for himself. Let this story be a reminder for all of us, and let us digest its lessons. Not everything that we desire is good for us, and not everything we think is bad is bad for us. The one who truly relies on Allāh in the face of hardship or ease will be prepared, knowing that both came from Allāh. In times of hardship, the Muslim will be patient. In times of ease, the Muslim will be grateful. Let that be your approach when getting your clarity from *al-istikhārah*.

4. Always keep in mind that the best time to pray Istikhārah and other *nāfila* prayers is during the last third of the night. In the famous hadīth narrated by Abu Hurairah, the Messenger of God said,

$$يَتَنَزَّلُ رَبُّنَا تَبَارَكَ وَتَعَالَى كُلَّ لَيْلَةٍ إِلَى السَّمَاءِ الدُّنْيَا$$

$$حِينَ يَبْقَى ثُلُثُ اللَّيْلِ الآخِرِ يَقُولُ مَنْ يَدْعُونِي فَأَسْتَجِيبَ$$

$$لَهُ، مَنْ يَسْأَلُنِي فَأُعْطِيَهُ، وَمَنْ يَسْتَغْفِرُنِي فَأَغْفِرَ لَهُ$$

> When it is the last third of the night, our Lord, the Blessed, the Superior, descends every night to the heaven of the world and says, "Is there anyone who invokes Me (demand anything from Me), that I may respond to his invocation; Is there anyone who asks Me for something that I may give (it to) him; Is there anyone who asks My forgiveness that I may forgive him?"[79]

In brief, Salātul Istikhārah has many virtues and in the journey of pursuing marriage, it serves as a vital tool for your protection. The first step is to be in a state of humility when confronted with the will of Allāh. It is extremely important to understand that reality. The reality is that you, the human, know nothing in the presence of Allāh. It should be comforting to know that Allāh is in control of all of our affairs because indeed, Allāh will never send us to our destruction; only we can do that. Always rely on Allāh, and always center your decision-making process on Allāh's pleasure and guidance.

---

[79] Sahīh Al-Bukhāri, Hadīth #6321.

CHAPTER 6

The Danger of Social Media

> The Facebook application has 2 billion active users around
> the world. Google's YouTube has 1.5 billion. These numbers
> are comparable to Christianity and Islām ... They are
> too big and too global to be held accountable.
> —Roger McNamee in *USA Today*[80]

I have found recent articles concerning marriage, romance, and relationships to be unsettling. Stories of men and women leaving their spouses for people they met online have kept me up at night as an imam. Whether we like it or not, this age of technology in which we live has influenced us greatly, for the worse and for the better. Couples spend more of their time chatting, tweeting, and texting with friends, sometimes even with total strangers, than they do with their significant others. American businessman Roger McNamee cited a 2013 study that found that the average person checks his or her smartphone 150 times a day! He follows this statistic by saying, "People spend 50 minutes a day on Facebook. Other social apps such as Snapchat, Instagram and Twitter combine to take up still more time." Based on these facts, it's safe to say that this phenomenon is a total distraction from the marital relationship and indeed a cause of major destruction.

---

[80] Robert McNamee, "The Google, Facebook Menace," *USA Today* (August 8, 2017).

When positive communication is replaced by social media, the intimacy and the relationship itself is in danger. If you truly love someone, then give that person your undivided attention. Cherish the moments you have with your spouse and your family because life is short. Twitter and Facebook trends are temporary, like the trends of today. Your family is forever. Why do we put ourselves in positions that we will later regret? The scariest fact about all of this is that Roger McNamee is an extremely successful businessman who was an early adviser for Facebook. He stated that despite his investment in the Internet monopoly, he was terrified by the damage being done by these Internet giants. He argued, "Like gambling, nicotine or heroin, Facebook and Google … produce short-term happiness with serious negative consequences in the long term." May Allāh protect us from the realization that we spent so much of our time on our phones that we missed out on the golden opportunities to communicate with our loved ones. Amīn.

Couples, Keep Your Phones Far Away from the Bedroom
We live in a world where couples, while lying in the same bed together, are communicating on social media with outsiders. In Arabic we say 'ajeeb (strange). Couples, keep your phones away from the bedroom, or it will cause someone to eventually leave the bedroom.

In my state of residence, New York, there is absolutely no leniency for those who text while driving. They are ticketed with points on their driver's licenses, which raises their insurance rates, and are given a hefty fine. This is because many innocent people have died due to the negligent behavior of texting drivers. Although texting while in a marriage is not physically fatal, on a spiritual and intimate level it is. Do not allow your marriage to be killed by Twitter, Facebook, Instagram, Snapchat, WhatsApp, and all the other distractive social media networks.

Let's be clear: Social media has its great benefits, and it is not *haram*. However, if consumed with imbalance, harm will be great. I have a suggestion, something I have observed more disciplined marital relationships practice: At the dinner table, couples and their children place all their devices in a designated area in the home and "unplug" themselves from the distractions in order to immerse themselves in the family discussion. Another suggestion from professionals is to designate hours of your day for specifically responding to social media and then being offline for the rest of those hours. Things of great benefit require the appropriate amount of discipline as well. Remind yourself that human interaction should never be trumped by social media interaction. Anything that impedes real-life communication in a marital relationship must never be entertained, for it is indeed a recipe for disaster. To save ourselves and our relationships from destruction, we must know when to be online and when to be offline.

The Dangers of Sexting Your Spouse

To the women of our world, because this problem has become not only regional but pandemic, sharing your nakedness with your man via communication devices such as your computer or phone is perhaps one of the most dangerous and riskiest things you can do. Only Allāh knows how many marriages and relationships have been destroyed by this behavior. Read the news; many companies sell our information to others. Likewise, your information and pictures could be sold. Why? Because none of us reads those fine-print terms and conditions. Your nakedness is your honor, and your honor is your nakedness. What are you to do if your phone with all those pictures is lost or stolen? What are you to do if hackers invade your privacy and access your nakedness? It is best to protect yourself from such vulnerability, and the world of the Internet is indeed one of vulnerability. Many companies hire cybersecurity analysts to protect their information. Remember you are not a company and cannot afford that type of security, so secure yourself by avoiding stupidity. Sexting is not only immoral but an act of stupidity. I have witnessed marriages collapse beyond repair due to sharing nakedness.

Mass Circulation and the Dangers of the Screenshot

Another danger is the power that social media has to circulate information to a mass amount of people in an extremely short time. How many people have ruined their lives by recording a simple fifteen-second voice message to someone and then finding their stupidity forwarded to hundreds of people in a matter of seconds? How many people, out of anger, expressed themselves immaturely and later found that their text conversation became a screenshot that was distributed to their community, causing public embarrassment? I have met people who had to relocate due to their self-inflicted wounds. We live in a world of *lā secret*; nothing is private anymore.

A minor mistake could lead to a disastrous end. It is extremely frightening because it is as if the curtain of Allāh that shields our sins from the public eye has been weakened through social media. To say something wrong in person is safer for you than to have it as a text or voice message. How many politicians have been destroyed for being reckless online? How many employees have lost their jobs for their behavior online? How many youth have recklessly exposed activities by documenting their sinful lifestyles online? Where is the shame? Those who are forgiven are those who are sincerely regretful and ashamed of their actions. How can they possibly be forgiven when they shamelessly and arrogantly go online into the public realm and disclose our major shortcomings? To my humble sisters I say be careful where you take off your clothes. Be careful with whom you indulge in private conversation and interaction. Honor is extremely important, and when your reputation is destroyed, it is almost impossible to redeem yourself. Of course, Allāh is the Oft-Forgiving to those who repent sincerely. With your shortcomings out in the open, however, humankind may not forgive, even though Allāh has forgiven. This is because His mercy is perfect, while humankind's is not. This may bring consequences that people must face for the remainder of their lives. Therefore, be extremely cautious of what you allow your phones to capture. A hadīth that comes to mind is authenticated by both the great imams Al-Bukhāri and Muslim. It is narrated by the great companion, Abu Hurairah, where he states that the Prophet ﷺ said,

كل أمتي معافًى إلا المجاهرين، وإن من المجاهرة أن يعمل الرجل بالليل عملاً، ثم يصبح وقد ستره الله عليه فيقول: يا فلان عملت البارحة كذا وكذا، وقد بات يستره ربه، ويصبح يكشف ستر الله عنه (متفق عليه)

Every one of my followers will be forgiven *except those who expose (openly) their wrongdoings.* An example of this is that of a man who commits a sin at night which Allāh has covered for him, and in the morning, he would say (to people): "I committed such and such sin last night,' while Allāh had kept it a secret. During the night, Allāh has covered it up but in the morning he tears up the cover provided by Allāh Himself.[81]

The environment in which we live is influenced by the digital age, so we need to equip ourselves with new cautionary standards. We need to add to our *hayā,* or modesty, by being more aware of what we share publicly. Our beautiful wives and daughters post photos of themselves looking their best while sick-minded people are watching. We need to be conscious and cautious with that reality by not providing our enemies with ammunition to attack us.

One positive point with regard to the danger that comes with social media is that it helps us somewhat learn *taqwa,* which means God-consciousness. If we were to walk cautiously on social media out of fear of being exposed, it is not far for us to learn the reality that Allāh is watching at all times. When approaching social media, approach it with the mentality that you could be publicly exposed at any time. Make sure the viewers are not given anything to demonize you because Shaytan is working day and night to destroy us all. Social media is his newest and most strategic offensive. May Allāh protect us all. Amīn.

The Challenges of Long-Distance Relationships

Loyola University professor John Powell writes in his book, *The Secret of Staying in Love,* "Human beings are composites of: body, mind, and soul. They have needs on all three levels of their existence. Their needs and appetites are: physical, psychological, and spiritual. Frustration at any one of these levels can produce agony in the whole organism."[82] If this is true,

---

[81] Sahīh Al-Bukhāri, Hadīth #5025; Sahīh Muslim, Hadīth #6069.

[82] John Powell, *The Secret of Staying in Love* (1974), 5.

married men and women whose spouses are unavailable for some reason will face serious challenges. Long-distance relationships or unavailability of the partner through situations like incarceration or seeking financial independence abroad cause spouses (especially women) three kinds of challenges:

1. waiting
2. cheating
3. leaving

For the woman, the challenge of waiting comes in the form of a dilemma. A woman who continues to wait for her husband as she ages must realize that her fertility weakens. Her chance of becoming pregnant is lower, and this is something that definitely requires consideration. Additionally, as the woman waits, her husband is aging too. Statistically, men are more likely to have weakened sexual health as they age. The male disorder known as erectile dysfunction often comes with age. If the woman chooses to wait for her husband, protecting faith and honor is extremely vital.

The trial of waiting is indeed a real one. Although divorce is not the end of the world, it should be a lesson. If the woman cannot wait for her husband because of her needs, she should leave humbly and respectfully in order to protect her image and her honor, which, if destroyed, cannot be brought back.

When finding a new partner, make sure all the necessary precautions have been taken to avoid the challenges of the past. It would be a great loss for the woman to have left her first husband only to marry a replica of the same man. As for those women who claim to be married but simultaneously violate the trust by seeing other men, fear Allāh. Turn back from this path immediately or else face the unfortunate fate of public exposure of your deeds. Cheaters are always caught in the end, and there is never an excuse to save them.

For those men who, while working elsewhere, have left their loyal and loving wives back home, respect yourselves and honor that trust. A long-distance relationship is enough of a trial, but if the man cheats while abandoning his family, Allāh will not overlook such a heinous crime. The prayers of the oppressed are always answered, and destruction will come very soon. We are to be honest with ourselves if we cannot handle long-distance relationships. By Allāh, it is better to leave than to commit one of the worst sins, adultery. For those men who have, for whatever reason, no way to return home, direct communication is key. Give your wife options, and do not hide such information from her.

The underlying theme of all this is self-accountability and self-awareness. The breaking of trust is never an option. If that thought ever comes to mind, understand that it may be time to let things go with that relationship. Indeed, Allāh is all-Aware of our affairs. We pray Allāh protects us from such trials and tribulations. Amīn.

I share this with you to educate. Many of us marry people while not understanding their future plans of relocating and without consideration of our plans. A prevalent problem in most countries is men moving abroad to support families back home. Although providing for the family is a noble cause, it is not the ideal situation and will come with major challenges. Women, make sure you are aware of these scenarios because I grieve along with you when I see you hurting from the challenges that come from long-distance relationships. Knowledge is truly power. We counselors will never stop providing knowledge for the sake of the collective community's protection. We ask Allāh for His *taufeeq* (success). Amīn.

Because imams are the leaders of their community, it is most commonly accepted that these spiritual leaders get to officiate marriage ceremonies. Based on this reality, there is a moral responsibility upon the spiritual leadership to do something that will increase couples' chances of marriage survival, as well as—more importantly—helping to increase an environment of happiness. This environment can be achieved through appreciation, respect, and care for each other.

An initiative of training and an educational discussion on the Islāmic principles of marriage are vital if the relationship is to work. Indeed, the wedding and its ceremonies are but a day or two; marriage is for a lifetime. A strong foundation is necessary for the marriage to succeed. That should come from all of us, individually and collectively. Although Islāmic marriage is a system with divorce as an option, such a step is only warranted when incompatibility and harmfulness arise. When done, it must be executed equitably. If divorce occurs, we must plan properly and then move on with optimistic thinking.

With that in mind, premarital counseling usually consists of a minimum of three sessions. The total time involved is approximately five hours. Topics that will be discussed in these sessions are the following:

1. Islāmic marriage
2. responsibilities
3. marriageability traits
4. how to resolve differences
5. divorce and its consequences
6. advice from seasoned couples

Premarital counseling is more essential in our modern day than at any other time in human history. With the challenges only increasing by the week, counselors need to equip our youth with the tools to protect their honor and future marriages, as well protecting their families from disintegration.

When I conduct premarital counseling sessions I ask couples what they think is true about love. I get a variety of great answers, some mediocre answers, and some that are downright terrible. As a teacher, however, I see people's mistakes as a chance to guide them. So many young people think that love is dangerous, a headache, or horrific, and they have other naive understandings of love. Love, however, is patience, kindness, care, and appreciation. A challenge that comes from love is balancing affection and mercy. Some young people are short-sighted and want to choose spouses who will be good for them temporarily. With age, however, their benefit will fade. That is why my job as an imam is to open the consciousness of these youth, help them avoid shallowness, and seek depth in their future spouses.

We all know the saying "Love is blind." Premarital counseling is here to give you eyeglasses so that your blindness does not cause you great harm in the long run. Blind love causes spouses to overlook serious flaws in the name of love. Such recklessness will cause the love often talked about to burn out quickly. Center your pursuit of love in the lens of spirituality, without neglecting your physical and mental needs. Premarital counseling does not have all the answers, but with its proper guidance, our young peoples' marriages stand more of a chance against today's turbulent times. May Allāh protect us all. Amīn.

CHAPTER 7

Marriage in Islām

هُوَ الَّذِي خَلَقَكُم مِّن نَّفْسٍ وَاحِدَةٍ وَجَعَلَ مِنْهَا زَوْجَهَا لِيَسْكُنَ إِلَيْهَا

It is He who created you from one soul and created from it its mate that he might dwell in security with her.

—Qur'an 7:189

Definition of Marriage in Islām

An-Nikah is the Arabic word for marriage. Linguistically, it means to tie, to make a knot, contract, to join, and unite. In a literal sense, that is what marriage is all about—the joining of two individuals. In Islām, the definition of *an-nikah* is connected to the literal definition. *An-Nikah* is the marriage contract between both individuals and their respective families. It documents the family's offering of the bride and the groom's acceptance of the offer. From the Islāmic perspective scholars of fiqh have defined marriage as clearly having two components:

1. *Ma'unun-Nikah*—the ability to provide for the family, and this is more specific to the husband.

2. *Al-Wat-u*—the ability to consummate the marriage, and this concerns both partners.

The Desire to Marry

Since the creation of humankind, with the first man—our father, Adam—Allāh constituted marriage between men and women. As mentioned in the very beginning, Surah Al-A`arāf has given us an explicit understanding of the very first marital relationship. The verse below, based on our predecessors' interpretation, discusses the purpose of the very first human union between our father, Adam, and mother, Hawwa.

هُوَ الَّذِي خَلَقَكُم مِّن نَّفْسٍ وَاحِدَةٍ وَجَعَلَ مِنْهَا زَوْجَهَا لِيَسْكُنَّ
إِلَيْهَا فَلَمَّا تَغَشَّاهَا حَمَلَتْ حَمْلًا خَفِيفًا فَمَرَّتْ بِهِ فَلَمَّا أَثْقَلَت
دَّعَوَا اللَّهَ رَبَّهُمَا لَئِنْ آتَيْتَنَا صَالِحًا لَّنَكُونَنَّ مِنَ الشَّاكِرِينَ

> It is He who created you from one soul and created from it its mate that he might **dwell in security with her**. And when he covers her, she carries a light burden and continues therein. And when it becomes heavy, they both invoke Allāh, their Lord, "If You should give us a good [child], we will surely be among the grateful." (Qur'an 7:189)

Through this verse, Allāh taught us the essence of marriage. Marriage is the union of two souls, and when the souls tie a knot with one another, they form a sense of security. The relationship is a partnership in which the husband carries the burdens of his wife, and the wife carries the burdens of her husband. This relationship of give and take guides them to Allāh's blessing them with a child, an offspring that will take from both in genetics and nurturing. Furthermore, when hardship becomes too tough, they call upon Allāh because within their relationship is the undying principle of *tawakkul*, an ultimate reliance in Allāh. They navigate through life by *shukr*, the attitude of gratitude.

Sexual desire is an innate characteristic, which, if not protected, will cause unbelievable harm that will destroy man beyond repair. This is why Allāh, through the Qur'an, sets regulations upon men to protect them from self-destruction due to their sexual desires. Allāh teaches sexual ethics for both men and women in this passage of Suratun-Nur:

قُل لِّلْمُؤْمِنِينَ يَغُضُّوا مِنْ أَبْصَارِهِمْ وَيَحْفَظُوا فُرُوجَهُمْ ۚ ذَٰلِكَ أَزْكَىٰ لَهُمْ ۗ إِنَّ اللَّهَ خَبِيرٌ بِمَا يَصْنَعُونَ

[Prophet], tell believing men to lower their glances and guard their private parts: that is purer for them. God is well aware of everything they do. (Qur'an 24:30)

First and foremost, let us observe the length of this verse. Only a little over a line long, this verse instructs the men who claim to believe how to protect themselves and purify their hearts from the challenges of our world; more specifically, sexual desires. As mentioned, this is arguably one of the most powerful desires in human behavior. Therefore, sexual attraction begins with the human eye glancing at the opposite sex's physical characteristics. This is why Allāh instructs men to reduce their vision, which also means to lower one's gaze. Moreover, we can take away from this verse that protection from these desires comes from the individual. The individual, although faced with these challenges, is responsible for how he conducts himself. Now let's continue this passage in the Qur'an, where Allāh addresses the believing women:

وَقُل لِّلْمُؤْمِنَاتِ يَغْضُضْنَ مِنْ أَبْصَارِهِنَّ وَيَحْفَظْنَ فُرُوجَهُنَّ وَلَا يُبْدِينَ زِينَتَهُنَّ إِلَّا مَا ظَهَرَ مِنْهَا وَلْيَضْرِبْنَ بِخُمُرِهِنَّ عَلَىٰ جُيُوبِهِنَّ ۖ وَلَا يُبْدِينَ زِينَتَهُنَّ إِلَّا لِبُعُولَتِهِنَّ أَوْ آبَائِهِنَّ أَوْ آبَاءِ بُعُولَتِهِنَّ أَوْ أَبْنَائِهِنَّ أَوْ أَبْنَاءِ بُعُولَتِهِنَّ أَوْ إِخْوَانِهِنَّ أَوْ بَنِي إِخْوَانِهِنَّ أَوْ بَنِي أَخَوَاتِهِنَّ أَوْ نِسَائِهِنَّ أَوْ مَا مَلَكَتْ أَيْمَانُهُنَّ أَوِ

التَّابِعِينَ غَيْرِ أُولِي الْإِرْبَةِ مِنَ الرِّجَالِ أَوِ الطِّفْلِ الَّذِينَ لَمْ

يَظْهَرُوا عَلَىٰ عَوْرَاتِ النِّسَاءِ ۖ وَلَا يَضْرِبْنَ بِأَرْجُلِهِنَّ لِيُعْلَمَ مَا

يُخْفِينَ مِن زِينَتِهِنَّ ۚ وَتُوبُوا إِلَى اللَّهِ جَمِيعًا أَيُّهَ الْمُؤْمِنُونَ لَعَلَّكُمْ

تُفْلِحُونَ.

And tell believing women that they should lower their glances, guard their private parts, and not display their charms beyond what [it is acceptable] to reveal; they should let their headscarves fall to cover their necklines and not reveal their charms except to their husbands, their fathers, their husbands' fathers, their sons, their husbands' sons, their brothers, their brothers' sons, their sisters' sons, their womenfolk, their slaves, such men as attend them who have no sexual desire, or children who are not yet aware of women's nakedness; they should not stamp their feet so as to draw attention to any hidden charms. **Believers, all of you, turn to God so that you may prosper.** (Qur'an 24:31)

When reading and reflecting upon the above verses of Suratun-Noor, observe the length difference. When Allāh addresses the women, the length of recitation is very different. Indeed, it will take you at least three times as long to recite the verse that addresses women as the verse that addresses men. This causes one to ask, why does Allāh place more importance in the sexual ethics of women? The answer to this question is that man is born out of woman, and therefore, if women are not protected, society will be unsafe as well. Moreover, mankind is fallible, and so Allāh addresses that reality at the end of the verse with a message of hope: "Turn to Allāh in repentance." This is not exclusive to women; it's for all the believers, in order for society to prosper.

With the two verses in Suratun-Noor in mind, author and psychologist James Dobson cites the research studies of social anthropologist J. D. Unwin. In Dr. Dobson's book *Emotions*, he comments on J. D. Unwin's profound work *Sexual Regulations and Cultural Behavior*. Unwin's work was affirmed by Allāh over 1,400 years ago. Dobson notes,

Mankind has known intuitively for at least 50 centuries that indiscriminate sexual activity represents both an individual and a corporate threat to survival." And history bears this out. Anthropologist J.D. Unwin conducted an exhaustive study of the 88 civilizations which have existed in the history of the world. Each culture has reflected a similar lifestyle, beginning with a strict code of sexual conduct and ending with the demand for complete "freedom" to express individual **passion**. Unwin reports that every society which extended sexual permissiveness to its people *was soon to perish*. There have been *no exceptions*."[83]

I would like the last line to echo in your mind: *no exceptions*. To save humanity from this societal destruction, Allāh created the institution of marriage in order to allow humankind to multiply without corruption.

Allāh said in An-Nisā,

وَإِنْ خِفْتُمْ أَلَّا تُقْسِطُوا فِي الْيَتَامَىٰ فَانكِحُوا مَا طَابَ لَكُم مِّنَ النِّسَاءِ مَثْنَىٰ وَثُلَاثَ وَرُبَاعَ ۖ فَإِنْ خِفْتُمْ أَلَّا تَعْدِلُوا فَوَاحِدَةً أَوْ مَا مَلَكَتْ أَيْمَانُكُمْ ۚ ذَٰلِكَ أَدْنَىٰ أَلَّا تَعُولُوا

> And if you fear that you will not deal justly with the orphan girls, then *marry* those that please you of [other] women, two or three or four. But if you fear that you will not be just, then [marry only] one or those your right hand possesses. That is more suitable that you may not incline [to injustice]. (Qur'an 4:3)

Al-Jamhoor, the majority of scholars are of the view that the commandment in *fankihoo* is for permissibility (*lil ibāhah*), as in, "(permissible for you is to) eat and drink." You do not *have to* marry one, let alone more than one. However, *you may*; and to marry is encouraged by the Sunnah. That is

---

[83] James C. Dobson, *Emotions* (2014), 66.

what the scholars of the majority opinion are arguing. However, there is the minority opinion, which is to be respected, as they are scholars within our ummah of diversity. The *zhāhiris*, or the literalists, in the scholarly community argue that the *amr* (commandment) is an obligation in the ayah and not just permissibility. This means, marriage, in general, is *mandatory*.

In our history, there arose a major misconception of this ayah, which was that through this ayah, it is justifiable to marry more than four wives. This distorted understanding came from two others:

1. The argument is based on the reality that our beloved Prophet married nine wives. This is a factual statement, but scholars remind us that although he married nine wives, the Prophet was no ordinary man, and there are rulings that pertaining only to him. For example, the Prophet would fast for a period of three full days—no food or water; this is called *siyāmul-wasāl*. Since the ummah would love to emulate the Prophet in all that he does, there came a point where some in the community wanted to practice this three-day fast, but the Prophet forbade them from doing so. When the community inquired why, as the Prophet himself practiced it, the Prophet clearly explained that this was documented through the narration of Abdullah bin Umar in a hadīth found in Sahīh Muslim, where the Prophet said clearly,

$$\text{إِنِّي لَسْتُ مِثْلَكُمْ إِنِّي أُطْعَمُ وَأُسْقَى}$$

"I am not like you; I am fed and supplied drink (by Allāh)."[84]

This sets the precedent for scholars to classify some of the Prophet's acts as exclusively permissible for him. The Prophet is not like us. Yes, he is human, but in spiritually and in many other ways, he is undoubtedly superior to us. His marrying nine wives is an exception simply granted to our beloved Prophet of God.

---

[84] Sahīh Al-Bukhāri, Hadīth #1962.

2. وَثُلَاث: Arabic letter 'و' may be used for addition. That is why some, with their twisted understanding, made the argument that Allāh was telling us that we can marry 2+3+4, which totals nine wives. It is quite apparent to the rational mind that this understanding is a quite a stretch from the authentic meaning of the verse. This misconception, however, happened in our peoples' history. To affirm what has been said against this misconception, I quote the eminent scholar of *tafseer* (Qur'anic interpretation) Al-Qurtabi: "Understand that the ayah *does not imply the permissibility of marrying nine women* as understood by those whose understanding of the Qur'an and Sunnah are perverted from the path of our predecessors, claiming that the 'و' is for addition; supporting their distortion with the argument that the Prophet married nine wives." To further affirm the statements above, the seventh-century (Hijri) scholar al-Hamdhani, in his book *'Irābul- Qur'an* (*The Grammar of Qur'an*) stated, "The و is used as a substitution (or option). It is stating that 'marry three *or* four' and this is the opinion of the *ijma'* (majority of Muslim scholars) except those whose statements are not recognized." This is the opinion of almost every respectable Muslim scholar, people who have studied the religion extensively.[85] May Allāh forgive and guide us all. Amīn.

Polygamy or Polygyny?

$$فَانكِحُوا مَا طَابَ لَكُم مِّنَ النِّسَاءِ مَثْنَىٰ وَثُلَاثَ وَرُبَاعَ ۖ فَإِنْ خِفْتُمْ أَلَّا تَعْدِلُوا فَوَاحِدَةً$$

"Marry whichever [other] women seem good to you, two, three, or four. If you fear that you cannot be equitable [to them], then marry only one" (Qur'an 4:3).

Definitions are extremely important to Muslims. Often when discussing the matter of marrying more than one wife, some Muslims use the term

---

[85] Al-Hamdhani, *The Grammar of Quran*, vol. 2 (2006), 205 (Surah 4:3.

polygamy. However, when we analyze the definition of this word, we realize that it means "marriage in which a spouse of either sex may have more than one mate at the same time." According to Islam, polygamy, by definition, is incorrect because marriage in which a spouse may have more than one mate at the same time belongs to males. Although it is enough to just say that this is what Allah instructed, logic as well explains why this is the case. If a woman has multiple husbands, who then becomes the legitimate father of her children? Yes, we live in the era of DNA testing, but that environment would cause a world of confusion. The correct term is *polygyny*, a term compatible with Islam. Islam, however, places conditions on it. Polygyny is "the state or practice of having more than one wife or female mate at a time." Islam allows a man to marry one, two, or three but no more than four wives at a time.

When addressing the matter of polygyny, we must understand a very crucial fact. Marrying of even one wife is an encouraged Sunnah with a set of obligations and rights, let alone marrying more than one. And this is why the best man after the Prophet ﷺ, Abu Bakr As-Sidiq (RA), married only two wives at a time in a culture where polygyny was predominant. It goes to show that if a man of his status chooses two when he can marry an additional two, there are more factors involved in choosing suitable wives. The great companion was not unable to financially afford the responsibilities of four wives; he was regarded as one of the wealthiest companions. The great companion was filled with noble qualities, so it was not as if he would have been incompetent as a husband, emotionally and spiritually, for the women. It was the satisfaction he had in his two wives, Asma bint 'Umais and Habibah bint Kharija. He was not concerned with other women because he was content with these two righteous women.

Imam Ibn Al-Jauzi, one of the great scholars of the sixth Islamic century, offered interesting and insightful advice, which is found in his book *Saidul Khatir*. He argues, "Be mindful of the women." He then states, "One of the greatest of harms that affects a man is marrying too many women … even if he is able to marry all the women of Baghdad, if a woman foreign to him from out of town arrived, he would think she has something that all his Baghdadian wives do not have."

Later in his book he discusses the "reasonable man" by suggesting, "The reasonable person will stick to one woman as long as she fulfills his needs. Moreover, there is no doubt that in this woman there will be a characteristic that he does not like, however he will work with majority of virtuous qualities rather than focus on her one shortcoming."[86] When reading the passage in Ibn Al-Jauzi's work, I reflect upon the tradition of Abu Bakr As-Sidiq, whose life perfectly supports the statements of the great scholar. Marriage is all about responsibility and accountability. It is not about the quantity (how many) but the quality of the marital relationship.

Polygyny in the West

In Western societies, polygyny is a culturally unacceptable practice. It is surrounded by misconceptions in the Western world, as well as many of the societies claiming to be Muslim. Nonetheless, its legal status in the West is clear; polygyny is outlawed, and therefore, as Muslims living in the West, we must respect the law of the land. Furthermore, as humble advice to imams living and leading in Western societies, our goal should be to preserve the families of our communities. Be diligent in cooperating with your nation's laws, and remember that marriage in Islam is by majority viewpoint, an encouraged Sunnah, and not an obligation; this is an extremely important distinction to make. Due to its optional status, polygyny can be compromised for the sake of complying with the law of one's land. Marriage to one is not equivalent to the practice of marrying more than one. In Islamic law, the former is prioritized much more than the latter.

Considering Sexual Attraction with Marriage

Sexual instinct is innate. Allāh has provided us with marriage to regulate this instinct. Marriage is a beautiful institution and is extremely encouraged for all who are capable. Sometimes it is considered a taboo to discuss the natural sexual attraction that men and women have for one another; I do care about and understand that mentality. However, the reality is that the consequence of our not discussing this issue is far more serious, especially

---

[86] Abdu-Rahman Ibn Al-Jauzi, Saidul Khātir (1999), 441.

when this book is about marriage. Is it not a fact that Allāh created man and woman to be attracted to one another? Marriage is how to go about such attraction. Do not allow people to demonize or forbid what is made permissible for you. A hadīth that affirms this point is told by one of Prophet Muhammad ﷺ's dear servants, Anas bin Mālik. He narrates a lesson-packed story:

أَنَس بْنَ مَالِكٍ ـ رضى الله عنه ـ يَقُولُ :جَاءَ ثَلَاثَةُ رَهْطٍ إِلَى
بُيُوتِ أَزْوَاجِ النَّبِيِّ صلى الله عليه وسلم يَسْأَلُونَ عَنْ عِبَادَةِ
النَّبِيِّ صلى الله عليه وسلم فَلَمَّا أُخْبِرُوا كَأَنَّهُمْ تَقَالُّوهَا فَقَالُوا
وَأَيْنَ نَحْنُ مِنَ النَّبِيِّ صلى الله عليه وسلم قَدْ غُفِرَ لَهُ مَا تَقَدَّمَ
مِنْ ذَنْبِهِ وَمَا تَأَخَّرَ. قَالَ أَحَدُهُمْ أَمَّا أَنَا فَإِنِّي أُصَلِّي اللَّيْلَ أَبَدًا.
وَقَالَ آخَرُ أَنَا أَصُومُ الدَّهْرَ وَلَا أُفْطِرُ. وَقَالَ آخَرُ أَنَا أَعْتَزِلُ
النِّسَاءَ فَلَا أَتَزَوَّجُ أَبَدًا. فَجَاءَ رَسُولُ اللَّهِ صلى الله عليه وسلم
فَقَالَ   أَنْتُمُ الَّذِينَ قُلْتُمْ كَذَا وَكَذَا أَمَا وَاللَّهِ إِنِّي لَأَخْشَاكُمْ لِلَّهِ
وَأَتْقَاكُمْ لَهُ، لَكِنِّي أَصُومُ وَأُفْطِرُ، وَأُصَلِّي وَأَرْقُدُ وَأَتَزَوَّجُ
النِّسَاءَ، فَمَنْ رَغِبَ عَنْ سُنَّتِي فَلَيْسَ مِنِّي .

A group of three men came to the houses of the wives of the Prophet (ﷺ) asking how the Prophet (ﷺ) worshipped (Allāh), and when they were informed about that, they considered their worship insufficient and said, "Where are we from the Prophet (ﷺ) as his past and future sins have been forgiven." Then one of them said, "I will offer the prayer throughout the night forever." The other said, "I will fast throughout the year and will not break my fast." The third said, "I will keep away from the women and will not marry forever." Allāh's Messenger (ﷺ) came to them and said, "Are you the same people who said so-and-so? By Allāh, I am more submissive to

Allāh and more afraid of Him than you; yet I fast and break my fast, I do sleep and I also marry women. So he who does not follow my tradition in religion, is not from me (not one of my followers)."[87]

This hadīth is also found in other hadīth books, including Sahih Muslim. It is extremely relevant to our times. So often we forbid ourselves the luxuries that even the Prophet himself enjoyed. When we derail from his Sunnah, we fall into extremism, whether in the far left or the far right.

Marriage, the most beautiful, oldest, and biggest institution known in human life, must also be recognized as the biggest responsibility a human can take on in his or her lifetime. As previously mentioned, the husband must be able to provide for the family, and both spouses must be able to provide one another with the necessary sexual satisfaction. Abdullah bin Mas'ood, one of the great scholars in the field of Qur'an, said, "We were with the Prophet (ﷺ) while we were young and had no wealth whatsoever." So Allāh's Messenger (ﷺ) said,

$$\text{"يَا مَعْشَرَ الشَّبَابِ مَنِ اسْتَطَاعَ الْبَاءَةَ فَلْيَتَزَوَّجْ، فَإِنَّهُ أَغَضُّ لِلْبَصَرِ، وَأَحْصَنُ لِلْفَرْجِ، وَمَنْ لَمْ يَسْتَطِعْ فَعَلَيْهِ بِالصَّوْمِ، فَإِنَّهُ لَهُ وِجَاءٌ".}$$

O young people! Whoever among you can marry, should marry, because it helps him lower his gaze and guard his modesty (i.e. his private parts from committing illegal sexual intercourse etc.), and whoever is not able to marry, should fast, as fasting diminishes his sexual power.[88]

This hadīth is found in nearly all authentic hadīth collections.

The word *Al-Ba-ah* refers to the responsibility that comes with marriage. This responsibility is defined by two components: (1) providing shelter

---

[87] Sahīh Al-Bukhāri, Hadīth #5063.

[88] Sahīh Al-Bukhāri, Hadīth #5066; Sahīh Muslim, Hadīth #1400.

144

for the family, and (2) the consummation of the marriage through sexual intercourse. Both go hand in hand. The eminent scholar of hadīth, Imam An-Nawawi, acknowledges that both are essential components of marriage and are inseparable.[89] Therefore, whoever can provide accommodation and consummate a marriage may marry. However, if the husband is unable to accommodate the financial needs of the household, and either spouse cannot accommodate the sexual need of the partnership, then they should follow the advice of the Prophet and fast. For more information, read Imam Ibn Hajar Al-'Asqalāni's *Fat-hul Bāri*.

Islāmic Ruling on Marriage

Scholars have long agreed that the Islāmic ruling on marriage is based on the individual case of the person. They have categorized these cases into five categories:

1. **Marriage is an obligatory act.** This ruling is for those who genuinely fear the risk of committing *zina* (fornication) with the ability to provide for the wife. For individuals in this case, marriage is the only proper solution and should be carried out as soon as possible.

2. **It is unlawful to marry.** This ruling is for those who cannot provide for the spouse, nor can they consummate the marriage— the two things that are necessary for marriage. Interestingly enough, however, the great scholar Ibn Hajar Al-Asqalani, in his *Fat-hul Bāri*, argued that if the bride knows prior to the marriage that her husband is impotent or has no desire for women, but she agrees to marry him anyway, their marriage is lawful.[90]

3. **It is discouraged to marry.** This ruling is for those who have a deficiency that will affect the partner, both physically and emotionally. Examples could be a serious mental illness, such as bipolar disorder or schizophrenia, two of many conditions that can make a marriage difficult for the other.

---

[89] An-Nawawi, *Sharh Sahīh Muslim*, vol. 9 (1987), 183–184.

[90] Ibn Hajar Al-'Asqalāni, *Fat-hul Bāri*, vol. 10 (1996), 135–136.

4. **It is encouraged to marry.** This ruling is for those who *can* marry. What are you waiting for? Get married because it will help protect you from dishonor and misconduct. Do not think you are too good for the advice of our Prophet.

5. **It is lawful for those who are safe and comfortable without it.** It is permissible to be single, of course, even if you have the capability to marry, as long as you can ensure that you will remain uncorrupted. One reason for this ruling is the example of young sons beginning in their careers. Although they absolutely have the means to get married, they choose to focus their priorities on their parents first. This is a noble and respectable path to take. However, marrying while also taking care of the parents is the noblest. And Allāh knows best.

Decision to Marry

The best and wisest decision you will ever make (after choosing your faith) is to carefully and intelligently choose a mate who cares about you and the relationship. I repeat that statement many times in this book because marriage is a lifelong commitment, and the two people will live in that commitment under the same roof. It begins with sharing happiness and sorrows, good days and bad days. Most important, marriage is building that house with the bricks of love, care, and compassion. Both individuals are expected to pass their heritage to their children and grandchildren. Is this reality scaring you? If so, perhaps you are not ready for this responsibility.

In Islām, however, we believe in the principle of *husnuz-zann*—the benefit of the doubt, the positive thinking one should have toward others. Therefore, I will assume good from you and say that you are scared due to being smart. Reasonable human beings get frightened when they understand how challenging a journey may be. Marriage indeed is a daunting task, especially when both come from different upbringings, and their lifestyles begin to merge and blend in nongraceful fashion. This can be an absolute disaster if the couple is ill equipped with regard to the responsibilities of marriage. So it is important for the potential bride and groom to *know* exactly what they are getting themselves into.

In *Marriage and the Family*, Dr. Thomas and his colleagues argue that "choice of a mate is perhaps the most important decision that a person will ever be called upon to make."[91] The statements of Dr. Thomas and his colleagues, however, are too general. For Muslims, choosing the appropriate mate is perhaps the most important decision after choosing one's faith. Moreover, as an imam who has seen too much, I advise you to choose wisely, or else you will be ruined, along with your children. They may never forgive you for your disastrous choice of marrying a toxic parent, who not only destroyed his/her life but also destroyed the lives of his/her own children through individualism, emotional immaturity, and toxicity. We are to fear Allāh and to put our trust in Him, yet not be stupid. Always approach things with knowledge, and never go into matters blindly.

How to Choose the Right Mate

The Prophet has given standard criteria for choosing the right mate. He is quoted to have said, "Choose him/her who is pious and surely you will prosper."[92] *Piety*, in this narration, is not separated from good manners. Therefore, our being mindful of the Creator guides us in understanding our roles as individuals in a relationship, along with living the life of righteousness, regardless of the challenges of the time. *Physical attraction* is important to marriage as well. We are created equal but not identical. Even identical twins have distinctions. Physical attraction may differ from one person to another. Different people find different qualities appealing. Tall women attract some men, while other men prefer short women. Likewise, some women are attracted to tall men, while some prefer short men. Be careful when you generalize what constitutes beauty or attraction. A hadīth that should guide the rest of this section is narrated by Jabir bin Abdullah, that the Prophet ﷺ taught the companions:

---

[91] Dr. Thomas, *Marriage and the Family* (1955), 25.

[92] Sahīh Al-Bukhāri, Hadīth #5090.

إِذَا خَطَبَ أَحَدُكُمُ الْمَرْأَةَ فَإِنِ اسْتَطَاعَ أَنْ يَنْظُرَ إِلَى مَا يَدْعُوهُ
إِلَى نِكَاحِهَا فَلْيَفْعَلْ. " قَالَ فَخَطَبْتُ جَارِيَةً فَكُنْتُ أَتَخَبَّأُ لَهَا حَتَّى
رَأَيْتُ مِنْهَا مَا دَعَانِي إِلَى نِكَاحِهَا وَتَزَوُّجِهَا فَتَزَوَّجْتُهَا. "

> When one of you asked a woman in marriage, if he is able
> to look at what will induce him to marry her, he should
> do so." He (Jabir) said: "I asked a girl in marriage I used
> to look at her secretly until I looked at what induced me
> to marry her. I, therefore, married her."[93]

This hadīth has great lessons in it:

1. When it is time to pursue marriage, have some introspection. You
   should seek within yourself the "why" behind your choice. There is
   nothing wrong with going for physical attraction, but when coupled
   with brilliant attributes in the realm of piety, you have found yourself
   an excellent choice to commit to for the rest of your life.
2. Jabir bin Abdullah's input in this hadīth shares an interesting lesson as
   well. Regarding his own pursuit of marriage, he said, "I used to look
   at her *secretly* until I looked at what induced me to marry her." What
   you can take from this is that when you sincerely intend to marry, you
   have the liberty of really looking at your potential spouse to make
   absolutely sure that you are attracted to him or her. But woe to the
   sick-minded who simply want to look for their gratification. Allāh is
   well acquainted with our affairs.

Based on the previous hadīth, the great imam Abdur Rahmān Al-Jauzi (d.
597 H) said, nearly a millennium ago, "Whoever is interested in bearing
a child and satisfying his sexual desire, let him be selective in choosing a
mate by first and foremost looking at her and follow his feelings." Al-Jauzi
concluded, "It is indeed meaningless, if the physical attraction contradicts
the inner self."[94] This means that it would be a great disservice to you
and your spouse to marry if you are not attracted to him or her. Intimacy

---

[93] Sunan Abi Dawūd, Hadīth #2082.

[94] Abdu-Rahman Ibn Al-Jauzi, *Saidul Khātir* (1999), 50–54.

is a crucial pillar in marriage and to not be attracted to your spouse is a monumental roadblock to intimacy. Al-Jauzi's words can be found in his work *Saidul Khātir*. This concept concerns husbands and wives to the same degree. Both spouses have the right to enjoy and benefit in the marriage. Furthermore, Imam Al-Jauzi warned against basing all of your decision to marry on attraction because it will not last. As previously mentioned, look for an ideal mate who has righteousness intertwined with physical beauty in order for you to prosper.

Remember, searching for a marriage partner is a very difficult process because of *pretenders*. We are surrounded by ungodly men and women who disguise themselves as righteous men and women when they are internally more evil than they appear. The predator will do anything to get its prey. This is why, like the wolf, the wicked will hide in sheep's clothing. These are the people who, on most occasions, are eloquent; they mimic and speak the language of the righteous but are venomous and will attack to kill or destroy during your silence and innocence. You must use common sense and patience when detecting falsehood. Most important, ask Allāh ﷻ for guidance and protection because pretenders are very sleek and difficult to detect.

Serious precautionary measures must be taken in choosing a mate so that you do not regret later your erroneous decision. Therefore, use your intelligence wisely. It is the most powerful gift from the Creator, and it will guide you to a correct decision.

Compatibility can't be overemphasized in this process—the qualities and characteristics shared by both mates. When choosing your ideal spouse, look for the similarities, as mentioned in premarital counseling. Is this potential spouse on the same religious level as you are? When it comes to cultural differences, are you able to work well with yours, or is there some key conflicting understandings? Are you into spicy food, and your potential spouse likes nonspicy food? Do you speak the same language, and if not, will it be a problem for you? These are necessary questions to ask yourself before entering the relationship. There is nothing wrong with being different from your spouse, but it is only natural to require some aspects of the relationship to be mutually understood and accepted. The Prophet encouraged diversity in marriage. Nevertheless, we must be prepared for the challenges that come with staunch differences. On that note, some Muslim jurists are of the opinion that *kafā-ah*, or compatibility, is necessary in choosing a mate.

Basic Principles and Qualities of an Ideal Mate

I cannot overemphasize that choosing your partner is the most important decision you will make in life (after faith, of course). A bad choice will not only affect you as an individual but will affect the stability of the entire family, which will bleed into the future generations to come. Additionally, a disaster in one family is a disaster in the community at large. Therefore, my dear sisters, choose the father of your children wisely; he should be a righteous guardian, a caring friend, a responsible adviser, and a protector. Your children will remember you as a responsible mother who did not worship her desires but rather was a phenomenal lady who did what was right in this life and the hereafter.

To my dear brothers who have been blessed with the position of husband, this is not a game. If you fail in this stage of your life, the life of your future children and grandchildren will become tainted with misery and destruction. Therefore, choose the mother of your children wisely; do not turn only to emotions in choosing a mate. Maintaining a healthy and sound relationship must be your priority.

By what standard do we measure quality spouses? Here are four points to keep in mind when seeking a spouse:

1. Inner characteristics—Find someone who is a righteous role model; someone who is disciplined, respectful, and responsible and who believes in family values. Let's not forget the previously mentioned hadīth narrated by Abu Hurairah: "A woman may be married for four qualities: for property, rank, beauty and religion; get the religious one and prosper."[95]

---

[95] Ibn Hajar Al-'Asqalani, *Bulugh Al-Maram*, hadīth widely agreed upon.

The Prophet also said,

$$\text{"الدُّنْيَا مَتَاعٌ وَخَيْرُ مَتَاعِ الدُّنْيَا الْمَرْأَةُ الصَّالِحَةُ"}$$

"The whole world is a provision, and the best object
of benefit of the world is the pious woman."[96]

2. Outer being—The heart is extremely important, but appearance matters too. Anas bin Mālik narrated about a sahabi named Mugheerah bin Shu'bah, who wanted to marry a woman. The Messenger ﷺ first instructed Mugheerah, "Go and look at her, for that is more likely to create love between you." Mugheerah followed the Prophet's instruction and later mentioned how well he got along with the woman.[97] Additionally, we already visited the hadīth of Jabir, where Allāh's Messenger said, "When one of you proposes to a woman, if he is able to look at what will induce him to marry her, he should do so."[98] Although it is agreed that religious and moral values are the basic foundation of marriage, physical attractiveness is still an important quality to bear in mind.

3. Your spouse's upbringing also needs to be acknowledged. The environment in which a person is nurtured plays a vital role in how he or she will act and react in a relationship.

   • Environment at home—Did your spouse grow up in an abusive home? If so, his/her experiences can cause him/her to be psychologically affected in negative and sometimes positive ways. A positive example would be someone who was physically abused and due to that experience will never physically harm his/her future spouse and children. However, the victim of physical abuse often becomes the victimizer. These are things that we need to

---

[96] Sahīh Muslim, Hadīth #1424.

[97] Ibn Mājah, Hadīth #1938.

[98] Reported by Ahmad and Abi Dawūd, and Imam Ibn Hajar said, its men are reliable and authenticated by Al-Hākim. Found in the Book of Marriage chapter of *Bulugh Al-Maram*.

be aware of so we can make the best choice of a spouse. If the problems are fixable, let us remedy them, but if not, it is a blessing that the person is a potential spouse and not an actual one.

- Environment outside—What kind of community did your spouse grow up in? Are his/her friends problematic or resourceful? These things need to be considered as well. As mentioned earlier in the saying of the Prophet, "A man is of the religion of their friend." Understand that when choosing your spouse, his/her influence on you is great. Therefore, you have to be selective.

- Expectations based on environment—Do not allow the media to shape your marital identity. Hollywood has done enormous damage to many people's understanding of romance and marriage. It has taught us to forgive less because we have been programmed to witness "perfect" marriages. In times of marital conflict, do not let your heart be troubled. Go about your days together with compassion, grace, love, and peace. Most importantly, pray for each other, and seek Allāh's protection. Indeed, He is the best Protector. Allāh says, "He wishes to accept your repentance, but those who follow their desires, wish that you should deviate tremendously away from the right path" (Qur'an 4:27). The media and other toxins have derailed humankind so much already, but don't let your marriage suffer from their impact.

4. Parents will continue to play a very important role in the lives of their children after marriage. Therefore, it is encouraged that they help the new couple with their experience of marital life and continue to guide and protect them.

- Parents must teach young married children responsibility and accountability. Marriage is about responsibility, which must not be neglected; the consequences of such negligence are enormous.

- Parents must discourage both partners in the couple from disrespecting each other. Teach them the values of patience and mercy.

- Parents must be guided by the principle of investigation before decision. Do not take sides, period. Investigate the problem, and help the couple in solving it.

- Parents must encourage communication between the couple. It is more important to understand than to condemn.
- Parents must be willing to help the couple, physically and emotionally.
- Parents must do whatever it takes to solve the existing problem within the family; if they are unable, they should involve a noble, righteous person.
- Parents must be honest when they are the problem solvers and not side with their child by default in the relationship's conflicts. Parents must help to bridge any existing chasm between the couple.
- Parents must establish a symbiotic relationship between both families.
- Most important, obedience to Allāh must be the utmost priority.

As parents, we are to advise but not *impose*. Families have been destroyed by the imposition of parents who still treat their married children like babies. Parents must always avoid being a problem because that is *triangulation*— when parents decide to be part of the marital life of their children and overstay their welcome.

Conditions of an Ideal Marriage

1. **Dowry.** In Arabic, *dowry* comes in many names, such as sadāq, sadaqah, mahr, nihla, and ajr. In Islām, the man is required to provide the offered bride a dowry. This gift has no limit and can consist of anything as long as the bride accepts it, and of course it must be a lawful gift. Although it may be delayed—as, for example, a sum of money in the form of installments—it is encouraged that part of be given before the marriage is consummated. Extravagancy is discouraged in this regard. Allāh said,

$$\text{وَآتُوا النِّسَاءَ صَدُقَاتِهِنَّ نِحْلَةً ۚ فَإِن طِبْنَ لَكُمْ عَن شَيْءٍ مِّنْهُ}$$

$$\text{نَفْسًا فَكُلُوهُ هَنِيئًا مَّرِيئًا}$$

"And give the women [upon marriage] their [bridal] gifts graciously. But if they give up willingly to you anything of it, then take it in satisfaction and ease" (Qur'an 4:4).

Allāh ﷻ also said,

$$وَلَا جُنَاحَ عَلَيْكُمْ أَن تَنكِحُوهُنَّ إِذَا آتَيْتُمُوهُنَّ أُجُورَهُنَّ$$

"And there is no blame upon you if you marry them when you have given them their due compensation" (Qur'an 60:10).

To give you a better picture of the importance of the dowry, there is a hadīth narrated by Ibn 'Abbas, where the Prophet prevented Ali from consummating his marriage with Fatimah until he gave Fatimah *something*. Ibn 'Abbas narrates that the Prophet ﷺ said,

$$أَعْطِهَا شَيْئًا، قُلْتُ: مَا عِنْدِي مِنْ شَيْءٍ. قَالَ "فَأَيْنَ دِرْعُكَ الْحُطَمِيَّةُ". قُلْتُ : هِيَ عِنْدِي. قَالَ "فَأَعْطِهَا إِيَّاهُ."$$

"'Give her something.' I said: 'I do not have anything.' He said: 'Where is your Hutami armor?' I said: 'It is with me.' He said: 'Give it to her.'"[99]

It is important to note that dowry is not a price paid for the purchase of the bride. If she chooses to end the relationship, she could return the dowry, and it is all over. In an abusive relationship, however, she is not required to return anything.

2. **Al-Waliyy.** The *waliyy* is the one who offers the bride in marriage to the groom. Waliyy is linguistically defined as "to be close" and "near." Islāmically, the waliyy is the guardian of the bride and the male support system for her. What are the conditions for one to be a waliyy? The person must be (1) a Muslim, and (2) a close male relative.

---

[99] An-Nasāi, Hadīth #3375, graded as *Sahīh* (authentic).

These conditions are of such great importance to the foundation of marriage that the great scholar As-Suyooti shares with us that the Prophet said,

$$لَا نِكَاحَ إلَّا بِوَلِيٍّ$$

"There is no marriage without guardian."[100]

When the father is available, no one deserves to be a waliyy except for him, unless he permits otherwise. When the father is unavailable and the paternal grandfather is still alive, then he assumes the position of *wilāyah*. When neither is available, there are many scholarly opinions and some disagreement on who should take this role. Some scholars argue that the waliyy should be the bride's brother; some say her uncle. Others argue that her son—if she was married before and is a mother—is the next in line.

When all are unavailable for whatever reason, there is a *wakeel*. Wakeel means to trust, to confirm, dispose affairs, lean upon, and rely upon. The wakeel is often the imam or a righteous male elder in the community. Who better to be her support system than the leadership of the community, who will protect her rights, which is the purpose of *wilāyah* and *wikālah*? To be an authorized wikālah, consult those of the position of wilāyah to avoid confusion.

Some will ask why a woman needs a guardian but not a man. As a man and a father, I would like to share some perspective. Many women are more emotional beings than men, and many sick-minded men have played on that trait for many centuries to inflict pain on women. When a woman comes to me in my role as an imam with love in her eyes, telling me, "Oh, I love him so much! He is the best! He will never hurt me. He is caring," I smile, but, with all due respect and honesty, I am not buying it until I see it for myself. Why would I judge someone without further investigation? I understand that he is innocent until proven guilty. Unfortunately, what comes with the job of counseling is witnessing things the hard way. Some women sing the praises of

---

[100] At-Tirmidhi, Hadīth #1101, graded *Sahīh* (authentic).

their future husbands but later curse the man and divorce him, and vice versa. As a father, I need to see what kind of man to whom I am giving away my daughter. Men recognize men, and women recognize women. How often does a man follow the advice of his mother when she doesn't like the woman he wants to marry? Love can be blind, and it is important to have clear-thinking support systems to protect us from regrettable commitments.

The Catfish: the Era of Great Pretenders

Regarding long-distance marriages or choosing a spouse through outlets such as matchmaking sites, the concept of *wilāyah/wikālah* (guardianship or representative) is sometimes neglected. So often in my office I see disasters from those who sought those types of marriages. It is not an overgeneralization to say that quite often there are negative surprises—or what some youngsters call a "catfish." The concept of a catfish—someone who creates a false online identity— perfectly describes the horror story I would like to share. I had a younger female counselee who told me that she was on a matchmaking site and was interested in a handsome, thirty-year-old man from Africa. Unfortunately for the young woman, this man actually was fifty-five years old. She had agreed to marry him, and when he picked her up from the airport, he walked with a cane! The poor lady thought that this man might be the father of her new husband, but when they got home, he made it very clear that he was not the father but her husband. Let this story be a lesson to those who neglect the important role that *waliy* must have.

What exactly is the Islāmic ruling for those who are deceived and tricked into marriage? If the woman chooses to stay, there is no problem, but if she chooses to leave, the marriage is void. And Allāh knows best. The young woman in the story chose the latter.

3. **As-Shāhidain.** The word *shahida* means to be a testimony to a fact, one who is present, and one who bears witness. During the *nikah* (marriage ceremony), there must be a minimum of two witnesses. This is to protect both parties from any ambiguities and accusations. In Abu

Mālik's book *Sahīh Fiqhus-Sunnah*, he explains one of Ibn Abbas (may Allāh be pleased with him)'s statements, where he says, "There is no marriage without two just witnesses and a rightly-guided guardian."[101] Although this is a companion's statement and not the Prophet's, his level of scholarship is so great that most scholars established his statement as authoritative.

4. **Al-Eejāb Wal Qabool.** This is the giving and acceptance of the bride. The guardian (al-waliyy) will serve as a representative for the bride. He is to give her away based on the agreed-upon conditions between the bride and the groom. The groom also will accept his wife based on the conditions agreed between them. Both parties accept responsibility and accountability by bringing good and averting evil.

The Shared Marital Rights

Islām has put much emphasis on the family structure. Husband and wife, despite their biological differences, are equally responsible. Marriage has components and principles to govern it. The chief principle is the marital partnership; each member of this relationship must try to give his or her utmost best in a collaborative effort for the interest of the entire family.

A relationship built on personal interests at the expense of the partnership will weaken the marital ties. It is indeed a team, and each member must be respected and his or her role appreciated. It is about *us*, and not *me*. Most relationships end chaotically because of egotism and self-centeredness. We are all, without exception, responsible. The culture of putting one another down in all aspects of life must be eradicated; if not, we are indeed far from the unique bounties of Allāh.

- In a healthy relationship, both husband and wife are committed to act in accordance to the teachings of the Qur'an and the Sunnah, with the proper understanding of the term.

---

[101] Abu Mālik, *Sahīh Fiqh As-Sunnah*, vol. 3, 150.

- Each must treat the other uniquely, with affection and recognition. In the final analysis, they both are responsible for their actions and happiness.
- Both must understand that their relationship is a lifetime commitment.

The basic principle that governs a healthy relationship is enshrined in Al-Baqarah:

$$\text{وَلَهُنَّ مِثْلُ الَّذِي عَلَيْهِنَّ بِالْمَعْرُوفِ ۚ وَلِلرِّجَالِ عَلَيْهِنَّ دَرَجَةٌ ۗ وَاللَّهُ عَزِيزٌ حَكِيمٌ}$$

And due to the wives is similar to what is expected of them, according to what is reasonable. But the men have a degree over them [in responsibility and authority]. And Allāh is Exalted in Might and Wise. (Qur'an 2:228)

Ibn Abbas said, "I make myself look good for my wife as she does likewise; I also hate to request all my rights over her, because doing so may necessitate all her rights over me." Allāh said women have rights over their husbands.[102]

The basic components of an ideal Islāmic marriage are as follows:

1. **Marital partnership.** Marriage is not a dictatorship, nor is it a relationship shared between more than the couple; it is a partnership between husband and wife. A relationship with the mind-set and ideals of a partnership is essential to an Islāmic marriage. We are in this together. We care for each other.[103]
2. **Abide by the laws of Allāh.** The marriage must be centered around the instructions of Allāh and the tradition of His Messenger. How can a marriage be blessed by Allāh if it is not connected to Him?
3. **Treat one another uniquely and with respect.** Your spouse is your main supporter, your greatest confidant, and your teammate in caring for and raising children. That relationship is a unique one and requires unique treatment. It is one of *mawaddah* and

---

[102] Ibn Kathir, *Tafsīr Ibn Kathir*, vol. 1 (1982), 271.

[103] Qur'an 30:21.

rahmah—treating your spouse with the necessary affection and mercy, as in the verse previously mentioned in Suratur-Rum. In order for the marital relationship to be long lasting, spouses must always treat each other with love and respect.

4. **Accountability.** Unlike the single man and woman, married people do not live carefree lives. They have many duties that are based on the physical, financial, emotional, and spiritual needs in a relationship. With this in mind, married men and women need to be aware of their responsibilities and excel in completing them. Mediocrity is unacceptable in a marriage because other people are on the line. Spouses and—more importantly—children need the couple to always be on their best game. Maintaining a healthy relationship should be the couple's priority; it is not about *me* alone but *us*. Hold yourself accountable before holding others accountable. Remember, you are not only accountable to yourself and your spouse but, most importantly, in the sight of Allāh. Therefore, spend your time wisely.

5. **Responsibility.** The wisdom behind putting accountability before responsibility on this list is to share with one another the importance of the mind-set before the actual work. Without a mind-set of accountability, spouses will not execute their responsibilities with perfect effort. We can never ensure perfect results, but we are in control of how much work we put in it. Part of the definition of our world is "responsibility. Some of our scholars call our world *Dāru-Takleef,* and it literally means "the world of responsibility." Our scholars have called our world *Dār A'mal* as well, literally meaning "the world of action." Neglecting our responsibilities is definitely a major problem for the relationship and for the family at large. Avoid all interruptions that will cause you to be irresponsible. Help your relationship before helping others.

6. **Commitment.** To be in a state of commitment is the understanding of when and how to execute a responsibility. We cannot be responsible if we are not fully invested or committed in the work that we are doing. And what is more important than to be committed to the well-being of your family, household, and relationship? Commitment brings excellence. Therefore, avoid procrastination—the habit of putting off intentionally the doing of something that should be done.

7. **Understanding.** There will be times where couples will disagree with one another, but the marriages that survive are when each spouse listens to the other's side and works toward developing a mutual satisfaction with one another. No thinking, no thanking; think before you act.

8. **Communication.** Similar to the relationship between accountability and responsibility, a desire to reach understanding is an essential mind-set for effective communication. Communication is not just talking with each other; it also is actively listening to one another and working toward solutions. Communication is both verbal and nonverbal. This suggests that married couples need to have a decent level of emotional intelligence to be able to pick up on the nonverbal forms of communication, such as body language, tone of voice, and facial expressions. Positive communication is needed in a healthy relationship. Therefore, you need to know when and what to say before you can be an effective communicator.

9. **Humility.** Humans can be very arrogant, claiming to have all the answers, especially men, in terms of their masculine identity. In marriage, however, success is connected with humility. Put your false sense of superiority aside, and work genuinely with your partner toward solving matters. It's important to remember that you are not always right. A solution can be achieved sometimes through the collaborative process.

10. **Protection.** In Surah Al-A'arāf, Allāh comments that marriage is about shielding one another (Qur'an 7:189). Marriage is a relationship that is all about protecting and supporting the other. The business of the home should stay there and not reach the community. The honor of your spouse is your honor and your family's honor. This mentality of absolute inclusion—the idea that your wife's pain is your pain, and vice versa—is vital to the psychology of the relationship. Therefore, the interests of your spouse are your interests and must be protected. This is how you achieve the highest status of security. To be in a relationship built on trust with your spouse will create a supportive environment for both the husband and the wife as you navigate through hardship and ease.

Marital Responsibilities

In the following section, we will discuss the responsibilities of couples and what each can do to help build a strong, impenetrable, and safe relationship for the benefit of all. At the beginning, Allāh created man and then his partner. The reason was to attain tranquility. Therefore, let's start with what the Creator Himself started with—man or husband. Allāh said,

الرِّجَالُ قَوَّامُونَ عَلَى النِّسَاءِ بِمَا فَضَّلَ اللَّهُ بَعْضَهُمْ عَلَى

بَعْضٍ وَبِمَا أَنْفَقُوا مِنْ أَمْوَالِهِمْ

"Men are the protectors and maintainers of women, because Allāh has made one of them to excel the other, and because they spend to support them from their means" (Qur'an 4:34).

Men's Responsibility

- **Fear of Allāh**. Many men use their patriarchy to promote and propagate a huge amount of injustice. It has become so widespread and popularized in some cultures that others view it as a phenomenon endorsed by Islām.

One of the cruelest crimes is to program people, from childhood, to believe they are inferior to their fellow human beings. Conspiring to keep our women on the bottom of society's pyramid is unethical and unprofessional. We must understand that Allāh created us equal but with different responsibilities. We as a people, however, have truly lost our way when we, the creation, think we can tell the Creator who is superior and who is inferior; who is the ruler and who is to be ruled. Men and women are equal in the sight of Allāh. Due to our biological differences, however, we are given roles that complete the family and society at large. Men are given extra responsibility. Unfortunately, we are so engrossed in worldly desires and possessions that we tell Allāh who is superior and inferior or when, where, and how we are going to serve Him.

This is where we are. When will we change and give women their utmost rights?

- **Knowledge of self.** To gain in the knowledge of self, we must have the courage to seek it and the humility to accept what we may find, no matter how daunting. This means learning our predominant faults and working toward remedying them. Improvement is necessary if we are to succeed.

- **Spending quality time.** We live in a world of income and entertainment. Although working and enjoying leisure time alone or with friends is important, you must dedicate time to your spouse. Family values must be a first priority in your life and have to override all other responsibilities. Managing your time to include your spouse is a must. Unfortunately, due to the age of technology, instead of spending quality time with our families, many of us spend time on social media.

- **Good companionship.** Be kind, friendly, and sympathetic with your wife. It is important to appreciate her duties and to show some mercy when she makes mistakes. Only then can you expect mercy when you make mistakes, and you *will* make mistakes. As mentioned, the husband is to mother the wife. Carry her burdens; be her go-to person when she has a lot on her mind and needs to unwind. In the ideal marriage, your wife should be your best friend, and vice versa.

- **Sound provision.** No rational or understanding person will leave his wife or his family starving. Any man who starves his family does not deserve the honor of being called a husband or a father. Allāh said, as is repeated many times in this book,

$$ لِيُنفِقْ ذُو سَعَةٍ مِّن سَعَتِهِ ۖ وَمَن قُدِرَ عَلَيْهِ رِزْقُهُ فَلْيُنفِقْ مِمَّا آتَاهُ اللَّهُ ۚ لَا يُكَلِّفُ اللَّهُ نَفْسًا إِلَّا مَا آتَاهَا ۚ سَيَجْعَلُ اللَّهُ بَعْدَ عُسْرٍ يُسْرًا $$

Let a man of wealth spend from his wealth, and he whose provision is restricted—let him spend from what Allāh has given him. Allāh does not charge a soul except [according to] what He has given it. Allāh will bring about, after hardship, ease. (Qur'an 65:7)

- **Fairness.** Treating your wife honestly and impartially is the only way to deserve the same treatment in return. Justice is a dynamic characteristic that must never be compromised. Allāh said,

$$اعْدِلُوا هُوَ أَقْرَبُ لِلتَّقْوَىٰ$$

"Be just; that is nearer to righteousness" (Qur'an 5:8).

- **Building a unique spiritual home.** A strong spiritual home will protect you from harm. A spiritual home is built on healthy soil from which individuals can grow and mature and be responsible human beings. Its house is electrically powered and protected by the light of Allāh. Those living in such a home have clear guidance during happiness and struggle and will do whatever they can to protect one another. Such a home is a sanctuary and not a war zone.

Women's Responsibility

- **Fear of Allāh.** In all situations, it is important to be a unique and disciplined mother, while simultaneously being a virtuous wife. Doing so requires a lot of effort and commitment. Additionally, a mother or a wife is indeed an institution on her own; if she "graduates" competent and God-fearing children, the society benefits, and, by the will of God, all is safe. As a wife, strive to seek the pleasure of Allāh if you want to be rewarded in both lives. The pursuits of life without Allāh is asking for trouble in both lives.

- **Be a virtuous wife.** There is nothing like a righteous, virtuous wife. The Prophet affirms this statement by saying,

$$\text{إِنَّمَا الدُّنْيَا مَتَاعٌ وَلَيْسَ مِنْ مَتَاعِ الدُّنْيَا شَىْءٌ أَفْضَلَ مِنَ الْمَرْأَةِ الصَّالِحَةِ}$$

"This world is but provisions, and there is no provision in this world better than a righteous wife."[104]

The virtues are elaborated in a saying of the Prophet, found in the collection of Ibn Majah:

$$\text{وَإِنْ نَظَرَ إِلَيْهَا سَرَّتْهُ}$$

When her husband looks toward her, she pleases him.

$$\text{إِنْ أَمَرَهَا أَطَاعَتْهُ}$$

When he advises her to do something she follows as long as it is lawful and not harmful to the family.

$$\text{وَإِنْ غَابَ عَنْهَا نَصَحَتْهُ فِي نَفْسِهَا}$$

When he is absent from home, she protects herself.

$$\text{وَمَالِهِ}$$

And protects the family's property when he is not present.[105]

Additionally, a virtuous wife and mother must be committed to giving her children and the children of her husband the necessary guidance

---

[104] Sunan Ibn Mājah, Hadīth #1855, graded Sahīh.

[105] Ibn Mājah, Hadīth #1857.

toward a successful future. Regardless of whether they are her biological children, she must help give them proper nurturing, which includes proper discipline. A parent or stepparent should never participate in abusing. Doing so will hurt her in the future when those abused children have become adults and perhaps are successful.

How to Solve Differences

When any two individuals are placed together with a common goal, disagreements are bound to happen. How you handle these disagreements is what distinguishes between successful couples and couples that fall apart. Disagreements are a natural phenomenon; they are inescapable obstacles. This is marriage, however, and not a game. This is not about winning or losing as an individual; this is about the success or failure of a partnership. The success depends on both spouses' willingness to solve their differences for the collective benefit. Again, this has nothing to do with eloquence or who wins the argument; it's about saying and doing the right thing.

No matter how much you love and respect each other, no matter how long you have been together, there *will* be things on which you will disagree. Allāh said,

$$ وَلَوْ شَاءَ رَبُّكَ لَجَعَلَ النَّاسَ أُمَّةً وَاحِدَةً ۖ وَلَا يَزَالُونَ مُخْتَلِفِينَ - $$

$$ إِلَّا مَن رَّحِمَ رَبُّكَ ۚ وَلِذَٰلِكَ خَلَقَهُمْ $$

> And if your Lord had willed, He could have made mankind one community; but they will not cease to differ. Except whom your Lord has given mercy, and for that He created them. (Qur'an 11:118–119)

Allāh is informing us of something critical. He *could have* made us all the same because, indeed, He is the all-Capable. It is by His mercy, however, that He created us differently in creed, color, and culture. People will always have different perspectives and views. Our diversity is what makes us so great as a species. We eat different foods, live under different cultures, and speak different languages, but through Islām, we pray the same way, recite Qur'an the same, and submit to the same Creator. Yes, there will be times when we forget and fall into disunity. A reminder to all is that our differences do not have to be threatening. To the husband and to the wife, differences keep us on our toes. If the husband thinks one way, and the wife thinks another, perhaps a better way, with both ideas merged, can be produced through discussion. This was the wisdom of Allāh when creating Adam and Hawwa, the foundation of our diversity.

In an ideal relationship, a husband and wife must be "ACCRA":

Appreciative. Saying "thank you" takes you a long way. This plants seeds of love and gratitude for one another, strengthening the roots of teamwork. Appreciation is said to be the secret of success.

Credible. When you say you will do something, your word is solid. This sparks a vibe of mutual trust and belief in one another, which is essential.

Courageous. The world of marriage is daunting at times, but it requires man and woman to rise to the occasion and shine. Despite the hardships that spouses face, they are committed to do the work of love. They are committed to work together as a team and leave behind their egotistic views and personal interests for the welfare of the family.

Responsible. Husband and wife must take their responsibilities seriously. Marriage is not a game. If one loses, there is great disaster.

Accountable. There will be times when responsibilities may be neglected, and mistakes will be made. However, what fixes everything is owning up to it and improving yourself to ensure that it won't happen again. Spouses must be self-disciplined and must continue to improve themselves as they grow together.

One of the most powerful things you can do to protect your marriage is to learn constructive ways to handle conflict and disagreement. Some methods are as follows:

- Be responsible.

- In order to be responsible, keep the family's interests in mind at all time.
- Justice must never be compromised, and therefore, spouses must be fair to one another. Mistakes will be made.
- Ours is the approach of being forgiving. If we want to be forgiven when we err, mercy is key.
- Satan's role must be understood. Take note of this powerful hadīth narrated by Jabir bin Abdullah:

"إِنَّ إِبْلِيسَ يَضَعُ عَرْشَهُ عَلَى الْمَاءِ ثُمَّ يَبْعَثُ سَرَايَاهُ
فَأَدْنَاهُمْ مِنْهُ مَنْزِلَةً أَعْظَمُهُمْ فِتْنَةً يَجِيءُ أَحَدُهُمْ فَيَقُولُ
فَعَلْتُ كَذَا وَكَذَا فَيَقُولُ مَا صَنَعْتَ شَيْئًا قَالَ ثُمَّ يَجِيءُ
أَحَدُهُمْ فَيَقُولُ مَا تَرَكْتُهُ حَتَّى فَرَّقْتُ بَيْنَهُ وَبَيْنَ امْرَأَتِهِ -
قَالَ - فَيُدْنِيهِ مِنْهُ وَيَقُولُ نِعْمَ أَنْتَ."

Iblis places his throne upon water; he then sends commanders (for creating conflicts on earth); the nearer to him in rank are those who are most notorious in creating conflict. One of them comes and says: "I did so and so." And he says: "You have done nothing." Then one amongst them comes and says: "I did not spare so and so until I sowed the seed of discord between a husband and a wife." The Satan goes near him (to embrace him) and says: "You have done well."[106]

This explicitly shows us what Satan is all about; it is the destruction of man. Notice that the evil deed that impressed Satan the most was the destruction of one's family. Therefore, I repeat, *know Satan's role*. There is nothing more beloved to him than the disintegration of love between the family, for that will directly contribute to the disintegration of love between humankind.

---

[106] Sahīh Muslim, Hadīth #2813b.

- In order to see Satan's plots against the family structure, be emotionally mature. Be someone who investigates instead of assumes, and foster feelings of trust between each other. These are the methods that will protect the family structure, a system that has kept humankind alive from its beginning.

Communication

Being able to communicate fairly is a must in all human relations. Remember that our success or failure is a result of our ability or inability to communicate well. It is as important as food and water; communication is nourishment for the spirit and the soul. Words are not easily forgotten, so be careful with what you say. Some people have tongues sharper than arrow tips, and some have tongues that heal souls better than medicine. Words can be categorized as positive or negative.

Positive Words

- أعوذ بالله من الشيطان الرجيم (Seek refuge with Allāh from Satan.)
- Words of appreciation. How often do we thank one another? When was the last time you complimented your wife's cooking or your husband's generosity? As mentioned, saying "thank you" takes you a long way.
- Words of patience: There will be times when your spouse uses words that hurt. This does not mean you should add fuel to the flame. This is a time for you to use words that calm the situation. Sometimes, no words at all but active listening and patience can de-escalate the situation.
- Words of clarity. Obviously, a major form of positive communication is telling the truth to your spouse and being clear with your concerns. When something is bothering you, through wisdom, speak clearly and boldly about it. Positive communication is all about being straightforward with your concerns. If you do not speak your mind, Satan will use this to destroy you from the inside, while your spouse has no clue what is going on, except that you seem to be a careless spouse.
- Perfect time and environment. Wisdom is communicating with the right words at the right time and place. If you cannot communicate with

wisdom, your marriage will be in trouble. True wisdom is understanding the perfect timing and environment and then communicating with the best choice of words.

- Stay on the topic. How many people, when disagreeing, bring up past arguments that have nothing to do with the topic of discussion? This creates escalation of the original argument and is simply a bad idea. Therefore, we are to stay on topic and confront its issue head-on, without beating around the bush. Escalation can cause triangulation.

Negative Words

- Intense emotions. Never communicate out of intense emotion; you *will* regret it later. People, out of anger, may scream out *tualaq*, meaning divorce. And after the third time, they can never get their wives back (according to the law). The husband's foolish screaming may have felt good at the moment, but when he is home alone with no wife, his reason will kick back in, and his heart will be filled with intense regret for his short-sightedness. When you are angry, be silent, according to the Prophet.

- Escalation. When spouses disagree with one another, the worst thing one of them can do is escalate the argument. People usually do this to imply they are angrier and stronger than the other. This is a very petty and emotionally immature way of acting. And it's not suitable behavior toward your lifelong partner.

- Invalidation. Sometimes an angry spouse tries to follow the positive communication approach of being clear with his or her concerns. An example is saying, "You do not spend as much time with me anymore." This shows that the spouse has respectfully addressed his or her concern and has opened himself/herself to genuine dialogue. The most despicable thing the other spouse can do is to invalidate that concern by saying things such as "Oh, it's not that big of a deal," or "You women are so emotional!" These and other nonsensical statements can cause your loved one to feel like she is not being taken seriously. The worst part about invalidation is that it exposes a subconscious understanding that one has of the other. This understanding is "I do not think your opinions matter." This can plant deep seeds of resentment that can never be uprooted and removed.

169

- Negative interpretation. There is nothing more annoying than when one always assumes the worst of the other. Having negative interpretations of the other exposes a deep, subconscious understanding that you have of the other. This understanding one has "I think everything that you do is negative by default." Once again, if your spouse realizes this, seeds of resentment will be planted deep in the relationship's soul, never to be uprooted or removed.
- Assassination of character. You must never assassinate the character of anyone, let alone your spouse. We often discuss physical abuse in the household, but often we ignore the reality of verbal abuse. When angry, the husband curses his wife, and vice versa. This emotionally immature behavior reflects the character of abusive spouses. They are unable to discuss what bothers them with reason and proper communication, so they resort to insults and humiliation. Psychologists say this is a display of low intelligence.

Here is a hadīth that we should all reflect upon, found in the collection of At-Tirmidhi:

عن أكثر ما يدخل الناس الجنة ؟ قال:" تقوى الله وحسن الخلق". وسئل عن أكثر ما يدخل الناس النار، قال:" الفم والفرج ".

> Messenger of Allāh (ﷺ) was asked about the deed that would be foremost to lead a man to Jannah. He replied, "Fear of Allāh and *the good conduct*." Then he was asked about indulgence that will admit a man to hell (fire), and he answered, "*The tongue* and *the genitals*."[107]

The Prophet is showing us that words are equally as dangerous as promiscuity and sexual deviation. However, how often do you hear scholars warn against the dangers of the tongue? Tongues can be very dangerous. Families as well as nations have been destroyed through leaders' abuse of the tongue.

---

[107] At-Tirmidhi, Hadīth #2004.

If you are unable to solve a disagreement by yourselves and help is needed, be extremely careful in choosing arbitrators. Allāh said,

$$وَإِنْ خِفْتُمْ شِقَاقَ بَيْنِهِمَا فَابْعَثُوا حَكَمًا مِّنْ أَهْلِهِ وَحَكَمًا مِّنْ أَهْلِهَا إِن يُرِيدَا إِصْلَاحًا يُوَفِّقِ اللَّهُ بَيْنَهُمَا ۗ إِنَّ اللَّهَ كَانَ عَلِيمًا خَبِيرًا$$

And if you fear dissension between the two, send an arbitrator from his people and an arbitrator from her people. If they both desire reconciliation, Allāh will cause it between them. Indeed, Allāh is ever Knowing and Acquainted [with all things]. (Qur'an 4:35)

Allāh is teaching us that fair representation is key to reconciliation between two people, especially spouses.

In this passage of the Qur'an, Allāh mentions only one representative (not representatives) to avoid spreading false information. False information, if not checked and investigated, will destroy the honor of both spouses, as well as their extended family. Also, an arbitrator must be conscious, God-fearing, and well informed of the existing problem. The main goal is to bring peace to the couple through reconciliation.

Islāh, as used in the verse, has multiple meanings; among them are improvement, repair, and remedying. For this reason, choosing an arbitrator must be done with the mind-set of improving the relationship and bringing peace to those involved, not hatred or hostility. So the couple must be very selective in choosing who will represent their interests.

CHAPTER 8

Marital Issues

What does the ideal marriage look like? The ideal marriage, in its most general and simple terms, consists of a few things. These terms and concepts come from Islām and the social implications that have come from it. It is important to remember that no two marriages are similar and that these parts of marriage are simple guides of what make up a marriage. These parts are as follows:

- A husband and wife who are reasonable. This means a man and woman working together, with realistic expectations of each other and equally contributing to making the marriage work. Both members of the marriage put the relationship first when making decisions. It is "we" before "me." They are practical. For example, the wife does not expect the husband to surprise her with a Mercedes-Benz when he doesn't even have a bicycle. The husband should not expect to receive a perfect smile and good-morning greeting every morning. Things have to be practical, or else, like a Hollywood romance movie, the marriage will be short lived.

- A husband and wife who are responsible. Both the husband and wife prioritize the relationship. They work together to accomplish tasks as a team. They do what they feel is necessary for their relationship to succeed. This is important because if one is doing more than the other, there is an imbalance, and the dynamics of respect begin to change.

- A husband and wife who are accountable. When a couple is accountable, they accept blame when they are at fault. They understand that it is not a competition and that they are working together. They focus on positives and humbly learn from their errors and mistakes, and they attempt to correct them and to change in order to prevent similar mistakes in the future. This is for the sake of the relationship and for bettering each other.

- A husband and wife who are committed. The relationship comes first. They do the work of loving, protecting, assisting, caring, and forgiving one another. This is for the interest of the family, which is pleasing to Allāh.

- A husband and wife who act upon equal partnership. It's true that the man and woman have different roles in a marriage, and both parties are expected to do different tasks, but one cannot contribute more effort to the relationship than the other. One cannot feel that the other does not carry the same weight, or that person may become disinterested with the other. Appreciation brings more appreciation.

Intimacy and What Puts It in Danger

There are many forms of *intimacy*. When it comes to relationships, the strongest form of intimacy comes from the marital bond between man and woman. The type of intimacy formed from marriage is a powerful desire that is regulated by sharī'ah through the act of marriage. However, as powerful as it can be, it is also a difficult topic to discuss in our ummah. It is typically ignored or intentionally forgotten, and because of this, many problems arise.

The sexual desires of an individual are often a taboo topic. Many pretend they do not exist, but behind closed doors, they commit many sins in this realm. In order to prevent these sins, we must educate ourselves and learn exactly why they are wrong. Islām teaches *haya*, meaning modesty or shyness. Modesty is a well-discussed topic in the discourse of Muslim scholars, and there is a great wealth of textual evidence regarding it. However, there is a fine line between sexual perversion and sexual awareness. This is an important aspect of human life, and if there is a lack of awareness on it, the consequences are severe. There is a hadīth narrated by the mother of the believers, Umm Salama, in which she says that the Prophet ﷺ said,

$$\text{إِنَّ اللَّهَ لاَ يَسْتَحِي مِنَ الْحَقِّ}$$

"Verily, Allāh does not feel shy to tell the truth."[108]

To even begin to discuss the matters of sex from an Islāmic perspective, two *fiqhi*, or jurisprudential principles, that should stay in one's mind are as follows:

First:

$$\text{الضرر يزال}$$

"Harm must be eliminated."

According to Islāmic scholars, this is one of the basic principles agreed upon in Islāmic *fiqh*, or jurisprudence (see chapter 3). This principle addresses many issues, perhaps half of all matters in Islāmic law.

Second:

$$\text{الأصل في الأشياء الإباحة}$$

Al-Aslu fil-ashyaai al-ibaahah
"The basic ruling of things is permissibility."

This principle, although widely accepted (but not unanimously used) in *fiqhi* scholarly discourse, was not discussed in chapter 3 due to its highly comprehensive nature. To briefly explain, this legal maxim expresses that

---

[108] Sahīh Al-Bukhāri, Hadīth #6121.

all matters are *halāl* (permissible) until proven *haram* (forbidden). The way to prove the *haramic* nature of something is through textual evidence. Matters of faith, however, are a much different field because it is required that they be explained through clear-cut, textual evidence. Beliefs such as *tauheed* and rituals are explained vividly through Qur'an and Sunnah. This principle, however, discusses matters that perhaps are not explained specifically in the Qur'an and Sunnah, such as cultural foods and dress. These matters are all, by standard, lawful until proven otherwise (if the food has something unlawful or the clothing is immodest).

Allāh says in Surah Al-Baqarah,

$$\text{هُوَ الَّذِي خَلَقَ لكُم مَّا فِي الْأَرْضِ جَمِيعًا}$$

"It is He who created for you all of that which is on the earth" (Qur'an 2:29).

Additionally, Allāh says in Surah Al-Jāthiyah,

$$\text{وَسَخَّرَ لكُم مَّا فِي السَّمَاوَاتِ وَمَا فِي الْأَرْضِ جَمِيعًا مِّنْهُ ۚ إِنَّ}$$
$$\text{فِي ذَٰلِكَ لَآيَاتٍ لِّقَوْمٍ يَتَفَكَّرُونَ}$$

"And He has subjected to you whatever is in the heavens and whatever is on the earth—all from Him. Indeed, in that are signs for a people who give thought" (Qur'an 45:13).

Therefore, based on this principle of permissibility, the scope of unlawfulness in Islāmic law is extremely restricted and short, while the scope of lawfulness is extremely vast. This is because in order to make something *haram*, one needs clear-cut, textual evidence to prove its illegality, while most things are naturally *halal*, whether mentioned in textual evidence or not. The Azhari scholar Dr. Yusuf Qaradawi quotes a hadīth authenticated by Imam An-Nawawi. (For those who would like to read it on their own, it is the thirtieth hadīth in his forty-hadīth collection.) The Prophet ﷺ said,

"إِنَّ اللَّهَ تَعَالَى فَرَضَ فَرَائِضَ فَلَا تُضَيِّعُوهَا، وَحَدَّ حُدُودًا فَلَا

تَعْتَدُوهَا، وَحَرَّمَ أَشْيَاءَ فَلَا تَنْتَهِكُوهَا، وَسَكَتَ عَنْ أَشْيَاءَ رَحْمَةً

لَكُمْ غَيْرَ نِسْيَانٍ فَلَا تَبْحَثُوا عَنْهَا"

> Verily Allāh ﷻ has laid down religious obligations
> (*fara'id*), so do not neglect them; and He has set limits, so
> do not overstep them; and He has forbidden some things,
> so do not violate them; and *He has remained silent about*
> *some things, out of compassion for you, not forgetfulness—so*
> *do not seek after them.*[109]

"Out of compassion for *you*"—this is Allāh, brothers and sisters! In this
powerful hadīth, the Prophet is teaching us that Allāh has informed us
of the necessary good and bad. However, too much inquiry will lead us to
total destruction, as with many nations before us. Allāh does not forget; let
us not pretend to play Allāh by restricting that which was not restricted.
We must do our best, however, to avoid questionable things.

With that brief fiqhi lesson, let us return to the purpose of this book, which
is to preserve the family structure through guiding married couples and
those seeking marriage with the proper tools to preserve them. Regarding
sex, Qur'an and Sunnah has encouraged the halal and made the haram
clear to the believers. That said, Islām encourages "PPI"—playing, praying,
and finally, intercourse.

Playing

The Prophet ﷺ encouraged foreplay between spouses. There was a
conversation between the Prophet and his student and dear companion,
Jabir bin Abdullah, that has been recorded for the benefit of our ummah.
Jabir informed the Prophet that he just got married to an elderly woman.
Out of surprise, the Prophet proceeded to ask,

---

[109] An-Nawawi, *Forty Hadīth*, 103, Ad-Daraqutni reported, graded *hasan*.

هَلاَّ جَارِيَةً تُلاَعِبُهَا وَتُلاَعِبُكَ

"Why didn't you marry a young girl so that you might play with her and she with you?"[110] The Prophet ﷺ asked this question with genuine concern for his companion, but soon after he inquired, Jabir explained his situation of losing his father and needing an elderly woman to assist him in taking care of his younger sisters. Nevertheless, the Prophet's question can be understood as implying that marrying at a young and healthy age to a spouse of the same youthfulness is preferable for the well-being of the marriage. However, this is the general implication, and not every person's experience is applicable to that of Jabir bin Abdullah's, may Allāh be pleased with him.

Ibn Hajar Al-Asqalani did intensive work on this hadīth; some of the scholars gave a different interpretation on the word *li'āb* (playfulness), whereas *lu'āb* is "saliva," which implies the kissing of one's spouse in the lips and tongue.[111] Moreover, before the more serious sexual acts, it is preferred to engage in foreplay with your spouse. This is proven through the great Hanbali scholar Ibn Qudama Al-Maqdisi in his classic work, *Al-Mughni*, in which he cites a hadīth of the Prophet ﷺ. In his eighth volume, Ibn Qudama reported, "Do not begin intercourse until she has experienced desire, like the desire you experience, lest you fulfill your desires before she does."[112] Although, we do not have the direct citation of the hadīth, Ibn Qudama Al-Maqdisi is a great scholar who is well respected and trusted. With this hadīth in mind, it also explains to all that penetration is not the only component of sexual intercourse between husband and wife. It implies that there are other components, such as foreplay.

Although the Prophet ﷺ lived more than 1,400 years ago, he understood the importance of foreplay, and that is due to the divine guidance of Allah ﷻ. Nowadays, science plays a part in explaining why foreplay before intercourse is so important. According to Stefan Bechtel, in his work *The Practical Encyclopedia of Sex and Health*, "Normally an aroused woman will produce enough natural lubrication to make intercourse silky and

---

[110] Sahīh Al-Bukhāri, Hadīth #5080.

[111] Ibn Hajar Al-Asqalani, *Fat-hul Bāri*, vol. 10 (1996), 153.

[112] Ibn Qudama, *Al-Mughni*, Hadīth #136.

---

sweet ... usually she requires a good bit of foreplay before she's actually ready for intercourse."[113] These conversations do not happen in the Muslim community because we have mistaken irrational suppression for modesty. Unfortunately, the effect of that mistake is that mostly the women suffer. As a counselor, I have heard many complaints from some who have expressed hatred for sexual intercourse. When hearing these complaints, the words of Bechtel come to mind. Perhaps, due to the lack of foreplay, which causes for a lack of natural lubrication, the sexual intercourse between the husband and wife becomes painful for the woman. Moreover, when the wife does not want to engage in sexual relations in the future, the husband invokes passionately the famous hadith narrated by Abu Huraira that the Prophet ﷺ said,

إِذَا دَعَا الرَّجُلُ امْرَأَتَهُ إِلَى فِرَاشِهِ فَأَبَتْ، فَبَاتَ غَضْبَانَ عَلَيْهَا، لَعَنَتْهَا الْمَلَائِكَةُ حَتَّى تُصْبِحَ

"If a husband calls his wife to his bed (i.e. to have sexual relation) and she refuses and causes him to sleep in anger, the angels will curse her till morning."[114]

However, what we have failed to ask ourselves is why? What we have failed to do is assess the source of these problems. Will the merciful Lord punish for no reason? The answer is a resounding no. Furthermore, sexual education in our communities is a necessity. It is necessary for the Muslim couple in order to improve their sexual life, and it begins with two things: (1) positive thinking and (2) positive communication.

When we engage in our lives with positive thinking, positivity manifests itself in our every day interactions. When we think of and communicate with our spouses positively, our relationships thrive. These matters of foreplay, although dismissed as menial in the eyes of some, can be a major asset in the prosperity of one's spousal relationship. May Allah guide us to be merciful and positive with our spouses. Amīn.

---

[113] Stefan Bechtel, *The Practical Encyclopedia of Sex and Health* (1993), 186.

[114] Sahīh Al-Bukhāri, Hadīth #3237.

Praying

Before sexual intercourse, the Messenger of God encouraged couples to invoke Allāh through *du'a* (supplication). This *du'a* is found in both Al-Bukhāri and Muslim. This is to protect couples from any satanic influences that might affect them or their children. The wisdom behind the praying aspect of sex is to connect all positive marital relations with Allāh. All benefit comes from only Him, and it is for us to seek Him and His blessings. Therefore, to maintain a spiritual connection and to bless the relations that spouses have with one another, especially during sexual intercourse, it is recommended by the Prophet to invoke this *du'a*. Its purpose is to protect and preserve the couple and their future offspring.

بسم الله، اللهم جنبنا الشيطان وجنب الشيطان ما رزقتنا،
فقضى بينهما ولد لم يضره

In the Name of Allāh. O Allāh! Keep us away from Satan and keep Satan away from what You have bestowed upon us; and if Allāh has ordained a child for them, Satan will never harm him.[115]

Intercourse

One must understand that sexual intercourse is one of the major pillars that holds the marital relationship. Moreover, when defining sexual intercourse, we are discussing penetration, when the penis of the male penetrates the vagina of the female. From the Islāmic perspective, here is what the Prophet ﷺ has said:

أَقْبِلْ وَأَدْبِرْ وَاتَّقِ الدُّبَرَ وَالْحِيضَةَ

"From the front, the back, avoiding the anus, and menstruation."[116]

---

[115] Sahīh Al-Bukhāri, Hadīth #141; Sahīh Muslim, Hadīth #1434a.

[116] At-Tirmidhi, Hadīth #2980.

This hadīth, narrated by Ibn 'Abbas, the cousin of the Prophet, was honored by the Prophet with the title *hibrul-ummah*, or the "Scholar of this Ummah." This hadīth clearly states that penetration of the vagina from front or back is absolutely *halāl* (lawful). However, during times of menstruation, vaginal penetration is strictly forbidden (*haram*). Although condemned by Islām over 1,400 years ago, scientists have affirmed what was already understood in Islāmic sexual ethics. Author Stefan Bechtel, in his work *The Practical Encyclopedia of Sex & Health*, wrote, "Having sex during menstruation directly exposes the male to bacteria. As protective mechanism against bacterial invasion, the vagina stays acidic. But during menstruation, blood's higher alkalinity slightly reduces the vagina's acidity, making it more susceptible to vaginal infections."[117]

Additionally, as clearly stated in the hadīth, anal penetration is strictly forbidden. A reminder is that Allāh has His infinite wisdom when setting prohibitions on humankind. Whether we, as a species, derived the reason now or never, most certainly it was for the well-being of our species that it was made forbidden. Sexual intercourse in Islām is not strictly purposed for procreation. The Prophet taught us that it is also for the pleasure and enjoyment of the couple. With everything positive, however, is a set of standards:

- Hygiene. The Prophet ﷺ, in his famous hadīth, said,

الطُّهُورُ نِضْفُ الإِيمَانِ

"Purification is half of Faith."[118]

- Good communication. Allāh, in Surah Al-Baqarah, instructs man by stating,

وَقُولُوا لِلنَّاسِ حُسْنًا

"And speak to people good [words]" (Qur'an 2:83).

---

[117] Stefan Bechtel, *The Practical Encyclopedia of Sex & Health* (1993), 207–208.

[118] At-Tirmidhi, Hadīth #3519, graded *hasan*.

Always speak positively with your spouse; additionally, speak to your spouse without ambiguities. Communicate your expectations respectfully, especially when it comes to sexual relations.

- Collaboration. Always think with a team-oriented mind-set. With regard to the context of sexual relations, try your best to be empathetic with the other. Perhaps your spouse is not in the best state of mind or is too fatigued one day. Do not impose, but communicate with respect.
- Safe environment. This should be a given, but when having sexual relations with your spouse, make sure there is a sense of privacy. There should be no third party whatsoever, directly or indirectly, present. This means especially the children, as this may cause psychological issues in the future, whether young or old.
- Respecting partner's nakedness. From the Islāmic perspective, your spouse is the only individual with whom you should share your nakedness. Regardless of the situation, *never* share each other's sexual life with anybody else because it is textually proven that it is an abomination. As narrated by Sa'eed Al-Khudri, the Prophet ﷺ said,

$$إِنَّ مِنْ أَشَرِّ النَّاسِ عِنْدَ اللَّهِ مَنْزِلَةً يَوْمَ الْقِيَامَةِ الرَّجُلَ يُفْضِي$$

$$إِلَى امْرَأَتِهِ وَتُفْضِي إِلَيْهِ ثُمَّ يَنْشُرُ سِرَّهَا$$

The most wicked among the people in the sight of Allāh on the Day of judgment is the men who goes to his wife and she comes to him, and *then he divulges her secret.*[119]

Marriage is a relationship dependent on trusting one another. When one cannot trust the other, especially in matters of intimacy and sexual relations, a great calamity will befall this couple in a short matter of time. Previously when discussing the dangers of social media and technology in the bedroom, we did not discuss the phenomenon of sick men or women secretly recording their partners during sexual intercourse. This kind of behavior is not only *strictly prohibited* but also is an abomination.

---

[119] Sahīh Muslim, Hadīth #1437.

> Brothers and sisters, do not underestimate the importance of the sexual relationship between spouses. It is the very reflection of their relationship with their spouse. Fogarty diagnosed, "A very small percentage of sexual dysfunctions arise from physical causes. Despite this small percentage, every person with such a problem should have a complete physical examination. Another very small group have sexual problems, which are largely due to lack of knowledge about sex and the organs of sexuality … The largest proportion of sexual problems results from a deterioration in the personal relationship between husband and wife."[120]
>
> **In Brief**
>
> 1. Marriage is a collaborative effort between spouses.
> 2. Both are responsible and accountable and are committed to do the work of love.
> 3. Sexual relations between spouses are not dirty or impure as long as they are done within the boundaries.

Ghusl (The Ritual Bath)

After penetration, which is the defining characteristic of sexual intercourse,[121] Islām requires both spouses to wash themselves in a ritual bath known as *ghuslul-janābah*. This is based on the ayah in Surah Al-Maidah:

$$وَإِن كُنتُمْ جُنُبًا فَاطَّهَّرُوا$$

"And if you are in a state of *janabah* (sexual impurity), then purify yourselves" (Qur'an 5:6).

---

[120] Eileen G. Pendagast, *The Family* (1992), 125.

[121] Other times where ghusl is required are ejaculation, menstruation, and blood after childbirth. Strongly recommended times are every morning of Jumu'ah (Friday).

Ibn Hajar Al-Asqalani says that the "essence of *ghusl*" is "pouring water on the entire body, with clear distinction between that which is ritual and that which is customarily act, coupled with clear intention." To elaborate, for the ghusl to be accepted as such, they must intend it to be ghusl and not just a "customary" shower, as the scholar stated. Al-Asqalani quoted Imam Ash-Shāfi'ie's *Al-Umm*, which stated, "Allāh legislated the *ghusl* or the ritual bath in a general sense. How one performs it is not discussed in the Qur'an, therefore, as long as the entire body is bathed, the ghusl is sufficient."[122]

Imam Ash-Shāfi'ie is one of the great scholars, and being the father of Al-Usūlul-Fiqh (the principles of Islāmic jurisprudence), his opinion is widely respected. It is, however, the minority opinion in the vast discourse of Islāmic scholarship. What the majority of scholars believe is that there are steps to performing *ghusl*. I will summarize them as follows:

1. Intention to perform this ritual.
2. Start by washing the hands.
3. Wash the private parts.
4. Perform *wudu* (ablution), and delay washing of the feet.
5. Wash the entire body, from right to left, head to toe.
6. Wash the feet.

Two things to keep in mind during ghusl are as follows:

1. Press your hands well on your washed body to ensure full cleanliness.
2. Use water in moderation. (Islām is a religion of conservation, not excess.)

Islām is a religion of evidence and proof; please read the following:

عَنْ عَائِشَةَ، زَوْجِ النَّبِيِّ صلى الله عليه وسلم أَنَّ النَّبِيَّ صلى الله عليه وسلم كَانَ إِذَا اغْتَسَلَ مِنَ الْجَنَابَةِ بَدَأَ فَغَسَلَ يَدَيْهِ، ثُمَّ يَتَوَضَّأُ كَمَا يَتَوَضَّأُ لِلصَّلاَةِ، ثُمَّ يُدْخِلُ أَصَابِعَهُ فِي الْمَاءِ،

---

[122] Ibn Hajar Al-Asqalani, *Fat-hul Bāri*, vol. 1 (1996), 480.

فَيُخَلِّلُ بِهَا أُصُولَ شَعَرِهِ ثُمَّ يَصُبُّ عَلَى رَأْسِهِ ثَلَاثَ غُرَفٍ بِيَدَيْهِ، ثُمَّ يُفِيضُ الْمَاءَ عَلَى جِلْدِهِ كُلِّهِ.

It was narrated by `Aisha:

> Whenever the Prophet (ﷺ) took a bath after *janabah* he started by washing his hands and then performed ablution like that for the prayer. After that he would put his fingers in water and move the roots of his hair with them, and then pour three handfuls of water over his head and then pour water all over his body.[123]

Sahīh Al-Bukhāri, Hadīth #248.

CHAPTER 9

The Uncomfort Zone

After discussing the dos and don'ts of Islāmic sexual ethics, I would like to discuss the challenges of our times in the realm of sexuality. As mentioned, the age of technology and social media has greatly influenced our species, for the best and for the worst. With regard to the great sexual challenges of our times, three come to mind:

- **Pornography.** Pornography is the display of sexually related images and videos. Even more dangerous is its nature of being unrealistic and mind-altering. Pornography is a toxin that harms the mind. As psychiatrist Terry Kupers of the Wright Institute in San Francisco wrote in his book *Revisioning Men's Lives*, "Pornography serves to create distance. Memories of the couple's weekend love making fade into the background as he imagines sex with each of the women on the screen."[124] For a married man, unrealistic and unfair expectations flood the mind from pornography, and because of this he will never be satisfied with reality. An addiction will form, and his mind will be gone. Dr. Kupers quotes an organization known as Men Against Pornography, which provides a checklist for signs of addiction to pornography, including dissatisfaction with a sexual partner's physical appearance or how she expresses herself sexually. In order to have sex with someone, the addict needs to remember images or scenes from

---

[124] Terry Kupers, *Revisioning Men's Lives* (1993), 81.

pornography. Additionally, he may isolate himself and become less outgoing.

Islām forbids this deviation because of its severely negative effects in the psychological, physical, and emotional realm, as well as spiritual. I have counseled a couple whose sexual relations became extremely weakened. I came to realize that when the wife was unavailable, the husband would view pornography. Due to that, he had weakened his sexual desire. Most men who consume porn are running away from their responsibilities because they have become possessed, mentally, searching for this "perfect" mate—a woman who doesn't age or menstruate, and whose body is for sale. Oh Lord, protect us.

To cure such people, they must be willing to cure themselves first. Californian psychiatrist and sex expert David Reuben wrote that the "inability to perform sexual intercourse adequately is only a symptom. Every sick penis is attached to a sick man. Cure the man, cure the penis. To put it another way, if the mind works right, the penis works right."[125]

Hypersexualization in the Media

We often forget how subliminal sexual messages are on our computers and televisions. Like a gateway drug, the television and the personal computer are gates of exposure to hypersexualized material from an early age. Pop-up advertisements on the computer sometimes promote sexually suggestive messages, and television commercials promote products by portraying women as sex objects. Unfortunately, this is too common. Speaking from the Islāmic perspective, it is recommended to unplug yourself a healthy amount of time from exposure to multimedia, despite its benefits. What it feeds the brains subliminally is truly detrimental to your spiritual health. That is why I recommend three things in the face of these challenges:

---

[125] David Reuben, *Everything You Always Wanted to Know about Sex* (1970), 21.

1. Lower your gaze. This concept is found in the Qur'an. Allāh ﷻ instructs the believers to lower their gazes in order to protect their chastity. We've mentioned Surah An-Nur previously.

2. Don't watch TV with provocative images. With all the images that are fed to us, it is crucial that we minimize our intake from such detrimental sources.

3. Fast. The Prophet ﷺ advised young single men to fast, and this was narrated by a great companion 'Abdullah bin Mas'ood:

$$\text{"يَا مَعْشَرَ الشَّبَابِ مَنِ اسْتَطَاعَ مِنكُمُ الْبَاءَةَ فَلْيَنْكِحْ}$$

$$\text{فَإِنَّهُ أَغَضُّ لِلْبَصَرِ وَأَحْصَنُ لِلْفَرْجِ وَمَنْ لاَ فَلْيَصُمْ}$$

$$\text{فَإِنَّ الصَّوْمَ لَهُ وِجَاءٌ"}$$

The Messenger of Allāh said to us: "O young men, whoever among you can afford it, let him get married, for it is more effective in lowering the gaze and guarding chastity, *and whoever cannot then he should fast, for it will be a restraint (wija) for him.*"[126]

• **Masturbation.** This is the second sexual challenge that tries humankind. Masturbation is sexual stimulation designed to produce an orgasm through any means except sexual intercourse. The term comes from the Latin word *masturbari*, which means to pollute oneself.[127] Note that this is not the Islāmic root letters; this is recognized even in Latin as a form of pollution that affects the human mind. If the mind is affected negatively, it affects the entire body. The majority of Islāmic scholarship deems masturbation as unlawful. However, we live in the world of diversity, and there is a minority opinion that should be respected. The minority viewpoint argues from the concept of "the lesser of two evils" regarding masturbation versus fornication. Fornication clearly is the greater evil for students, immigrant workers, and prisoners with no wives; masturbation *may* be

---

[126] Sahīh Al-Bukhāri, Hadīth #5066; Sahīh Muslim, Hadīth #1400.

[127] David Reuben, *Everything You Always Wanted to Know about Sex* (1970), 152.

---

lawful for them. However, even scholars of the minority opinion argue that this statement should never be abused. This minority opinion is popularized by the great Azhari scholar Dr. Yusuf Qaradawi, who bases his arguments on the great founder of the Hanbali school of jurisprudence, Imam Ahmad bin Hanbal.[128] And Allāh knows best. In surah Al-Mu-minoon, Allāh ﷻ begins by saying "The Believers are successful." Following that, He discusses in the fifth ayah an important point, which is perfect to conclude with:

$$\text{وَالَّذِينَ هُمْ لِفُرُوجِهِمْ حَافِظُونَ}$$

"Who guard their private parts (their chastity)" (Qur'an 23:5).

• **Oral sex.** Stefan Bechtel defines oral sex as any kind of sexual contact involving the mouth; this includes kissing.[129] Oral sex is divided into two categories: (1) kissing and (2) oral sex relating to the genitals.

Islām is a faith of personal hygiene, and we simply cannot discuss these serious matters until we know the health of the mouth. When discussing oral health, the following questions come to mind:

1. Is your mouth healthy?
2. How many times a day do you brush your teeth?
3. Do you wash your hands and shower regularly?

In *USA Today*'s March 2016 edition, the article "Healthy Mouth Healthy Body" shared the following:

> Your mouth serves as a window into potential issues elsewhere in the body, as dental health and overall health are often connected ... diseases that affect the entire body may first show up through lesions or even bad breath ... Research shows that more than 90% of systemic diseases, such as diabetes, cancer and heart diseases, have oral manifestations." Additionally, in Bechtel's encyclopedia,

---

[128] Dr. Yusuf Al Qaradawi, *Al-Halāl wal-Haram* (2004), 153.

[129] Stefan Bechtel, *Practical Encyclopedia of Sex and Health* (1993), 218.

he states that "there are more bacteria in the mouth than on the vagina or on the penis. A much more serious worry is the risk of contracting STDs.[130]

While kissing the body is Islāmically acceptable, kissing genitals is a very serious, objectionable act.

Bechtel concludes by expressing that "there are more bacteria in the mouth than on the vagina or on the penis. A much more serious worry is the risk of contracting STDs." If Bechtel's conclusion is correct, then why do we indulge in an act that will hurt our health in the long run?

Allāh warned,

$$\text{وَلَا تَقْتُلُوا أَنفُسَكُمْ ۚ إِنَّ اللَّهَ كَانَ بِكُمْ رَحِيمًا}$$

"And do not kill yourselves [or one another]. Indeed, Allāh is to you ever Merciful" (Qur'an 4:29).

Whatever you know that is harmful to the mind and body must be avoided completely. Therefore, based on this textual evidence, although it does not discuss the issue of oral sex specifically, if there is the probability of contracting a sexually transmitted disease (STD) through it, Allāh encourages us to avoid it. This is also based on the fiqhi principle mentioned earlier: "Harm must be eliminated." To be clear, I am not overgeneralizing the dangers of oral sex. I am addressing the factors that may cause sexual health issues, and oral sex is one of many causes, especially if we do not take care of our oral health. Allāh loves cleanliness. To be safe, avoid all pollutions. In brief, the act of oral sex is detested and, in the fiqhi terminology, *makruh*, based on the information mentioned above. This pertains to the healthy couple; as for the unhealthy couple or the unsure, it is forbidden (*haram*). And Allāh knows best.

---

[130] Stefan Bechtel, *Practical Encyclopedia of Sex and Health* (1993), 220–221.

Dr. Yusuf Al-Qaradawi on Sexual Relationships

During his visit to the United States, Shaykh Al-Qaradawi was asked about sexual relations, with regard to looking at and touching genitals during sex. He answered that Islām did not ignore matters related to sex, but it has set rules and regulations. He cautioned those who rush into calling an act *harām* (unlawful) but encouraged them properly investigate before taking a stand. Additionally, he reminded the audience to go with the balanced approach, and avoid harshness. Especially with converts/reverts, go easy.

He added that books of fiqh did not ignore such matters. An example he mentioned was *Ad-Durru Al-Mukhtār* of the Hanafi school, which is a book that expands and explains *Tanweed Al-Absār*. Dr. Qaradawi concluded with a story from the book:

The great student of Imam Abu Hanifa, Abu Yusuf, asked his teacher, "Is there any problem of legality regarding touching one's spouse's genitals for sexual arousal?" Imam answered, "No! I hope they have great reward for doing so." (Found in Ad-Durru Al-Mukhtār, vol. 5, 234)[131]

Sexual Health and Men

Erectile dysfunction. This disorder affects more than half of all men worldwide over the age of seventy.[132] This condition is when the penis becomes too weak to penetrate. Men suffering from this problem often are too ashamed to seek help. The causes of this disorder may be a physiological, psychological, pharmacological, or biological lifestyle or problems in their relationships. My humble advice is to stop medicating yourself, and seek a qualified physician for consultation. Moreover, eat healthier, and work out regularly.

---

[131] Yusuf Al-Qaradawi, *Fatāwa Al-Mu'āsarah*, vol. 2 (1991), 350–353,

[132] Rallie McAllister, MD, MPH, MSEH (2004), 71–72.

Azoospermia and Oligospermia. When couples are unable to conceive children, the problem may stem from either the man or the woman. It is therefore necessary to consult a doctor. When the man is unable to impregnate his wife, it may be due to no sperm (azoospermia) or low sperm cell production (oligospermia). No pointing of fingers.

Sexual Health and Women

Menopause. This is the time of life when women's ovaries stop producing eggs. Menopause may decrease sexual desire and causes vaginal dryness. Vaginal dryness may cause discomfort during sex. As couple, seek your doctor's advice.

Douching. Douching is the flushing of the vagina with water and commercial product for general cleanliness due to heavy vaginal secretions, which often produce uncomfortable odor.[133] The Prophet did advise that women should cleanse themselves after menstruation, including the use of the *misk* (natural perfume oils). Today, however, commercial perfumes are heavily concentrated chemical products that irritate the delicate tissues of the vagina and can even cause vaginal infections. Amy Cooper, an expert on the subject of human sexuality, notes, "Douching or using feminine deodorant sprays is unnecessary and perhaps even harmful."[134] Advice to our sisters for general cleanliness: To be safer, use water instead of a commercial product.

Sexual pain disorder. This is when women suffer pain during sexual intercourse. Often it may occur due to bacterial infections or allergies to certain ingredients in contraceptives. Schedule an appointment to see your doctor, and please avoid self-medicating.

---

[133] Stick to natural ingredients; by the will of Allāh, you will live longer.

[134] Amy Cooper, *The Everything Orgasm Book* (2010), 45.

Reproductive Technology

Science has created artificial methods of fertilization to help solve the problem of infertility, but some of the methods are objectionable, ethically and Islāmically. There is nothing wrong with relying on science, but some of the reproductive technology aimed at circumventing infertility breaks the set boundaries that Allāh has established for every believing man and woman:

AID, or artificial insemination by donor, is when the sperm of a donor is placed into the woman through a tube. This practice is objectionable because a third party is introduced into marital intimacy. From the point of view of Islām, it is adultery, a very grave sin.

IVF, or in vitro fertilization, is where a developing egg is surgically removed from an ovary, joined with concentrated sperm, and then placed in an incubator. The fertilized egg is then inserted into the uterus. This procedure, when done with the sperm of the husband and the egg and uterus of the wife, is Islāmically correct. But if a third party is involved, it is unlawful and may be dangerous.

Surrogacy is the practice of using a surrogate, which means *substitute*—a person who is hired to bear a child for a woman who is unable to bear a child herself. This process is unethical and un-Islāmic for the following reasons:

- The commercialization of babies
- The exploitation of women
- Total disconnection between the baby and its biological mother

This practice is beyond objectionable for the above-mentioned reasons and also because a third party is introduced into the intimacy, which means it becomes adultery. Who knows the diseases or health complications the baby may introduce to the family. I want to share the following story, which terrified me: A woman paid her own mother ten thousand dollars to carry her baby through surrogacy, using the sperm of her husband implanted in her mother's womb. After the baby was born, the amount of conflict that arose was beyond ten thousand dollars, as the mother refused to give up the child. If this story does not show how twisted this practice is, nothing can. No disciplined mother who carries a baby for nine months would be willing to surrender the child, not for any cost. What kind of world do we live in, where a mother would agree to bear her own grandchild, using the sperm of her son-in-law? I invoke the phrase that our Prophet instructed us to use during times like these:

إِنَّا لِلَّهِ وَإِنَّا إِلَيْهِ رَاجِعُونَ

"Indeed, to Allāh we belong and to Him we shall return."

Science is not the enemy, but Allāh has set clear boundaries that never are to be crossed. In the world of reproductive technology, what Islām makes unlawful is the third-party element. The husband and the wife should be the only participants in the making of the child. If a machine assists them, that's fine, but once a human third-party element is present, the legality of the process is out the window. This is because third-party element introduces *darar*—harm. Remember that harm must be eliminated—this is one of the most important principles in Islāmic jurisprudence. To conclude, Allāh says in Surah Ash-Shurā,

لِلَّهِ مُلْكُ السَّمَاوَاتِ وَالْأَرْضِ ۚ يَخْلُقُ مَا يَشَاءُ ۚ يَهَبُ لِمَن يَشَاءُ
إِنَاثًا وَيَهَبُ لِمَن يَشَاءُ الذُّكُورَ ۔ أَوْ يُزَوِّجُهُمْ ذُكْرَانًا وَإِنَاثًا ۖ
وَيَجْعَلُ مَن يَشَاءُ عَقِيمًا ۚ إِنَّهُ عَلِيمٌ قَدِيرٌ.

To Allāh belongs the dominion of the heavens and the earth; He creates what he wills. He gives to whom He wills female [children], and He gives to whom He wills males. Or He makes them [both] males and females, and He renders whom He wills barren. Indeed, He is Knowing and Competent. (Qur'an 42:49–50)

Allāh provides for some and deprives others. He does so in terms of wealth, status, education, and even in the form of children. I reflect on the story of Khidr, a great man to whom Allāh gave the insight of the unseen (a dimension that humankind cannot see, the realm of jinn and angels. Note: Many were not given this ability). Prophet Moses was instructed to follow Khidr and learn from him, but he was unable to tolerate the eccentric actions of his new mentor, who was instructed by God to kill an adolescent boy in front of Prophet Moses, causing Prophet Moses to fall into great shock.

فَانطَلَقَا حَتَّىٰ إِذَا لَقِيَا غُلَامًا فَقَتَلَهُ قَالَ أَقَتَلْتَ نَفْسًا زَكِيَّةً بِغَيْرِ نَفْسٍ لَّقَدْ جِئْتَ شَيْئًا نُّكْرًا

> So they set out, until when they met a boy, Khidr killed him. [Moses] said, "Have you killed a pure soul for other than [having killed] a soul? You have certainly done a deplorable thing." (Qur'an 18:74)

Prophet Moses, being unaware of what Allāh had shown Khidr, questioned the act and protested against it. This was because he did not understand at the time that this was the will of Allāh. Due to his consistently challenging Khidr's actions, they parted ways. Later, Khidr explained himself before letting Prophet Moses go:

وَأَمَّا الْغُلَامُ فَكَانَ أَبَوَاهُ مُؤْمِنَيْنِ فَخَشِينَا أَن يُرْهِقَهُمَا طُغْيَانًا وَكُفْرًا- فَأَرَدْنَا أَن يُبْدِلَهُمَا رَبُّهُمَا خَيْرًا مِّنْهُ زَكَاةً وَأَقْرَبَ رُحْمًا

> And as for the boy, his parents were believers, and we feared that he would overburden them by transgression and disbelief. So we intended that their Lord should substitute for them one better than him in purity and nearer to mercy. (Qur'an 18:80–81)

How many children, especially in these trying times, gain access to firearms and end up taking the lives of innocent children at their school? How many children have slaughtered their own parents, and how many children have caused their parents to be sentenced to life imprisonment? The world is a place of unpredictability, and our human brains cannot fathom all the realities within this earth. We just pray that Allāh protects us and our families. For those who are blessed with children, may Allāh bless them. For those who do not have children, may Allāh bless and guide them. There are always abundant blessings to be grateful for. And Allāh is all-Aware of what we can handle and what we should have. Therefore, have *tawakkul* (reliance in Allāh), and you will find yourself content with wherever you are in life.

Family Planning

When couples begin to navigate their marital journey, some choose to hold off on having children. The way they control that aspect of their relationship is through family planning, also known as birth control. There are two types of birth control: artificial and natural.

Artificial

Artificial birth control methods, especially those that affect the womb, should be absolutely avoided. These methods include surgical sterilization, also known as permanent birth control. This process is Islāmically incorrect. And honestly, no one can tell the future. What are people to do if they decide to terminate their fertility and then later desire children? That would probably be the saddest moment in that person's life. Most who have consented to that procedure have regretted it immensely later.

Natural

Natural birth control can include fertility observation. This is when women predict their periods of fertility and abstain from sex. Another natural method is coitus interruptus, the withdrawal of the penis from the vagina just before ejaculation. Withdrawal actually is a practice that was used during the time of the Prophet ﷺ. The companions of the Prophet asked the Prophet whether withdrawal of the penis was okay. He replied,

مَا عَلَيْكُمْ أَنْ لاَ تَفْعَلُوا مَا مِنْ نَسَمَةٍ كَائِنَةٍ إِلَى يَوْمِ الْقِيَامَةِ إِلاَّ وَهِيَ كَائِنَةٌ

"It does not matter if you do not do it, for very soul that is to be born up to the Day of Resurrection will be born."[135] This method, along with contraceptives, such as condoms and diaphragms, are permissible. However, the most recommended approach is withdrawal. The wife must agree in order for this to be acceptable. Remember the basic principle of harmlessness.

Abortion

Abortion is a very controversial topic. It is the deliberate act of ending a human pregnancy. Some argue for it, calling it "pro-choice"; on the other hand, others argue against it, calling it "pro-life." In Islām, we avoid rhetorical battles and strictly discuss these matters through our lens of the Qur'an and Sunnah. From the Islāmic perspective, when approaching anything, we begin with the questions of why and, if possible, when. Generally, abortion is unjustifiable from the opinions of Islāmic scholarship, except in the rare circumstance where the birth of the child will cause significant injury or fatality for the mother. This is based on one of the goals of sharī'ah known as *Hifzun-Nafs*, the preservation of life. Some argue that the fetus is a life, and of course it is, but the current life is more guaranteed to be preserved than the fetus. Therefore, the priority is to preserve the current life over the potential life. May Allāh protect us from such a trial. Amīn.

Moreover, abortion is discouraged after the first trimester and absolutely unlawful during the next trimester, unless it's to protect the life of the mother. Scholars have mentioned that if a woman was impregnated during the horrific crime of rape, then it is permissible to have an abortion. The forbidden doctrine in abortion, from the Islāmic perspective, comes from the hadīth found in Muslim, where the Prophet ﷺ says,

إِنَّ أَحَدَكُمْ يُجْمَعُ خَلْقُهُ فِي بَطْنِ أُمِّهِ أَرْبَعِينَ يَوْمًا ثُمَّ يَكُونُ فِي ذَلِكَ عَلَقَةً مِثْلَ ذَلِكَ ثُمَّ يَكُونُ فِي ذَلِكَ مُضْغَةً مِثْلَ ذَلِكَ ثُمَّ يُرْسَلُ

---

[135] Sunan Abi Dawūd, Hadīth #2172.

الْمَلَكُ فَيَنْفُخُ فِيهِ الرُّوحَ وَيُؤْمَرُ بِأَرْبَعِ كَلِمَاتٍ بِكَتْبِ رِزْقِهِ
وَأَجَلِهِ وَعَمَلِهِ وَشَقِيٌّ أَوْ سَعِيدٌ

The constituents of one of you are collected for forty days in his mother's womb in the form of blood, after which it becomes a clot of blood in another period of forty days. Then it becomes a lump of flesh and forty days later, Allāh sends His angel to it with instructions concerning four things, so the angel writes down his livelihood, his death, his deeds, his fortune and misfortune.[136]

This hadīth proves that life does not fully enter the fetus until *during* the first four months of the fetus' development, but for sure it has life *by* the completion of that period (*fa yunfakhu feehir-ruh*, "the soul is blown into it"). Based on this, scholars unanimously agree that abortion during and after the fourth month is reprehensible and is deemed as "taking the life of an innocent person," which is a grave crime. In brief, as the pregnancy develops over the nine-month period, the more seriously sinful abortion becomes.

Generally, abortion is abhorred; the more developed the pregnancy gets, the graver the sin. However, Allāh knows best, and therefore, there are very rare exceptions.

---

[136] Sahīh Muslim, Hadīth #2643b.

CHAPTER 10

Divorce

A reality in our modern day is that our marriages are suffering and even collapsing worldwide. When we analyze national statistics in the most powerful and advanced nation on earth, the United States, it is revealed that almost 2.5 million marriages are contracted there each year. When glancing at the nation's divorce rate from a historical lens, during the 1970s more than five hundred thousand couples divorced. During the 1980s, more than a million couples divorced. During the '90s, it was more than 1.8 million. Today, 65 percent of new marriages are bound to be terminated, while another 10 percent will stay together for various reasons but remain miserable. Therefore, a typical marriage in our modern day has a 75 percent failure rate![137] A terrifying reality like this keeps imams like me horrified and up at night. However, we are not to despair but have optimism. I personally believe that if single people educated themselves more on the realities of what makes a marriage so special, we could halt this horrific trend for divorce. This is because, in most cases, willingness to change is based on awareness. Theologian Fred Lowery wrote in his book *Covenant Marriage*, "I fear that in America today, the only standard is that there are no standards. The only rule is that there are no rules. The fences are down. The limits are gone. The boundaries are fading into the distant past."[138]

---

[137] Fred Lowery, *Covenant Marriage* (2002), 2.

[138] Ibid., 4.

Getting a divorce is not as easy as you might think. It's a very difficult process with enormous psychological and emotional effects. It will have an impact on several aspects of your life and can change your entire lifestyle. Before you begin the process of getting a divorce, you need to take some time to think about how it will affect your life and the lives of those involved. When parents divorce, the impact is painful, and its consequences are unimaginable. Women face serious problems postdivorce, and as for children, only Allāh will save them. American psychologist Judith Wallerstein says, "When parents divorce, they do put their children at risk of long lasting damage."[139] An article in *USA Today* noted, "For a lonely house, one can be an unhealthy number."[140] This means that humans are social beings. You cannot live in isolation. The more you isolate, the more depressed you get. This is especially true for children. They need the support and upbringing of both parents. A child raised by a single parent loses some aspect of discipline. About half of all children born today in the United States will live in a single-parent family at some point. According to the census figures released in October 2003, this translates into about thirteen million custodial parents in the United States.[141]

Two researchers, Paul Amato and Allen Booth, have provided important statistics and information to consider before divorcing. They state that "many people who divorce and remarry find their second marriage is no happier than their first."[142] This makes sense if we revisit what I said about women who face the challenge of leaving due to the unavailability of their husbands or due to erectile dysfunction. The reason behind making the same mistake is a lack of investigation and inadequate assessment of their spouses. When we leave our former loved one, we move on to the same type of spouse, and it obviously causes the same type of problems—or worse.

There are instances where divorce is an absolute necessity, and that is when a marriage is irretrievably dead. Therefore, to make sure that things are done correctly during those instances, let's visit Islāmic jurisprudence and the scholarly take on divorce.

---

[139] Judith Wallerstein, *The Good Marriage* (1995), 125.

[140] *USA Today*, Section D, August 27, 2007.

[141] Mary J. Boland, *Child Support* (2004), vii.

[142] Paul Amato and Allen Booth, *The Case for Marriage*, 147–148.

Components of Islāmic Divorce

1. **Al-Mutalliq.** "One who divorces," or the divorcer. According to Islāmic jurisprudence, this must be the legal husband, in a state of sanity, and doing it based on his own will, not forced. This is inspired by the great primary fiqhi principle of "all deeds are based on intention."
2. **Al-Mutallaqah.** "One who is being divorced," or the divorced. This pertains to the legal wife.
3. **Seeghatut-Talāq.** The statement of divorce. In Islām, this is very important because it expresses the evidence, if it was actually a divorce. These statements are categorized as *sareeh* (explicit) and *kināyah* (implicit). An example of an explicit divorce statement is "I divorce you!" Meanwhile, implicit divorce statements are those such as "Go to your parents!" or "Go home."

Talāqus-Sunnah vs. Talāqul-Bid'ah

Divorce is divided as Sunnatic versus Bid'i divorce. *Sunnatic* comes from the actual Arabic word of *Sunnah*, and it means that the divorce was in line with the tradition of the Prophet ﷺ and therefore legitimate in the eyes of Islāmic jurisprudence. So what does a *sunnatic* divorce look like? Observe the wisdom of Allāh; here are four conditions that make the divorce in line with the Prophet's instructions:

- The husband should divorce his wife when she is not menstruating.
- If the husband wishes to divorce his wife, he must not engage in sexual intercourse with her during that cycle when she is not menstruating.
- Two witnesses must be present when the statements of divorce are made.
- In Islām, after the husband divorces his wife three times, the marriage can never be reinstated until the wife remarries and consummates that marriage. Therefore, with that context in mind, the husband is not allowed to declare "divorce" more than once at a time.

One might ask why there are so many restrictions in the *sunnatic* form of divorce. This shows that Islām takes divorce very seriously, as marriage is a very sacred institution. Divorce is a very serious process, and in order for someone to divorce in the Islāmic perspective, she cannot be in menses and cannot engage in sexual intercourse afterward, when she is free from it. The divorcer needs two witnesses to be there, and the divorcer can say "I divorce you" only once. This is Allāh's unsubtle way of telling us that divorce is a last-resort type of approach and not something to be played with. With all these conditions in mind, if the husband still chooses to divorce *sunnatically*, the marital relationship is most likely facing some serious challenges. As long as it is not the marriage's third divorce, the relationship may be repairable.

The second kind of divorce is labeled *bid'I*, which comes from the Arabic word of *bid'ah*, meaning "innovation." In the Islāmic context, an innovation is not a positive term. This is because to innovate is to deviate from the perfect pathway that the Prophet ﷺ paved for his followers. Who are we to walk another path or even think that it's a superior one? Bid'ah, therefore, is the opposite of Sunnah. Symptoms of a bid'i divorce are as follows:

1. When a husband divorces his wife during her menses
2. When the husband has engaged in intercourse with his wife and divorced her during the same period of "purity"
3. When the husband divorces his wife with no witnesses
4. When the husband divorces his wife with more than one pronouncement (two or three).

Divorce with one or two of these characteristics is unsunnatic, but most Muslim jurists hold the view that it is valid and counted as divorce. In the instance that three pronouncements of divorce occur in one seating, the majority of our scholars are of the view that it is counted as one. Ibn Taimiyyah documented that some scholars argued that the law forbids three pronouncements at once in order to prevent the divorcer from regretting later.[143]

---

[143] Ibn Taimiyyah, *Al-Fatawwā Al-Kubra*, vol. 3 (1987), 290.

Allāh ﷻ in the Qur'an, in the chapter known as At-Talāq, which literally means "the divorce," says,

$$يَا أَيُّهَا النَّبِيُّ إِذَا طَلَّقْتُمُ النِّسَاءَ فَطَلِّقُوهُنَّ لِعِدَّتِهِنَّ$$

$$وَأَحْصُوا الْعِدَّةَ ۖ وَاتَّقُوا اللَّهَ رَبَّكُمْ ۖ لَا تُخْرِجُوهُنَّ مِن$$

$$بُيُوتِهِنَّ وَلَا يَخْرُجْنَ إِلَّا أَن يَأْتِينَ بِفَاحِشَةٍ مُّبَيِّنَةٍ ۚ$$

$$وَتِلْكَ حُدُودُ اللَّهِ ۚ وَمَن يَتَعَدَّ حُدُودَ اللَّهِ فَقَدْ ظَلَمَ نَفْسَهُ ۚ$$

$$لَا تَدْرِي لَعَلَّ اللَّهَ يُحْدِثُ بَعْدَ ذَٰلِكَ أَمْرًا$$

> O Prophet, when you [Muslims] divorce women, divorce them for [the commencement of] their waiting period and keep count of the waiting period, and fear Allāh, your Lord. Do not turn them out of their [husbands'] houses, nor should they [themselves] leave [during that period] unless they are committing a clear immorality. And those are the limits [set by] Allāh. And whoever transgresses the limits of Allāh has certainly wronged himself. You know not; perhaps Allāh will bring about after that a [different] matter. (Qur'an 65:1)

What is the "waiting period" that Allāh mentioned in this verse? The waiting period in the Arabic language is al-'iddah. The 'iddah is three menstrual cycles for women, and for those who do not menstruate for whatever reason, three months. The significance of menstrual cycles during the divorce is to ensure that there is no pregnancy without the divorced couple's knowledge. And for those who do not menstruate, usually due to age, this is a waiting period for psychological preparation in regard to this transition into a new life. If they choose to come back after the expiration of the waiting period, a new contract must be officiated with all the aforementioned conditions of marriage.

In the case of desiring to remarry after the third divorce, things get a little complicated. In order to remarry the divorced wife, she must marry someone else and consummate the marriage. Then if she divorces again, the former husband can remarry her. The takeaway lesson from this is that divorce is no playing matter. If a couple can repair their marriage, despite the challenges, it is better for them to passionately work toward resolution than to divorce, just to remarry continuously. Imagine how ridiculous it would be to get to the stage of wanting to remarry after the third divorce—a stage that leaves the wife with no choice but to remarry another man. Would it not have been better to fix the relationship before it got to such a point?

> Ours is not divorce-free marriage; that may not be pragmatic. However, when divorcing, do it right. In order to avoid being harmed, avoid harming.

Al-Khulu'

Khulu' linguistically means "to take off," and Islāmically, it is the women's right "to cancel" the marriage contract she has with her husband. After all, this is a contract of offering and acceptance, so if the woman seeks to cancel her marriage, then she must return the *mahr*, or dowry, which is the bridal gift given to her by her husband. This is based on the hadīth narrated by Ibn 'Abbas:

قَالَ جَاءَتِ امْرَأَةُ ثَابِتِ بْنِ قَيْسٍ إِلَى رَسُولِ اللَّهِ صلى الله عليه وسلم فَقَالَتْ يَا رَسُولَ اللَّهِ إِنِّي لاَ أَعْتُبُ عَلَى ثَابِتٍ فِي دِينٍ وَلاَ خُلُقٍ، وَلَكِنِّي لاَ أُطِيقُهُ. فَقَالَ رَسُولُ اللَّهِ صلى الله عليه وسلم "فَتَرُدِّينَ عَلَيْهِ حَدِيقَتَهُ" . قَالَتْ نَعَمْ.

The wife of Thabit bin Qais came to Allāh's Messenger and said, "O Allāh's Messenger! I do not blame Thabit for any defects in his character or his religion, but I cannot endure to live with him." On that Allāh's Messenger (ﷺ) said, "Will you return his garden to him?" She said, "Yes."[144]

---

[144] Sahīh Al-Bukhāri, Hadīth #5275.

The Prophet then granted her khulu', which is proven in a hadīth collected by At-Tirmidhi:

عَنِ ابْنِ عَبَّاسٍ، أَنَّ امْرَأَةَ، ثَابِتِ بْنِ قَيْسٍ اخْتَلَعَتْ مِنْ زَوْجِهَا عَلَى عَهْدِ النَّبِيِّ صلى الله عليه وسلم فَأَمَرَهَا النَّبِيُّ صلى الله عليه وسلم أَنْ تَعْتَدَّ بِحَيْضَةٍ.

> The wife of Thabit bin Qais was granted a Khulu' from her husband during the time of the Prophet. So the Prophet ordered her to observe an 'Iddah of a menstruation.[145]

In regard to the waiting period, there is scholarly disagreement as to how long it should be when the wife divorces her husband. Some are of the opinion that it is one month or one menstrual cycle; others argue for three months or three menstrual cycles. The former is my preference, due to strong arguments presented by Islāmic scholarship.

In brief, to help one know Islām's official opinion on divorce, the Prophet ﷺ says, in a famous hadīth found in Abu Dawūd, Ibn Majah, and others' collections:

أَبْغَضُ الْحَلَالِ إِلَى اللَّهِ تَعَالَى الطَّلَاقُ

"Of all the lawful acts *the most detestable* to Allāh is *divorce*."[146]

Therefore, couples struggling should not rush to divorce, due to reasons we mentioned earlier. Rather, have the attitude of positivity and harmlessness. How many times will man hate something, but Allāh has put enormous blessing in it? Even in the unfortunate scenario where couples have had enough of one another, and the damage is beyond repair, despair is the not the mind-set to have. If divorce is necessary, do it the right way, through harmlessness based on the guidance of the Prophet ﷺ.

---

[145] Jami' At-Tirmidhi, Hadīth #1185b, graded Hasan.

[146] Sunan Abi Dawūd, Hadīth #2178, authenticated by Hakim.

Divorce is painful, and often, it may be harmful. Think before you initiate divorce. You have no one but you to blame if things did not go as well as you predicted—unless your spouse is indulging in a seriously sinful and immoral deed. In that instance, be patient with the spouse and continue to pray for him. Do not approve of your family's disapproval of him. Ibn Taimiyyah once said, "A man should not divorce his wife just because his mother ordered that. He should be obedient to her and it is not an act of obedience to divorce his wife when asked to do so."[147]

Al-Hidāna

The elephant in the room when it comes to discussing divorce is the custody of the children. The Arabic word for custody is *al-hidāna*, and it is discussed in great lengths in the fiqhi community. When explaining chapter 2, verse 233 of the Qur'an, Imam Al-Qurtubi quoted several scholars. Ibn Al-Mundhir, one of those great scholars, said, "There is a consensus in all of Islāmic scholarship that if a couple divorces with a child, the mother is more deserving of custody as long as she is stays unmarried." Abu 'Umar, another great scholar, emphasized, "I do not know of any disagreement between the predecessors of our scholarship on the matter of an unmarried divorced mother's greater right to custody over the child than the father. As long as the child is immature and also, as long as the mother is righteous, the mother has more of a right to the custody of the child."[148]

As an imam, I see it is a struggle when couples divorce because the first target is the child. In most cases, fathers would like to separate their children from their mother, especially when emotions are involved and without looking at the interest of the child. An infant needs its mother more than anyone else. As mentioned, children are attached to their mothers, and mothers are willing to go to extra lengths for them, regardless of what occurred between her and the baby's father. How can a man compete with that? As the child develops and matures, the child may be given the option to choose which house. Additionally, no one said that because one parent has custody over the child that the other parent is obliged to be out of the

---

[147] Ibn Taimiyyah, *Al-Fatāwa Al-Kubra*, vol. 3 (1987), 331.

[148] Muhammad bin Ahmad Al-Qurtubi, *Al-Jāmi' Li-Ahkām Al-Qur'an*, vol. 3, 164.

picture. This is incorrect, and therefore, regardless of where they stand with each other, parents should not be blinded from seeing the interest of their child.

Divorce is really challenging, but at the same time, it is a reality that many face. The truth about divorce is that harm will be done. Nevertheless, advice to divorced couples is to go to great lengths to minimize the negative effects that stem from divorce in order to protect the welfare of all those involved, especially the children. Unfortunately, I have seen many divorced couples transmit their hatred to their innocent children. They may be children today, but in a few years, they will be adults who can distinguish right from wrong. Be aware of that now, or prepare yourself for the moral judgment of your children later. A child is to be cared for, regardless of bad blood between spouses.

CHAPTER 11

Children

Children are indeed a blessing and a gift from the Creator. Some couples are blessed with many children. Some parents have only daughters, while others have only sons; some have both, while other have none. Indeed, whether we are provided with children or no children is a trial from God. Read, if you wish, in Surah Ash-Shurā, where Allāh says,

$$
\text{لِلَّهِ مُلْكُ السَّمَاوَاتِ وَالْأَرْضِ ۚ يَخْلُقُ مَا يَشَاءُ ۚ يَهَبُ لِمَن يَشَاءُ}
$$

$$
\text{إِنَاثًا وَيَهَبُ لِمَن يَشَاءُ الذُّكُورَ - أَوْ يُزَوِّجُهُمْ ذُكْرَانًا وَإِنَاثًا ۖ}
$$

$$
\text{وَيَجْعَلُ مَن يَشَاءُ عَقِيمًا ۚ إِنَّهُ عَلِيمٌ قَدِيرٌ}
$$

> To Allāh belongs the dominion of the heavens and the earth; He creates what he wills. He gives to whom He wills female [children], and He gives to whom He wills males. Or He makes them [both] males and females, and He renders whom He wills barren. Indeed, He is Knowing and Competent. (Qur'an 42:49–50)

Many marriages have ended because of children or the lack of them. Often what causes the marriage's end is the latter. Every child has a father; in Islāmic jurisprudence, the child becomes an orphan when the father dies.

207

However, there are a lot of fatherless children in the world. This is not because of death but because many fathers abandon their children and neglect their responsibilities. They are less concerned with the welfare of the child and more concerned with satisfying their desires. In some cases, they indulge in relations with multiple women and have become, as one of my counselees once said, pointing to her ex-husband, "A sperm donor."

Likewise, every man has a mother, and in most (if not all) cultures, the responsibility of motherhood cannot be overemphasized. They are the foundation of raising competent leaders. But when mothers shirk from their responsibilities at home; and when children are neglected through an absent mother, no one can predict the horror that follows, and no one in the family is safe. Therefore, let's analyze two important pillars to the stability of the nuclear family:

1. Fathering or "husbanding"
2. Mothering or "wifing"

Why Start with Motherhood?

Motherhood is arguably the strongest emotional bond in all relationships, human and nonhuman. The mother is willing to save her children at the expense of her own life, and this is innate. Nothing equals the love of the mother, and sometimes she focuses more on the loving, nurturing, and protection of her offspring than on her role as wife. Sadly, an immature phenomenon is that most husbands refuse to accept this reality. Instead, they demand their share, fully without interruption, as if their wife's attention toward them comes before the children. When there are no children in a relationship, it is understandable that the love, nurturing, and protection are centered on both spouses. At this stage of the relationship, both are willing to do anything for the sake of love. However, when children arrive, things begin to shift, not only physically but also psychologically. Especially for mothers, the concentration is no longer on the husband or herself but on her children. This emotional connection is remarkable; she is willing to sacrifice anything and everything, including her marriage, to protect her children. Most husbands are not willing to reach that state of mind. Additionally, because of that, they lose a portion of their rights to the preservation of the children and the entire family.

The husband is more concerned first about "I-ness" and then "we-ness"; he is more focused on himself as the individual than the collective family's interest. He starts by asking, "Where is my food?" After he's fed, then he is concerned with whether the children are eating. Me first; then them second. The wife, on the other hand, thinks about "we-ness" and then "I-ness"; it's the collective family's interest and then herself. Only a few husbands are willing to sacrifice the "rights" previously given to them by their wives to their children, which, by the way, most wives do.

We must never underestimate the reproductive advantage of women. Giving birth to a child grants the mother a connection with the child for which there is no competition. Women are biologically made for reproduction, and due that reality, they possess a maternal instinct. Women are innately experienced, which means they have a natural attachment to their children that forms the foundation of effective mothering. Meanwhile, men lack a similar capacity to nurture. A woman's experience of pregnancy, labor, and nursing can never be overappreciated. There is an assumption that paternity is inherently social, while maternity is essentially natural.[149]

It is therefore a "natural" phenomenon that mothering outweighs *wifing*. Trying to change this is dangerous to the survival of the relationship because only a small percentage of wives may be willing to sacrifice their children at the expense of their marriage. Family therapist Thomas Fogarty, MD, writes regarding marital crisis, "If he really wants to impress her, he should do it by being the best father that he knows how to be. Because her major concern goes toward the children, she will be more impressed by his fathering than by his husbanding."[150] This is not simply an opinion but a psychological fact. Therefore, we must emphasize the important role a father has in parenting. Although, the mother does an innumerable amount of nurturing, there is room for the father to assist as well. Children absolutely need a responsible father.

---

[149] Brettell & Sargent, *Gender in Cross-Cultural Perspective* (1993).

[150] Thomas F. Fogarty, MD, *Marital Crisis* (1976), 325.

Reflect on the words of psychiatrist and pioneer in the field of family therapy Nathan W. Ackerman, who argued that "as the mother mothers the child, so the father mothers the mother. The mother, while caring for the young infant, needs care for herself."[151] The husband also has to understand that he has to be the caretaker of his wife, as she is the caretaker of their children. This mind-set will create a harmonious relationship between husband and wife, along with parents and children.

Husbanding

The modern father, if he is to contribute his rightful share to the reconstruction of our total society and fulfill his parental vocation, must accept the burden of authority. Within his little Kingdom, he must take a position of responsibility and thus help to overcome the prevalent notion of moral anarchy. He must resist the superficial notion of equality. He ought to know more than his child knows; he ought to be wiser; he ought to make decisions that are unchallenged. Then, when he wisely gives more freedom and helps to develop initiatives by degrees, these are more likely to be appreciated than abused. He will have the grace to forgive as well as the courage to admit failure on occasion, but he will never forget that the role of father is different from the role of child. He will not abdicate.[152]

These few words of wisdom could be summed up in the teachings of the Prophet more than fourteen centuries ago, when he said,

$$\text{وَالرَّجُلُ رَاعٍ عَلَى أَهْلِ بَيْتِهِ، وَهُوَ مَسْؤُولٌ عَنْ رَعِيَّتِهِ}$$

"A man is the shepherd of the people of his house and he is responsible for his flock."[153]

---

[151] Nathan W. Ackerman, *Manual for Group Premarital Counseling* (1971), 177.

[152] Lyle B. Gangsei, *Manual for Group Premarital Counseling* (1971), 181–182.

[153] Saḥīḥ Al-Bukhāri, Ḥadīth #893; Saḥīḥ Muslim, Ḥadīth #1829.

This popular hadīth is mentioned in more than seven places and in most books of hadīth. This stresses the importance of responsibility, which is inseparable from accountability. Husbanding and fathering will be meaningless without caring.

The Islāmic Etiquette of Preparing for a Child's Birth

Before preparing for the birth of a child, one first must choose the right spouse. When seeking the right spouse, one should look for two things: (1) Will the partner be a compatible and positive match? (2) Will the partner be a great parent? Imam Al-Bukhāri affirms this point in his book of marriage when he asks, "What type of women should one seek in marriage? What type of women is better for marrying? Also, what is recommended to select to have good offspring without obligation?" He answers this question through hadīth: "There is a clear statement of the Prophet; reported by Ibn Majah and authenticated by Al-Hakim from the narration of 'Aisha, that the Prophet said, 'Select right spouse to have good offspring, and marry competent women.'"[154]

Once a couple has been formed, what comes next? Mutual happiness must be established between the couple, as it will help create an environment of shared responsibility of affection for both during the fulfillment of their sexual desire and shared parenthood during pregnancy. Then, the couple should pray for a righteous child, before and after the pregnancy. In order for a praying couple to expect a positive result, three conditions must be met:

1. The establishment of a safe environment
2. The consuming from safe and lawful provision
3. The behavior of safe conduct

The Establishment of a Safe Environment

We always heard from our elders, "You want me to speak on your character? Show me your friends." A righteous child is a product of a safe environment. Sociologists have debated for years on the concept of nature versus nurture. Despite the debate still being discussed to this day, it is clear that the

---

[154] Ibn Hajar Al-Asqalāni, *Fat-hul Bāri*, vol. 10 (1996), 156.

nurturing of an individual is quite impactful. Parents should preserve their children by preserving a safe environment in the home, neighborhood, school, and community.

The Consuming from Safe and Lawful Provision

Previously, we established that what we expose ourselves to has a spiritual impact. Further, what we consume is important. What no one really talks about, however, is the importance of how it was acquired. Both are deeply connected. As an imam, I have seen innumerable examples of people who cared not about where their source of provision came from. Every case ended with losing everything.

In the context of marriage and preparing for childbirth, the concept of safe and lawful provision matters even more. What the mother eats is what the baby eats. For the embryo to grow into a responsible and pious human being, it begins with what it is fed from the initial stages. There is great blessing in provision that comes from lawful and safe means. Additionally, there is great disaster in the provision that comes from the unlawful and evil means. John Stott wrote, "By thirteen weeks, the completion of the first trimester, the embryo is completely organized, and a miniature baby lies in the mother's womb; he can alter his position, respond to pain, noise, and light, and even get a fit of hiccups."[155] In essence, it is extremely important to surround the child from its inception in a safe environment that is provided for through lawful means.

Safe Conduct

The final condition is with regard to the home and parenting. We all have heard the proverb, "Monkey see, monkey do." Our children are not monkeys, but they love the two who brought them to earth. They express their love by emulating their parents' example. Therefore, words and actions of parents are immediately transferred to the behavior of their offspring. A father who abuses his wife will transfer his abusive qualities to his son. It may not appear today, but tomorrow it will. A mother who

---

[155] John Stott, *Involvement* (1985), 201.

---

abuses her husband will transfer her abusive qualities to her daughter. It may not appear today, but when she gets married, it will.

On the other hand, the father who honors his wife will transfer this noble quality to his children. The son will learn respect for women, and the daughter will know a positive example of a partner for the future. The mother who honors her husband will show her children what a positive female partner looks like. We should never underestimate the power of how we conduct ourselves. It is either a tool for destruction or construction. The choice is ours.

Counseling Involving Children

When involving children in the therapeutic process, one should be able to identify and separate young children and adult children. Although they may be equal in terms of inheritance, during marital conflicts they should be treated differently because of their level of understanding and maturity.

Young Children

As an imam I have come to understand clearly that the parents' utmost duty is to properly prepare their children, inwardly and outwardly, to face the challenges of the world in which they live. Moreover, the world may be different from the world their parents grew up in. Therefore, to provide children with a guaranteed safe navigation in their world, proper nurturing and discipline must come from both parents. When? From before the children are born to their very last days as parents. When nurturing children, it is important to understand not only their environment but also their developmental stages. Younger children are not fully matured and not yet capable of understanding details. Therefore, parents must realize their level of understanding and communicate with them based on that. It is extremely foolish to expect them to understand on the same level that adults do.

Likewise, it is also reprehensible to directly and indirectly involve them in adult conversation. Raising children while making these kinds of foolish mistakes is far from helpful to their survival in our world of destruction and confusion.

Even more haunting is how the media plagues and controls what goes on in the minds of teenage children. Their agenda is the glamorization of ugliness. Parents who adopt uncritical thinking about freedom care less about what their children are seeing and hearing. They do not realize that what these children see and hear today is part of who and what they will become in the future. It contributes to their makeup. For this reason, when young children are involved in the counseling process, I advise, as a counselor, that all must avoid actions and statements that will cause severe harm to the young child. What they hear today may live with them for the rest of their lives. Although one may succeed in deceiving those young children today, as they grow up to become adults, things may change. Past and present events will be more explicit, and at that moment, when the truth is known, they may feel betrayed by the same people who claimed to love and protect them. In some instances, this betrayal causes a victim to devolve into the victimizer.

In my years of counseling, I have witnessed such children abandoning their own parents. Therefore, during the interview, young children are brought only as a last result. Young children who have no business in the interview must be excluded from the room completely, especially in an intensive atmosphere. Witnessing their mother's grievances may cause the child to grieve too and consequently hate the father. I once interviewed a teenager who was going through a tough time with his father. I asked him the reasons for his delinquency. When talking about his father, he expressed that his father hated everybody in the family; that his father never appreciated them but always glorified himself. After investigation, it became very clear that the teen had witnessed many altercations between his parents and, in most cases, sympathized with his mother because she expressed high emotions by grieving and crying, which caused annoyance and withdrawal from the children. Since this young man was the oldest of three, he felt it was his duty to protect his mother from the father, who he believed was the victimizer. That perception might not have been the whole truth, but it actually was with this case. You see, the irresponsible mother was always using her children as a tool against her husband by feeding them fabrications regarding their father, who I came to realize, after my inquiry, was a responsible, disciplined disciplinarian who was doing his best to provide nurturing and protection for all. May Allāh protect us. Amīn.

Things to Avoid

- Inviting young children into serious marital disagreements. Do so only if it involves them and is in a favorable environment.
- Exposing children to adult language and explicit toxic materials, such as profanity; that exposure is harmful to them and the relationship.
- Making children choose sides, which many parents do. Putting your children against your spouse is highly immature and is extremely divisive to the stability of the family.
- Babysitting a child during the counseling interview. It is not healthy for the child to be exposed to the very serious adult issues. Likewise, the counselee will lack concentration with the counselor if she is caring for a child.
- Any other kind of destruction, either from the parents or their children.

Adult Children

Adult children—whether they are adult children of the counselees or a part of the counselee interview—are treated as adults, without forgetting that they are deserving of the respect offered to them by the Creator. There are no restrictions regarding the amount and nature of information they could give or receive. Unlike young children, their rights are equal to their parents' rights, but children must demonstrate *respect* toward their parents. Moreover, parents must avoid abusing the tradition of a child's obedience. Whether a person is a parent or offspring, justice must never be compromised. Read, if you wish, in the famous ayah, in Surah An-Nisa:

يَا أَيُّهَا الَّذِينَ آمَنُوا كُونُوا قَوَّامِينَ بِالْقِسْطِ شُهَدَاءَ لِلَّهِ وَلَوْ عَلَىٰ أَنفُسِكُمْ أَوِ الْوَالِدَيْنِ وَالْأَقْرَبِينَ ۚ إِن يَكُنْ غَنِيًّا أَوْ فَقِيرًا فَاللَّهُ أَوْلَىٰ

215

بِهِمَا ۖ فَلَا تَتَّبِعُوا الْهَوَىٰ أَن تَعْدِلُوا ۚ وَإِن تَلْوُوا أَوْ تُعْرِضُوا فَإِنَّ اللَّهَ كَانَ بِمَا تَعْمَلُونَ خَبِيرًا

O you who have believed, be persistently standing firm in justice, witnesses for Allāh, even if it be against yourselves or parents and relatives. Whether one is rich or poor, Allāh is more worthy of both. So follow not [personal] inclination, lest you not be just. And if you distort [your testimony] or refuse [to give it], then indeed Allāh is ever, with what you do, Acquainted. (Qur'an 4:135)

When adult children and their parents are involved in the counseling process, the following must be a guide:

* Fairness must never be compromised.
* Respect must dominate the interview and the discussion.
* Awareness of the self and of the environment should be observed.
* Self-improvement must be the focus and not self-destruction.
* Patience and forgiveness must be exercised.
* At-Tawakkul, intrinsically rely on Allāh.

We also must be cognizant, during the interview process with adult children, of whether those children come from a previous marriage, current marriage, or are adopted (Islāmically).

Children from Previous Marriage

This category may be the most challenging of the three. There may be unaddressed external factors that these children inherited from the previous household before divorce or death. Perhaps these issues were not addressed adequately, and the lack of direct confrontation led to the very disintegration of that previous marriage. In most cases, these children come to the counseling session with the preconceived mind-set of "us versus them." This is most commonly the case when dealing with the father who remarried. It is necessary that the counselor meets with parents alone and, following that, meets with the children alone in order to calm things down. Another acceptable approach for counselors is to choose to meet with one parent and child at a time. Consequently, these approaches will bring everyone together because the environment is conducive for a counseling session that instills the values of the collaborative process. However, we live in a world of unpredictability, and the counselor must always be prepared to face crisis and accusations.

Here are some haunting statistics: Half of first marriages in the United States end in divorce. More than 75 percent of those divorced Americans remarry, and 84 percent of the women who become wives for the second time marry men with children. Forty percent of these women have children of their own. I share these statistics to help us to visualize the world in which we live. From a counselor's point of view, this is a recipe for a lot of complicated family conflict. Conflict will arise from the blending of families, the damaged remains of divorce, and so much more that is yet to be discovered. Moreover, one of the greatest problems I have witnessed stems from previously married men with children limiting the new wife when it comes to having children of her own.[156]

The stepfamily, if not disciplined, will create unnecessary tension between stepchildren and their stepparents. If not properly addressed, it may cause unimaginable harm to the relationship. It is a generalization say that all stepchildren hate stepparents. What may be true, though, is that many divorced parents, in order to win the love of their children, feed their children with wrong, contaminated, and poisonous information about the other. This satanic methodology creates tension for the children with regard to the new relationship they have with their biological parents.

This is more intense when the biological father marries a younger woman who is equal or closer to the children's ages. They may respect their father but not their stepmother, who they feel has come to benefit from or inherit what their family had built together. The original mother will plant seeds of animosity by saying to her children, "I am your real mother; do not listen to that woman." Surely her innocent children, who feel she is the victim of the divorce, will sympathize with her and will rebel against any type of discipline at home, especially when it comes from their stepmother. The

---

[156] Barbara M. Keenan, *When You Marry a Man with Children* (1992), 7–12.

external influence is huge and powerful because of the innate connection between mothers and their children.

In brief, there are serious consequences for the family and community at large when divorced parents exhibit the following:

- They are unwilling to be truthful to themselves and their children.
- They are unwilling to accept responsibility for their actions.
- They are unwilling to compromise.
- They are unwilling to enforce discipline colored with love. With the baggage that comes with stepfamilies, everyone will suffer due to the ramifications of conflicting information that parents give to children. These innocent children learn to lie at a young age and to be aggressive and unhappy in their own marital and family lives. This leads to hopelessness due to the helplessness of the past.

It must be emphasized that entering a new marriage after divorce is perfectly normal and fine. The more we learn about the challenges that stem from the stepfamily, however, the more equipped spouses and children will be in ensuring a harmonious environment.

All stepparents must avoid prejudices and all forms of discrimination. It is absolutely critical to treat all the children with respect and generosity. They may not appreciate it at first, especially stepchildren and their biological parents, but the focus is to please none but Allāh. Trying to please everybody is an unattainable goal; it is not only about now but also the future. To protect the family, everyone must be respected and treated as a member of the family and not as an outsider. From an Islāmic perspective, stepchildren or biological, these children are an *amāna* (a trust) and should never be neglected—period.

With all this in mind, the stepmother, specifically, needs to stand up for herself. Stepmothers, do not allow others to suppress your role in your marriage. Yes, it is your responsibility to take care of the children—stepchildren and your own—to the best of your ability, but there will be times when, no matter how colored with love you are, they will abuse it. Make sure to set some principles as you navigate this challenging role. These principles should govern with justice, coupled with mercy and should protect your honor. Barbara, an author, wrote a brilliant set of rights for wives and stepmothers, which I found resonated with what I previously stated:

1. I will be part of the decision-making process in my marriage and family always.
2. People outside the immediate family—including ex-wives, in-laws, or adult children—cannot make plans that affect my life without my consent.
3. I will not be responsible for the welfare of children for whom I can set no limits.
4. I must be consulted about which children will live with us, when they can visit, and how long they will stay.
5. I will not be solely responsible for housework. Chores will be distributed according to each family member's ability.
6. I must be consulted regarding all family financial matters.
7. Others may not violate the private space I have designated for myself in my home, nor use my possessions without my permission.
8. I will never be treated as an "outsider" in my own home.
9. My husband and stepchildren must treat me with respect.
10. Our marriage is our priority, and we will address all issues together.[157]

In most cases, children are used as a weapon against the other parent, and the stepparent is the victim of the unsolved problems that led to the divorce. Children who are caught in this intense situation must be helped. Counselor, be aware of the situation; accept the reality, and work toward a meaningful communication among the members of the entire family. Remember, we may not be able to help solve the problem, but make an effort and leave the result with Allāh.

Children from Present Marriage

Marriage scholars Elton and Pauline Trueblood made a thought-provoking statement: "The fortunate child is not the one who grows up in a world

---

[157] Lyle B. Gangsei, *Manual for Premarital Counseling* (1971), 38–39.

---

which has neither rules nor boundaries. The child needs boundaries, with an area of freedom within the boundaries. If he is to develop any sense of security."[158]

Phenix, in the same book, argues, "A child is to be accepted and cared for as a person, without regard to how well or how poorly he may live up to his parents' expectations and hopes for him. He is not a marketable commodity, to be bought up or written off, and measured by price. He is a unique person to be loved for himself, without measure or calculation of benefits."[159]

One of the biggest challenges in parenting is balancing discipline and freedom for the child. We cannot afford to allow our young children to make decisions without parental guidance, but we cannot be extremely dictatorial either. Corsini and Painter wrote, "Although all parents want good children ... very few children have good parents." The difference between a good parent and a bad parent is in which one chose to equip himself or herself with the necessary knowledge of raising children. Every child requires his or her physical and emotional needs to be satisfied, along with a spiritual nurturing. When one of these aspects is neglected, it affects the upbringing of the child.

Every parent wants to have ideal children, but according to Corsini and Painter, the "four R's" need to be incorporated:

Respect

We want our children to be respectful, but how often do we expose them to respect? Children learn from what they see their parents doing, so they can't learn to be respectful if parents are not respectful. A great Muslim scholar once said, "Every child is brought up based on the discipline of their parents."

---

[158] Lyle B. Gangsei, *Manual for Premarital Counseling*, quoted from Philip H. Phenix of Columbia University, 181.

[159] Lyle B. Gangsei, *Manual for Premarital Counseling*, quoted from Philip H. Phenix of Columbia University, 176 & 181.

Responsibility

We want our children to be responsible, but do we baby them, preventing them from learning? Children are naive and immature, but mistakes are their best teacher. I run a youth group, and I tell them that I love to see them make mistakes in my presence so that I can correct them, rather than their erring without my guidance. In order for children to grow, parents must hand them some kind of responsibility that will slightly push them out of their comfort zones. It is through that experience that they will learn the most about themselves and the world they live in.

Resourcefulness

We want our children to acquire resourcefulness. Being resourceful is being someone who is a source of benefit and assistance to all. However, children can't learn this if we do not give them the proper spiritual guidance, as well as push them to tackle the world's problems. I have given some of my adult youth the opportunity to give *khutbah* at one of my communities. These young adults, although excelling in their tasks, caused pushback from a few in our community. How can these young individuals become resourceful leaders if they are not put to the test?

To the older generations, we need to remember our purpose in leading. If we are unable to raise competent leaders of tomorrow, then we have failed in our responsibilities as leaders. Parents, we were children too. We became adults because of the proper nurturing of our elders. Therefore, it is the parents' duty to give that proper nurturing for their children. We do this in order for them to grow up to be resourceful to their surroundings, wherever they happen to be.

Responsiveness

We often long for our children to communicate with us. When picking them up from school or extracurricular activities, we ask them how their day went. Often they reply with short phrases, such as "Nothing much." Does this attitude cause us to reflect on what could have caused their lack of desire to communicate with us? According to Raymond Corsini and Genevieve Painter, authors of *The Practical Parent*, "Children become responsive when treated fairly with love and respect."

I love to share the story of my son, Rayyan. Every morning and every evening when I come back from work, my dear son greets me with "*Assalāmu Alaikum*, Dad." This may look like something minor, but his consistency in greeting his father has a profound emotional effect on both of us. I therefore believe that the greatest influence on a child to adopt good qualities, such as being responsive, is the parents themselves displaying these good qualities. Parents who always greet their neighbors will raise children who most likely will greet their neighbors. A parent who always shows warmness and love toward the other parent will raise children who will most likely express love and warmness toward their siblings, and so on.

In order to raise children to develop these ideal qualities—the four R's—make sure you, the parent, establish these qualities within yourself first. Children, especially in their early stage of life, love their parents so much, and children learn best by following what their role models do. Make sure your children are exposed to the best, outstanding individual of a parent possible. Children may not like your discipline because that is the nature of children, but surely every child needs discipline to achieve these qualities.

As parents, understand that your nurturing may not be appreciated today, but remain vigilant with your vision, for indeed when you are long gone your children will greatly appreciate your methodology. When I was growing up in the '70s, I thought my mother was extremely strict with me because of her methodology of discipline. Now that I am a parent of several children, I understand very well what she gave me, and today I truly appreciate it. May Allāh have mercy on Nana Hawwa. Amīn.[160]

Children and Mental Health

Parents, teachers, and leaders, collectively, are concerned about the nurturing of children in the new millennium. They are focused on how

---

[160] Raymond Corsini and Genevieve Painter, *The Practical Parent* (New York, Harper & Row: 1975), 7–8.

to better nurture the children and the leaders of tomorrow. It is therefore necessary, as mentioned earlier, to not only understand the environment but also to understand their influences in general and why they do what they do.

A counselor must be able to guide parents to help their children. Many children today are faced with multiple disorders, physically and mentally, such as ADHD, ADD, and others. Children diagnosed with such disorders have problems organizing themselves because the part of the brain that helps us organize doesn't work properly. This by no means implies that such children are unintelligent. They are just as intelligent as the other children, but they have difficulty with their judgment; they think fast but not fast enough. They are constantly in trouble because they just don't think before they act. The thinking, in most cases, comes after the action was completed. Additionally, mentors and teachers are still students when it comes to dealing with these challenges and can improve in their ability to approach these children.

There are three conditions that will help keep such children focused:

1. One-on-one sessions
2. Exposing them to new approaches
3. Engaging with them in things they are interested in

Although there is no cure for ADHD or ADD, these conditions can be successfully managed. Medication and discipline must go hand in hand to help those with the disorders. Therefore, the family must have a tool to help manage the symptoms. Support groups are very helpful. Likewise, part of the management strategy is to accept the responsibilities of our actions. There are no favors for anyone just because they have been diagnosed with certain disorders. Acceptable is acceptable; unacceptable is unacceptable to all and for all. Everyone must understand that they are responsible for their actions.

Therapy for Children with Psychological Problems

The therapeutic needs of children can never be overemphasized, especially children diagnosed with mental illnesses. When dealing with troubled children who constantly get into trouble with peers or parents, it is necessary to evaluate the child's psychological nature. *ABC World News* reported, "More than forty thousand people with mental illnesses commit suicide in America every year."

The cognitive restructuring technique recommends action as a way of breaking the reciprocal negative relationship between a person's thought, feelings, and behavior. Individuals' inactivity and social withdrawal feeds their feelings of worthlessness and thoughts that they deserve no better than what they have. To break this spiral of defeat, individuals must force themselves to be active by planning every hour, if necessary.[161]

Depression and anxiety disorders are very serious, and if not approached with the proper tools of treatment, severe consequences may occur. Therefore, as counselors, it is important to remember your role in assisting of the counselee. There are times where you have to refer your counselee to a doctor for the betterment of that individual.

In conclusion, counselors need to be equipped and made aware of the psychological issues in order to serve their counselees in the best way that they can, either by engaging with them through their counseling methods or, when the issues are too severe, referring them to a medical expert.

---

[161] Lawrence E. Shapiro, *The New Short-Term Therapies for Children* (1984), 88.

CONCLUSION

وَتَعَاوَنُوا عَلَى الْبِرِّ وَالتَّقْوَىٰ ۖ وَلَا تَعَاوَنُوا عَلَى الْإِثْمِ وَالْعُدْوَانِ ۚ وَاتَّقُوا اللَّهَ ۖ إِنَّ اللَّهَ شَدِيدُ الْعِقَابِ

"And cooperate in righteousness and piety, but do not cooperate in sin and aggression. And fear Allāh; indeed, Allāh is severe in penalty" (Qur'an 5:2).

Alhamdulillah, all praises are due to Allāh, and may peace and blessings be upon the Prophet. It is indeed a great achievement to acquire the necessary tools to help ourselves and humanity. This is the goal of Islām. As mentioned earlier, Qur'an and Sunnah are indeed our guides. And surely it is a perfect guide. In the preceding pages, we have mentioned support systems that provide care and nurturing to those who need them. We all need them. Moreover, those providing the nurturing need to maximize their ability to help, and this is my intention with this book.

As imams and leaders, we must understand that if change is ever to happen, it must come from the self. We also must understand that change has never been easy. Therefore, our practice must be justice coupled with mercy. We must do whatever we can to protect the confidentialities of those we are trying to help. Knowledge of the *dīn* and the profession is a must. To succeed in this profession, the mind-set needs to be on listening more and seeking more through questions. When counselors speak, they should speak positively and full of optimism.

To the young and energetic, looking to get married, I pray that Allāh blesses you. However, be cautious. Marriage is not what we see in the movies; finding a compatible lifelong partner requires a lot of self-development and assessment. This is one of the most important investments you can make in your entire life, and it must be done properly. To the young men, make sure you can provide for your wife because that is a major pillar in marriage. To the young women, make sure you know what kind of husband you are looking for. Make sure that this man is someone worth obeying and respecting. To both, we discussed in great detail the topic of sexual health. The importance of both spouses' health cannot be overemphasized with regard to the consummation of the marriage.

Most importantly, due to how technology has influenced our way of life, beware of social media. Although it has its many positive aspects, it also has its severely negative ones. As an imam, I have seen many things and realize that one of the greatest dangers to a family is the couple's inability to leave the smartphones out of their bedroom. Keep your smartphones out of the bedroom, and your household will be protected. Learn to prioritize your time with your family, and maintain self-discipline with regard to going on social media.

To conclude, to seek your future spouse, you need to be in tune with who you are first. Your knowledge of self must be actualized. Your standards must be based on realistic expectations, and then you will be ready to begin this transformational milestone. I pray for you and your future spouse. May Allāh chose the best for us all.

وَعَاشِرُوهُنَّ بِالْمَعْرُوفِ ۚ فَإِن كَرِهْتُمُوهُنَّ فَعَسَىٰ أَن تَكْرَهُوا شَيْئًا وَيَجْعَلَ اللَّهُ فِيهِ خَيْرًا كَثِيرًا

"And live with them in kindness. For if you dislike them - perhaps you dislike a thing and Allāh makes therein much good" (Qur'an 4:19).

When I reflect upon what you may need after digesting all that has been mentioned, I am sure some who thought of approaching marriage soon may now have reluctance in their hearts. Perhaps some have even been scared away because the dangers of entering a relationship blindly are so severe. At the end of the day, however, I would like to remind myself and the reader that the Prophet ﷺ married and encouraged us to follow his footsteps.

Islām legislated marriage for the purpose of bringing goodness to the individual and human society. It is an equal partnership with the aim of bringing security to all. As we take this responsibility, we have to be willing to see beyond our own needs. The world cannot be governed anymore by "I-ness" but rather "we-ness." The pursuit of self-pleasure at the expense of your partner is unacceptable in the marital relationship. During difficulty—and there will be difficulties—do the work of love by caring for one another. Unfortunately, our world today understands only the language of strong currency—Mercedes-Benz and Land Cruisers. It is to the point that love has become materialized before internalized. Blessed to the righteous, who understand that ours is both this life and the hereafter.

A reminder is that there will be problems, and when they arrive in the relationship, avoid as much as you can all triangulation.[162] To avoid the effects of triangulation, concentrate on achieving meaningful cooperation through effective, sincere, and positive communication. There may be times when divorce is the only solution because of incompatibility and self-destruction. However, harmlessness must never be compromised, especially when children are involved. Be appreciative, and receive appreciation in return.

لَا يَرْحَمُ اللَّهُ مَنْ لَا يَرْحَمُ النَّاسَ

"Allāh will not be merciful to those who are
not merciful to the people."[163]

---

[162] The interference of a third party in marital conflict affecting the couple, such as parents or in-laws.

[163] Sahīh Al-Bukhāri, Hadīth #6941.

Our *dīn* is a faith of mercy and compassion. Without such an attitude, how will humankind survive? Humans are fallible. We make mistakes. Sometimes these mistakes will affect others. Forgiveness is necessary for human survival. As Muslims, we must remember the Golden Rule: Do unto others as you would have them do unto you. The rule applies to your spouse, your child, your parents, your neighbors, Muslim or not Muslim. Ours is mercy for all and to all. Allāh ﷻ said in Surah Al-Anbiyā,

$$وَمَا أَرْسَلْنَاكَ إِلَّا رَحْمَةً لِّلْعَالَمِينَ$$

We have not sent you but as a Mercy to Humanity.
—Qur'an 21:107

To the parents, your children are indeed a blessing from Allāh to you. Therefore, they deserve your utmost care and nurturing, coupled with discipline. Your children will be your representatives when you are no longer around. Make sure they are positive representatives because surely they will demonstrate exactly what was taught in the home, whether positive or negative. To the counselors and leaders in general, live by example. Never exclude yourself from the advice you are giving, for indeed, the arrogant and unjust are always exposed. We ask Allāh to help us hear the positive reminder and implement it in the best way that we can. Indeed, our world is a reflection of how we treat one another.

Let us love one another, forgive one another, and be appreciative of one another.

$$سُبْحَانَ رَبِّكَ رَبِّ الْعِزَّةِ عَمَّا يَصِفُونَ - وَسَلَامٌ عَلَى$$
$$الْمُرْسَلِينَ - وَالْحَمْدُ لِلَّهِ رَبِّ الْعَالَمِينَ$$

Your Lord, the Lord of glory, is far above what they attribute to Him. Peace be upon the Messengers. And praise be to God, the Lord of all the worlds.

Amīn.

BIBLIOGRAPHY

Ali, A. Y. *The Meaning of the Holy Qurā n*. Beltsville, Md: Amana Publications, 2001.

Al-Qurtubi, Al-Jāmi' Li Ahkām Al- Qur'an.

Asad, M., & A. Moustafa. *The Message of the Qur'ā n: The Full Account of the Revealed Arabic Text Accompanied by Parallel Transliteration*. Bitton: Book Foundation, 2008.

Bechtel, S. *The Practical Encyclopedia of Sex and Health*. Emmaus, PA: Rodale Press, 1993.

Boston Women's Health Book Collective. *Our Bodies, Ourselves for the New Century: A book by and for women*. New York: Simon & Schuster, 1998.

Corey, G. *Theory and Practice Counseling and Psychotherapy*, 2005.

Corsini, R. J., & G. Painter. *The Practical Parent: ABCs of Child Discipline*. New York: Harper & Row, 1975.

Cox, K., G. J. Subak-Sharpe, & D. M. Goetz. *The Good Housekeeping Illustrated Guide to Women's Health*. New York: Hearst Books, 1994.

Dittes, J. E. (1999). *Pastoral Counseling: The Basics*. Louisville, Ky.

Dobson, J. C. *Emotions, Can You Trust Them?* Grand Rapids, MI: Revell Books, 2014.

Dobson, J. C., & G. L. Bauer. *Children at Risk: The Battle for the Hearts and Minds of Our Kids.* Dallas: Word Pub., 1994.

Gangsei, L. B. *Manual for Group Premarital Counseling.* New York: Association Press, 1971.

Guerin, P. J., & American Orthopsychiatric Association. *Family Therapy: Theory and Practice.* Lake Worth, Fla: Gardner Press, 1996.

Harris, G. A., & D. Watkins. *Counseling the Involuntary and Resistant Client.* College Park, MD: American Correctional Association, 1987.

Havner, V. *Playing Marbles with Diamonds: And Other Messages for America.* Grand Rapids: Baker Book House, 1985.

Hilali, M. T.-D., & M. M. Khan. *Interpretation of the Meanings of the Noble Qur'ân in the English Language: A Summarized Version of At-Tabari, Al-Qurtubî, and Ibn Kathîr with Comments from Sahih Al-Bukhârî: Summarized in One Volume.* Riyadh: Darussalam, 1996.

Ibn-al-Jauzi, A.-R. I.-A., & -S. M. Saiyid. *Said al-ḫāṭir.* al-Qāhira: Dār al-Ḥadīt, 1996.

Ibn Hajar Al-Asqalani, & M. I. Bukhari. *Fatḥ al-bāri bi-sharḥ ṣaḥīḥ al-imām Abi 'Abd Allāh Muḥammad ibn Ismā'īl al-Bukhārī.* Bayrut: Dār Aḥya' al-Turāth al-'Arabī, 1988.

Ibn Katheer, & M. A. Ṣabuni. *Mukhtaṣar tafsīr Ibn Kathīr: Mukhtaṣar li-Tafsīr.* Bayrut, Lubnan: Dār al-Qur'ān al-Karīm, 1981.

Ibn Qayyim Al-Jauziyyah, & H. A. Ṭahir. *Kitāb al-fawā'id.* al-Qāhirah: Dār al-Fajr lil-Turāth, 2002.

Ibn Taimiyyah, *Learning Philosophy: The Relief from Distress,* 2012.

Ibn Taimiyah, & M. A. Q. 'Ata̅. *Aḥka̅m al-zawa̅j*. Bayru̅t: Da̅r al-Kutub al-'Imi̅yah, 1996.

K̲h̲a̅n̲, V., & F. Kha̅nam. *The Quran*. New Delhi: Goodword Books, 2011.

Kupers, T. A. *Revisioning Men's Lives: Gender, Intimacy, and Power*. New York: Guilford Press, 1993.

Loury, G. C. *The Anatomy of Racial Inequality*. Cambridge: Harvard University Press, 2003.

Lowery, F. *Covenant Marriage: Staying Together for Life*. West Monroe, La: Howard Pub., 2002.

Maxwell, J. C. *The 21 Irrefutable Laws of Leadership: Follow Them and People Will Follow You*. Nashville, Tenn.: Thomas Nelson, 2010.

Mihanovich, C. S., G. J. Schnepp, & J. L. Thomas. *Marriage and the Family*. Milwaukee: Bruce Publishing Company, 1955.

Nadwi, A. A. *Al-Qawa̅`id al-fiqhiyah: Mafhumuha, nash'atuha, tatawwuruha, dirasat mu'allafatiha adillatuha, muhimmatuha, tatbiqatuha*. Damsyik: Dar al-Qalam, 2011.

Pacifico, C. *Think Better, Feel Better: A Practical Guide to Avoiding the Errors in the Thinking Process That Cause Negative Feelings*. San Diego: Libra Publishers, 1990.

Reuben, D. R. *Everything You Always Wanted to Know about Sex but Were Afraid to Ask*. New York: St. Martin's Paperbacks, 2000.

Sahi̅h International. *The Qur'a̅n: English Meanings = al-Qur'a̅n al-Kari̅m*. Jiddah: Abul-Qasim Pub. House, 2004.

Salim, K. -S. *Sahih Fiqh us-Sunnah*. al-Qahirah: al-Maktabah al-Tawfiqiyah, 2003.

Stone, H. W. *Strategy for Brief Pastoral Counseling*. Minneapolis, Minn.: Augsburg Fortress, 2001.

Sue, Donald Wing and David Sue, *Counseling the Culturally Diverse: Theory and Practice*, 1990.

Wehr, H., & J. M. Cowan. *A Dictionary of Modern Written Arabic: (Arabic-English)*, 1994.

ABOUT THE AUTHOR

Imam Abdul-Rahman Yaki is a native of Accra, Ghana. He was raised by two beautiful parents, Muhammed Atta Kakayatchi and Hawwa Abdullah, may Allāh have mercy on them. He began his beginner's education in traditional Islāmic studies with Ansāruddīn, both in Abeka and Fadama, Accra, Ghana. He began his secular studies in Abeka Middle School and continued his traditional Islāmic studies in Kaduna, Nigeria, where he learned traditional Māliki Fiqh. He enrolled in the Islāmic University of Say, Niger, and graduated from the Faculty of Islāmic Law. He returned home to be a tutor in the Institute of Islāmic Studies, located in Nima, Accra, which is affiliated with the organization Islāmic Research, which is when he began to work alongside his esteemed Ghanaian Islāmic scholar, Umar Ibrahim Imam, who is the leader of ASWAJ Ghana. He went to the United States on scholarship for a graduate program in Islāmic studies. After graduating with a master's degree in Islāmic law, he became imam in few communities in the Washington, DC metropolitan area. Currently, he and his beautiful family reside in Albany, New York, where he leads one of the largest Muslim communities in the Capital District, ICCD, along with Islāmic Research Center in Capitol Heights, Maryland. In addition, he serves as a full-time imam/chaplain with the New York State Department of Corrections and Community Supervision. He is the first imam to give Islāmic invocation in the New York State Senate and was invited to the February 2014 National Prayer Breakfast with former president Barack Obama.